FROM **KAI** TO **KIWI KITCHEN**

From Kai *to* Kiwi Kitchen

New Zealand Culinary Traditions and Cookbooks

Edited by **Helen M. Leach**

OTAGO

Published by Otago University Press 2010
PO Box 56/Level 1, 398 Cumberland Street
Dunedin, New Zealand
Fax: 64 3 479 8385, Email: university.press@.otago.ac.nz
www.otago.ac.nz/press

ISBN 978 1 877372 75 9

Printed in New Zealand by Astra Print Ltd, Wellington

Contents

Preface

Culinary history has attracted increasing attention over the past two decades. Both popular and academic books, as well as articles in journals and magazines, reflect the growth of research and public interest in research findings. Many types of historical resource can provide useful information for such studies, from personal diaries, menus, household inventories and account books, to recipe books, in both printed and manuscript form. Yet despite the number of cookbooks that survive, they have not been the primary focus of the majority of research projects. For a start, they do not directly reflect diet or consumption patterns in the past – many meals were (and still are) prepared without recourse to recipes. In addition, a recipe book written by a famous chef differs in content and purpose from a cookbook compiled by a fundraising committee and is hardly comparable. Library holdings of cookbooks are uneven, with authored, commercially published cookbooks better represented than compiled community efforts. For these reasons, the potential contribution of cookbooks to our understanding of culinary history has been slow to be acknowledged. Researchers have been uncertain how best to use them or what questions they were suited to answering.

However by 2003, cookbooks held in research libraries such as the Hocken Collections in Dunedin and the Alexander Turnbull Library in Wellington were increasing as a result of the recognition of their potential as a research resource. In addition, several private collections had reached a size that rendered them suitable for quantitative analysis. We now believe that several thousand cookbooks have been published in New Zealand since the 1880s. To me as one of the cookbook collectors, it seemed the right time to formulate a project that would make proper use of them. My background was that of an anthropologist with a long-established interest in the archaeology of gardens and domestic life, and a strong conviction that the anthropological notion of a tradition could provide a suitable framework for such study. Culinary traditions accompany migrants to new homelands and mark their identity. Traditions persist because of culturally embedded mechanisms of transmission, such as formal education and family custom. As well as being a written representation of a tradition's culinary repertoire, recipes are also sensitive markers of the socioeconomic conditions of their times. They are prone to modification, reflecting the arrival of new fashions and new technology, yet they also preserve connections with the past. They reflect international trends in ways of thinking about food, nutrition and identity. Above all, they offer a window on core domestic activities that are poorly represented in other historical resources.

In 2004, I asked Michael Symons (leading Australian food historian and author, then resident in New Zealand), Janet Mitchell (lecturer in Food Science at the University of Otago and trained dietitian) and Jane Teal (Christchurch archivist and cookbook collector) to help me put together an application to the Marsden Fund (administered by the Royal Society of New Zealand) for support for a project entitled 'The Development of New Zealand's Culinary Traditions'. The period to be investigated was the nineteenth and twentieth centuries, and the primary data would be recipes and the cookbooks in which they appeared.

We proposed to examine several themes, including the adaptation of British and Maori culinary traditions to colonial contact in the nineteenth century and the fate of the Maori tradition in the twentieth; the external influences on New Zealand cookery (previously thought to be predominantly British until after World War II); the ways in which cookery knowledge moved between and within generations; the impact of changing stove technology on methods and recipes; the uptake of nutritional advice in the community; major trends in perceptions of the cook's roles as modernism gave way to postmodernism from the 1960s; and cultural conservatism and innovation in different aspects of cookery such as meal courses and between-meals baking. The project provided support for PhD candidate Raelene Inglis (Anthropology), and MA candidate Sophia Beaton (Maori Studies). The work of two other students, Fiona Crawford (BA Hons, Anthropology) and Renée Wilson (BSc Hons, Food Science) also contributed to the project.

Success in the 2004 Marsden funding round allowed us to begin the project early in 2005. Most of the components were completed within the three-year plan, and we were given an extension for another year in order to publish the remaining papers, along with the three Macmillan Brown lectures that I gave on the overall theme during October 2008. This volume includes those lectures (Part I), in addition to four chapters from other team members and one from a food historian, Duncan Galletly of Wellington, who became closely associated with the project and offered much help to the Marsden team (Part II).

Three conferences or symposia were held in conjunction with our three-year project: the first (14–15 November 2005) was hosted by the Department of History, Victoria University of Wellington, and organised by Kate Hunter and Michael Symons; the second took place at the Research Centre for the History of Food and Drink at the University of Adelaide (3–4 July 2006) and was organised by Roger Haden; the third was hosted by the Departments of Anthropology and Food Science at the University of Otago (29 November to 1 December 2007) and was organised by the Marsden team. Chapters 4 to 8 in this volume incorporate and expand on material originally delivered at the 2007 symposium in Dunedin, while Chapters 2 and 3 provide an overview of the project's findings. Chapter 1 synthesises my earlier research into the culinary traditions of pre-European Maori and their Polynesian ancestors, conducted over many decades.

These meetings attracted other researchers currently working on the history of cookery in New Zealand and Australia and generated enough momentum for a fourth symposium, held in Christchurch in October 2008. During that year several important books appeared on the theme of New Zealand's culinary heritage and these in turn stimulated much public interest. The field of research has thus benefited enormously from the support of the Marsden Fund, and its future development looks assured. We are very grateful for the confidence the administrators and panelists of the Marsden Fund demonstrated in our project.

Many individuals assisted directly and indirectly with the work represented in this volume. The authors have thanked some of them in the acknowledgments following the chapters. I should like to add some further names here: for assistance in obtaining illustrations we should like to thank Nancy and Bryan Tichborne (Banks Peninsula), Ian Smith (Dunedin), Lois Daish and Beverley Shore Bennett (Wellington), Greig Roulston, Heather Mathie and Jenni Chrisstoffels from the National Library and Alexander Turnbull Library (Wellington), Mary Lewis and the staff of the Hocken Collections (Dunedin), the Consumer and Applied Science Administration at the University of Otago (Dunedin) and Anne McEwan of the Nelson Provincial Museum. A large number of illustrations were scanned from my collection of cookbooks. I wish to extend my gratitude to the many generous donors who passed on cookbooks or procured them on my behalf from fairs and second-hand outlets. The Department of Anthropology at the University of Otago generously provided a base for the project. Finally, I should like to acknowledge the input of Wendy Harrex our publisher at Otago University Press, Georgina McWhirter, copy-editor, and Fiona Moffat, the book's designer.

HELEN LEACH
2010

PART I

The Macmillan Brown Lectures, 2008

1

Maori Cookery before Cook

Helen M. Leach

You have decided to put on a dinner party for some close friends. What are you going to cook? That's a much harder decision since the choice appears endless. But is it? I am certain you won't be offering a horse-meat ragout, nor back steaks from a dolphin. You won't be calling in at the local pet shop for some tender young guinea pigs or puppies. So why don't we consume meat from these animals? Your answer might be along the lines of 'we just don't eat dogs or dolphins' or 'they are not food'. Such a response may not be particularly rational, in view of the fact that at various times such creatures have been eaten and in various places still are, but to an anthropologist of food your words reveal the constraining power of your culinary tradition.

CULINARY TRADITIONS

What is a culinary tradition? Is it the same as a cuisine? Some would say yes, but the word cuisine has some additional connotations that can lead to misunderstandings. Cuisine, for many people, stands for haute cuisine. This is why historian Michael Freeman wrote provocatively 'It is usually agreed that Americans are without a cuisine, but that the French ... have one' (Freeman in Chang 1977:144). A French commentator, Jean-François Revel was more inclusive, believing that domestic cooking traditions were also a form of cuisine (Revel 1982:19–22, 267). Revel called them 'popular' cuisine, that is to say, belonging to the people. In contrast, the American anthropologist Sydney Mintz once alienated a roomful of American students by stating the same conclusion as Freeman: that there is no such thing as American cuisine, just remnants of ethnic and regional cuisines becoming debilitated by commercialisation. In his view, the defining and most commonly eaten dishes of middle-class America were items like quiche, pizza, chicken breasts, hamburgers, and peanut butter and jelly sandwiches, but he was most reluctant to call them collectively a 'cuisine' (Mintz 1996:114, 117). Nevertheless they are recognisably American and have infiltrated the food habits of many other countries. You may not want to call them representative dishes of a people's cuisine but they cannot be ignored.

The alternative label is culinary tradition. Under the names 'food culture', 'food style' and 'food tradition' the concept was developed by the American archaeologist Kwang-chih Chang in the introduction to his seminal book *Food in China*, published in 1977. He noted that the Chinese food tradition and its regional cuisines is first determined by the available raw materials, and second by the underlying binary principle for composing a meal – the *fan* component consists of the starch staples, usually rice, and the *ts'ai* component is the rest, predominantly meat and vegetables. This principle affects the processes of preparing food, as well as the types of utensils used in cooking and serving. The Chinese tradition is characterised by flexibility, allowing it to adjust to wealth or poverty; it is also typified by certain beliefs about health, food hierarchies, frugality and over-indulgence. In Chang's opinion, a Chinese cook sent into an American kitchen would still prepare a Chinese meal regardless of a lack of Chinese utensils and whether or not Chinese ingredients were available (Chang 1977:7–8). This is because food cultures incorporate rules and principles that we learn, often unconsciously, as we grow up. They are passed down from one generation to the next. They guide our decisions and mark our identity.

When I use the term culinary tradition, I divide these unwritten rules into two sets. The first set relates to foods, for example:

- what items are classified as edible (including staple foods, secondary items like vegetables, and flavourings);
- how foods should be combined into dishes;
- what equipment should be used to prepare and cook them;
- what is believed about the properties and symbolic meanings of these foods.

The second set of rules help in the composition of meals and include:

- what dishes should be served, in what combinations, with what drinks, and in what order for particular occasions;
- when and where meals should be served;
- with what utensils;
- how people should behave at meals.

When you start to plan your dinner party you will call on your own culinary tradition to help you make decisions about all these elements – not just about the items on the menu, but the way you will cook them, the portion sizes, how you will set the table, when you will ask your guests to arrive, and so on. Without our culinary tradition to help, we would be overwhelmed by the possible choices.

A culinary tradition combines edible items, material culture or artefacts, customs and ideas. And as with other cultural traditions, it undergoes progressive change as it adapts to changes in food supply, new technology, social trends, and external influences. My ancestors used to eat cockscombs and 'lambstones' (testicles) in eighteenth-century England. Changing tastes have relegated these to the historical dimension of our culinary tradition. If a people migrate, their culinary tradition moves with them, but it needs to adapt quickly to the new environment, for on it depends the survival of its practitioners.

OUTLINE

In these first three chapters, the culinary traditions of the two main peoples to settle in Aotearoa New Zealand will be explored. Because both groups were migrants from distant homelands, their culinary traditions were placed under great pressure. The first chapter will show the dramatic challenges successfully faced by Maori over the first 600 years as they learned to survive in a very different environment from the tropical Pacific islands. The second will examine the encounter of Maori and Pakeha in the nineteenth century and the effect on both culinary traditions. The twentieth century will be the subject of the third chapter. Whereas migrating peoples were the key players until 1900, subsequently the migration of ideas had the more significant impact on our culinary traditions, an impact that some have interpreted as obliteration. I hope to show, however, that culinary traditions are so deeply associated with a people's sense of identity that they are powerful agents of resistance. They are capable of swallowing the foods and dishes of other cultures and regurgitating them as their own!

MAORI ORIGINS

Maori are descendants of Polynesians who from homelands like Samoa had earlier explored and settled islands in the eastern Pacific, such as the Society Islands, the Cook Islands and the Austral Islands. Their culture is described by archaeologists as Ancestral East Polynesian and it could be found on all the larger islands of East Polynesia by A.D.1000, except for Aotearoa. Because of our distance from central

East Polynesia and the disposition of winds and currents, there was less chance of encountering Aotearoa than some of the other islands. But such was the spirit of exploration of the East Polynesians that they finally reached our shores. The current estimate is that first settlement took place in the thirteenth century – the Polynesian rat, dependent on human transport, was widespread by A.D.1280 and is believed to have spread rapidly through the country within a short period of its introduction (Wilmshurst et al. 2008). These people were no castaways. They regularly travelled with crops and domestic animals and the expectation that they would find a new island to colonise.

THE CULINARY TRADITION IN THE MAORI HOMELAND

Using the archaeological evidence from the possible homelands of the Maori, together with our knowledge of the food traditions of East Polynesia recorded by early European visitors, it is possible to sketch out the culinary tradition of the Maori ancestors just before their departure. We should start with their foods. Their homeland was most likely a small high island in the southeast corner of Central Eastern Polynesia, with a volcanic core and fringing reef, like Mangaia in the Cook Islands. Gardening and fishing provided most of their foods. A few centuries before, they had stocked it with an array of domesticated plants and animals. These included three important tree crops: the coconut, breadfruit, and various types of banana. They also brought the tropical cabbage tree, and some fruit and nut-bearing trees (Leach and Stowe 2005:11). Coconut trees were planted around their coastal villages, bananas on the edges of garden plots, and breadfruit and other fruit trees wherever the soil was rich – often on the floors of inland valleys. Some Polynesian islands looked forested to the first European visitors but were really managed plantations of useful trees.

Root crops complemented the tree crops, because they were ready to eat much sooner, and could be harvested in the seasons when tree fruits were unripe. The most important root crops were the taro and the tropical yams, especially the greater yam. Taro likes wetter growing conditions than the yam and some varieties were grown in stream-fed pond-fields. A relative newcomer from South America was the kumara, or sweet potato; it matured faster and was more tolerant of drought than the other root crops. Yams were the preferred provisions on oceanic sailing canoes (Leach 2005:69). Fire was used to prepare the ground for yams and kumara, in a process referred to as swiddening, or slash-and-burn. On a well-watered island, it was less destructive than it sounds. Oceanic gardeners had too much capital tied up in their tree crops to let them be burnt in a bush fire. However, drought-prone islands and those with dry leeward valleys saw the replacement of forest species on their slopes and ridges by ferns and wiry grasses following periodic fires.

Compared to the number of crop species, very few domesticated animals travelled with the Polynesians: just pigs, dogs, and chickens. In the Polynesian culinary tradition, as in some Asian traditions, dogs were considered good food. Rats came along as commensals and they, too, were sometimes on the menu. We can't be sure that the founding canoes that reached Aotearoa still retained the full quota of animals because there is no evidence that two, the pig and chicken, ever landed here. Several small high islands in southeast Polynesia have remains of pigs only in the earliest layers of their archaeological sites, indicating that they were later killed off (Leach 2003a:446), so it is possible that the ancestors of the Maori shared the view that pigs were difficult to contain and were destructive when feral. Since Polynesian gardening was much more extensive than what we practise, fencing the plots against pigs would have been a major task. The alternative was fencing the pigs, which meant that they had to be fed, instead of foraging for themselves.

In the early decades following settlement, these tropical islands provided variety of diet, in the form of land and seabirds, along with fruit bats. Many species suffered the same fate as some birds were to in New Zealand: either local or complete extinction or severe reduction in numbers. The sea offered greater sustainability in food supplies, especially where islands had extensive fringing reefs. Periodically however, tropical cyclones damaged reefs, coastal villages and gardens. Survivors had to rebuild and replant, and endure food shortages over several months. For these disasters, Polynesians called on their knowledge of famine foods, harvesting plants that were normally left to grow in the bush because of their bitter taste, and processing them in special ways. This knowledge was part of the invisible cargo on the founding canoes.

FOOD PRINCIPLES

Before looking at the preparation and cooking of Polynesian foods, it is important to set out their principles for composing a meal (Leach 1989:132–3). Like the Chinese, Oceanic peoples used a binary food-classification system. Nearly all communities classified their starchy foods as *kai*, a word that can be traced back over 5000 years. This term encompassed both root crops and the starchy fruits like bananas and breadfruit. *Kai* was considered the essential foundation, without which a meal was not a proper meal. This starch staple also formed the bulk of the meal, as in the case of a chief's dinner observed by Sir Joseph Banks in Tahiti – it consisted of two or three cooked breadfruit eaten with one or two small fish cooked in leaf wrappers, then fourteen or fifteen ripe bananas and seven *vi* apples, and finally a starchy pudding made from a pounded breadfruit base (Oliver 1974:220–21). This was a substantial meal, dominated by the carbohydrates in the *kai* portion, with the fish supplying most of the protein. It was accompanied by coconut milk, and the fish was seasoned with salt water. The Polynesian term for the part of the meal that was not *kai* was *kiki* or *kinaki* (or another variant of this word). Quantitatively it constituted the relish or trimmings of the meal, but nutritionally it served to balance it. The large quantity of complex carbohydrates in this meal would have left the chief feeling comfortably full. Not surprisingly this feeling was an important criterion for judging the quality of a Polynesian feast. As the great New Zealand anthropologist Raymond Firth wrote of the Tikopians, 'True hospitality consists in placing before a man more than he can possibly eat and then commanding him at intervals to continue when he shows signs of flagging' (Firth 1957:114).

On the second voyage, Captain Cook described a chiefly meal that he saw consumed on Huahine in the Society Islands: a pint of kava was drunk first, followed by bananas and baked fermented breadfruit, and finally three pints of a pudding made from starchy fruits. Of course 'pudding' was the name given to this dish by Captain Cook and his officers. There is no single Polynesian term for these concoctions, but their names are repeated from island to island, an indication that many of the recipes have an antiquity of a millennium or more (Su'a 1987). The base ingredient was a starchy fruit or root crop, or occasionally pit-fermented breadfruit. The root or fruit was either cooked then pounded until it was completely smooth, or it might be grated before cooking and then kneaded. Stone food pounders were manufactured on some islands, along with large wooden slabs to serve as anvils. Heavy wooden bowls were also carved; in them a liquid pudding mixture received its final stirring. In viscosity Polynesian puddings ranged from pastes to a batter. Once the mixture was homogeneous it was enriched with coconut cream or nut oil, extracted by wringing it out of grated coconut flesh. Puddings were usually served hot. The thicker pastes were cooked in leaf-wrapped parcels in an earth oven, while more liquid puddings were cooked either in coconut shells in the oven or in a wooden bowl into which red-hot stones were dropped. Because of the work involved in preparing a pudding, they were frequently reserved for feasts, heads of households or other high-ranking people.

Feasts were normally the only occasions on which pigs, dogs or turtles were cooked. For successful cooking, these required large earth ovens, heat-retaining oven stones and much fuel. On many islands, women were not permitted to eat the resulting delicacies. Commoners' meals consisted of chunks of baked *kai* with a small *kinaki* of fish, shellfish, or greens. Ovens for daily meals were shallower, used fewer stones and might not even be covered by earth. Old mats were sometimes sufficient. Preparation of ordinary oven *kai* involved peeling or scraping the outer skin of the root or fruit, wrapping the chunks in large leaves and placing them in a small pre-heated oven. Some leaf-wrapped parcels of seafood might also be included, but fish was commonly broiled on a stick thrust into the ground beside a small scoop hearth containing glowing ashes. No pots were used in East Polynesian cooking after initial settlement, although earthenware pots had been part of the early West Polynesian kitchen of their ancestors. Stone potboilers dropped into a wooden bowl could heat a liquid through but not cook a solid chunk of taro, let alone a leg of pork (Leach 2007:53–4).

To a European, there seems to be more emphasis in the Polynesian culinary tradition on texture and the power to fill, than on flavour. No spices were observed, but that does not mean that the food was bland. Preserved breadfruit paste (known as *masi* or *ma*) became very acidic in the underground *ma* pits, and candlenuts also contributed a strong-flavored condiment. What we underestimate is the capacity of the leaf-wrappers and leafy oven partitions to impart a flavour to the food baked within them. For example the *nonu* tree, whose leaves were used in ovens throughout Polynesia, is lemon-scented, as evidenced by its botanical name *Morinda citrifolia*.

EARLY ADJUSTMENTS IN AOTEAROA

For whatever reason East Polynesians were undertaking voyages of colonisation a millennium ago, the remarkable fact for me is that those who reached Aotearoa stayed. Their large voyaging canoes were perfectly capable of return trips. As gardeners and cooks they must have experienced losses that were utterly disheartening. Let's suppose that they arrived in springtime in the welcoming arc between East Cape and Cape Reinga (as an autumn or winter landfall would probably have wiped out most of the crops). They had been used to a warm, humid climate with a temperature range between twenty and thirty degrees Celsius. What they found here were cooler nights than they had previously but ideal daytime temperatures for their crops – many parts of New Zealand can exceed thirty degrees on a summer's day. They planted their crops as the days lengthened, making sure that the taro was in the damp areas behind the dunes, and that the rest of the crops were in rich well-drained soils in coastal valley mouths. After a few months, the weather took a turn for the worse. Temperatures plummeted at night and they had their first experience of the white killer, frost. At this point their edible tree crops were fatally damaged, with just one exception, the tropical cabbage tree that could re-sprout from its underground taproot. Their yams and kumara showed withered tops but they could be lifted and stored in a house or pit until the weather improved. Yams die down naturally in tropical dry seasons, so there were precedents for lifting them and packing them into storehouses.

It is hard to appreciate the extent of their losses. Two of the lost tree crops, breadfruit and bananas, had been important providers of starchy *kai*, and the coconut had been the key ingredient in Polynesian puddings. It would be like removing potatoes, wheat and dairy foods from our modern diet and telling us to 'get on with it' (Leach 1987:22). However, three root crops survived this drastic relocation from the tropics to temperate Aotearoa – kumara, taro and yam – mainly because they reached maturity in from five to eight months. The bottle gourd coped for the same reason, while the tropical cabbage tree hung on in frost-free locations. Most crops were restricted to northern regions. Only the kumara succeeded further south, and its limit was Banks Peninsula (Leach 1984:69). Devising storage facilities such as pits and raised storehouses was the key to the remarkable persistence of Polynesian gardening in this country.

While the crops shrivelled and turned black in the unexpected winter cold, the people shivered. They had to make rapid improvements in housing and clothing to prevent hypothermia. Why they didn't abandon their colony and sail north is worth considering, for no other stone-age gardeners have ever successfully moved in a single migration out of the tropics or sub-tropics into a temperate landmass. In one bold voyage they had transported themselves, animals and crops at least thirteen crucial degrees of latitude. Then, not content with that step, they planted their crops and carried on exploring. Within a short time some of the founding group had built small villages in Murihiku, further south, adding a further ten degrees of latitude to their distance from their tropical homeland.

Three beneficial factors need to be taken into consideration, though they in no way diminish the achievement. The first is that the Polynesians had already demonstrated a powerful drive to expand and to colonise the eastern Pacific (Anderson 2002:32). The second is that they had a biological advantage over most tropical peoples. The open ocean that was the Polynesians' highway and

Of all the energy-giving plants that the ancestors of the Maori had grown in tropical Polynesia, only three root crops survived in temperate Aotearoa: the taro (top), kumara (centre) and greater yam (bottom). Of these, only the kumara could be grown in cooler regions, and then only as far south as Banks Peninsula. From H. Leach, *1,000 Years of Gardening in New Zealand* (1984), illustrations by Nancy Tichborne.

21

a source of some of their food is characterised by a high wind-chill factor. The biological anthropologist, Philip Houghton argued that in the course of their voyages, these seafarers were selected for their physiological ability to withstand the cold. Their physique was significantly larger and more muscular than is normally seen in people living in continental tropical regions (Houghton 1996). To them, a winter's night in Tamaki may not have felt much colder than a storm at sea in the tropics. The third factor relates to food. Humans living in high latitude areas where there are few wild plant foods derive much of the energy they burn to keep their bodies warm from fats and oils obtained from animals. The insulating blubber of sea mammals, and the seasonal body fat of land mammals and birds were vital sources to groups living in sub-arctic and sub-antarctic regions. Aotearoa offered what would have seemed like unlimited quantities of seals and large flightless birds in compensation for its cooler climate. Animals like sea mammals that were reserved for high-ranking men in the tropics were so plentiful here that everyone could partake. The cold winter temperatures and energy expended on hunting required a higher intake of kilocalories than in the tropics, but in the thirteenth century this land was awash with fuel, in the form of high energy fats and oils for human consumption and unlimited firewood to heat their houses.

Archaeologists working on New Zealand sites, especially in the south, have found that the ovens of early Maori are often larger than those of their tropical cousins. They had to have sufficient hot stones to cook large joints of moa or seal, as well as a thicker insulation of earth to maintain the temperature inside while the meat cooked. Smaller ovens for cooking kumara or fish continued to be made throughout the prehistoric period, as well as shallow hearths for spit-roasting small birds and opening shellfish. French observers described three cooking techniques for fish practised in the Bay of Islands in 1772. One was to wrap the fish in leaves and place them directly on the embers in a shallow hearth; another was to impale the fish on a stick and broil it; the third method, which was also applied to root crops, was to make a hole 45–60 cm across and 23–26 cm deep, build a fire in it to preheat the pit and oven stones, scrape out the embers, insert the fish in its wrappers, then cover it with earth and hot stones (Ollivier 1985:321–3). The dimensions of this oven are comparable to those in tropical village sites, but much smaller than those in early moa and seal hunters' villages. We can thus see that the basic cooking methods of the Polynesian culinary tradition were transplanted to Aotearoa, and where necessary adjusted for larger joints of meat and cooler surrounding temperatures.

Ovens made by the early Maori, such as this one excavated by Atholl Anderson and his team at the fourteenth-century village of Shag River Mouth (Otago), were often much larger than those of the tropics, in keeping with the massive joints of moa and sea mammal cooked in them. Courtesy Ian Smith, Anthropology Department, University of Otago.

Large-leaved plants suitable for wrapping food parcels were more common in the far north (Leach 2007:55–6) because their distribution is normally correlated with warm growing conditions. In the south the 'leaves' of the giant bull kelp provided a substitute. The family whom Cook encountered in Dusky Sound in 1773 cooked some of their fish in a kelp bag placed over a hardwood grill (Salmond 1997:57). A widely used alternative to a leaf wrapper or bag was a woven basket (Taylor 1855:392).

THE FATE OF THE PUDDING

You might expect that with the loss of three key ingredients in Polynesian puddings, coconut, breadfruit and bananas, this ancient type of dish would cease to be made and fade from memory. Captain Cook and his scientists didn't see any elaborate puddings being made in New Zealand, as they had in Tahiti. It was not until people began to record the Maori language more systematically and collect artefacts throughout the country that evidence of the continuation of the pudding emerged. Until recently we didn't realise the significance of the large carved wooden bowls and the heavy pounders from regions such as Taranaki. Few nineteenth-century scholars

23

undertook comparative linguistics, but one who did, Edward Tregear, noticed that Maori had a dish of mashed kumara whose name *roroi* was a cognate of one of the pudding names of tropical Polynesia, Samoan *loloi* (Tregear 1891:421). The Maori term was recorded in 1820, when the Northland missionary Thomas Kendall translated *roroi* as a sort of pudding (Kendall 1820:204), then in 1848 Richard Taylor (1848:101) described it as a 'kind of pudding formed of mashed kumara or potato'. Another missionary, the Reverend William Yate, saw a mixture being made up by a Maori cook from the flower bracts of the epiphyte kiekie (*Freycinetia banksii*) scraped and beaten to a pulp, some peaches and onions chopped up with a hatchet, some cooked potatoes and kumara, fuchsia berries and tutu juice, pig brains, some lard or seal oil, and some sugar. The ingredients were assembled in a piece of hollowed wood and then kneaded to a pulp with the hands (Yate 1835:111). Note the presence of the starchy root crops, and the lubricating ingredients, pig fat or seal oil and pig brains, which served as a substitute for coconut. Note also the finished texture achieved by kneading, and the hollowed wood serving as the bowl. Structurally, this was still a Polynesian pudding.

THE CARBOHYDRATE SHORTAGE

In comparison to their cousins on tropical islands, the early Maori had an abundance of animal food, so there was no question of any lack of protein or lipids in their diet. However the first settlers of Aotearoa were adapted to a regime that was based on carbohydrates from plant sources, and this was enshrined in the Polynesian *kai-kinaki* food classification. It was not starvation that faced these migrants but an unexpected shortage of palatable, filling, starchy tubers and fruits. With the tree crops succumbing to the cold, and the root crops having to be acclimatised to long summer days and provided with new types of insulated storage in the winter, it was very hard to put together the sort of meal that had daily sustained their ancestors for several thousand years. As I have shown, the foundations of tropical meals were chunks of starchy vegetables and fruits, while the flesh foods were the *kinaki* supplement. Large joints or whole animals were feast foods. For the Polynesian settlers of Aotearoa, every meal became a feast, until they began to crave the carbohydrates that had been their staple. For me, the equivalent torture would be serving me roast beef on its own for breakfast, baked fish for lunch, and barbecued chicken for dinner, day after day, week after week. In no time I would be begging for potatoes, rice or pasta. An added torment for the early Maori would have been to save enough of their kumara, taro and yams for replanting the following spring (Leach 1987:22). Even when the kumara had been adapted by selection for early maturing, followed by long storage, it was still not prolific enough to feed Maori in the North Island throughout the year, and was only available in Murihiku through trade and exchange. Taro and yam were even less tolerant of our temperate climate.

There was a solution, and it was already part of the Polynesian culinary tradition: to seek out wild or feral plants containing the scarce nutrients. On tropical islands the forest concealed arrowroot and coarse relatives of the taro and yam, which remained unharvested until a cyclone or drought affected food supplies. These plants needed special processing because of high levels of irritating or bitter substances in their flesh. There were also endemic tree ferns on the high volcanic islands that contained sugars or starches in their trunks and taproots. These were subjected to prolonged cooking. To accommodate the necessary quantity of oven stones, huge ovens were constructed up in the bush, a practice recorded for preparation of both the tropical cabbage tree for religious ceremonies, and the tree fern during food shortages. In the Marquesas Islands, the short-trunked tree fern known as *nahei* was baked for over twenty-four hours in such an oven. In his colorful account of 1799, the Reverend Crook wrote that

> Larger Stones are put into the Oven, for this purpose, than for any other. All the Wood of a large tree is laid underneath, and set on fire, when the whole is prepared. The heat is so intense, that the nearest trees are scorched, and their branches destroyed thereby. Sometimes, after the Oven is covered over, it bursts, and makes a report like a Cannon. (Crook 1799:67–8)

As the Maori ancestors searched the forests of the north for similar foods to relieve their cravings for sugars and starch, they came across one familiar fern, the *para*, the same species (*Marattia salicina*) as was used during times of scarcity in the Cook Islands, the Marquesas and Tahiti. The base of the petioles are the edible part, but the fern is hard to find in dense bush. They also encountered numerous tree ferns. Only two could be rendered palatable, both belonging to the genus *Cyathea*. The black tree fern (*Cyathea medullaris*) they named *mamaku* after its edible tropical relatives. Cook's botanist, Johann Forster thought it 'tasted like a Turnep or rather better'. The European explorers Charles Heaphy and Thomas Brunner were forced by hunger to prepare *mamaku* on four occasions on the West Coast and complained bitterly of the long wait before they could eat it: twelve hours for cooking and then a further twelve hours for the pulp to consolidate and cool (Leach 2003b:142–4). In comparison to *mamaku*, they found the *katote* (*Cyathea smithii*) was only just palatable and far from satisfying.

One tropical cultigen not mentioned earlier was the sugar cane. It failed to grow in Aotearoa, adding a further incentive to the search for substitutes. Young endemic cabbage trees (*Cordyline australis*) provided a labour-intensive alternative. Instead of chewing the freshly cut stems of sugar cane for a sweet treat, the only way of releasing the sugar in a cabbage tree is to cook its stems and taproots for at least as long as a tree fern, in a similar-sized oven. Archaeologists find clusters of large rimmed oven pits in many eastern regions where cabbage trees would have been more at home than *mamaku*. When cut open, the cooked stems of *ti* reveal crystals of fructose in a mesh of fibres: a light, high-energy food of special value to travelers (Leach 1986:134).

There were few other sweet foods to be found in Aotearoa. Sucking the nectar from flax flowers, or consuming fuchsia, bush lawyer or various *Coprosma* berries could never be more than a snack. What was needed was a plant where the sugars were easily extracted. As forest gave way to bracken after bush fires, a shrubby species also took advantage of the additional light, and was equally resistant to further firing. This was the tutu (*Coriaria* spp.) that tested Maori perseverance to the maximum. When it flowers in summer, the sepals appear like luscious berries, full of sweet wine-coloured juice. It would have been discovered at an early stage that though the juice is delicious, every other part of the tutu plant contains the deadly poisonous substance known as tutin, including the leaves, flower stalks and seeds. The death of family members following convulsions and paralysis should have deterred all subsequent trials of this plant, but remarkably it did not. Maori discovered that by straining the berries through a finely woven bag, the toxic parts could be separated from the delicious juice. Tutu juice became a highly valued ingredient in Maori puddings. Those of us who have inherited the Pakeha culinary tradition treat every wild plant as poisonous unless our mothers tell us that we can eat it. We should not assume that this maxim applied in the Polynesian tradition. I believe that the opposite principle was in operation throughout Polynesia: that every plant is potentially edible if you can work out how to process it.

Other toxic and indigestible plants were encountered in the Maori search for carbohydrate-rich foods, and one of these posed as much of a risk as tutu. Yet this fruit, the karaka kernel (*Corynocarpus laevigatus*), became so important in Maori cookery that seedling karaka trees were moved around the country and planted beside settlements, as far south as the limits of kumara gardening on Banks Peninsula. Botanist Chris Stowe and I have argued that the Maori began the process of domesticating this native tree, seeing it as a nutritious substitute

To compensate for the failure of tropical crops in many parts of Aotearoa, Maori harvested the starchy rhizomes of the wild bracken fern (top) and extracted sugar from the stems and taproots of young cabbage trees (bottom). From H. Leach, *1,000 Years of Gardening in New Zealand* (1984), illustrations by Nancy Tichborne.

27

for some of the tropical nuts lost in the relocation to Aotearoa (Leach and Stowe 2005). Untreated karaka kernels contain the bitter glucoside karakin that kills in a similar way to tutin. The bitterness was the danger signal to which early Maori responded, for they had a repertoire of techniques that had been used to detoxify bitter plants in the tropics. The first step was to subject the fruit to prolonged cooking, which broke down the karakin. Then baskets of cooked kernels were placed in a pool formed by damming a running stream. Over a period of weeks the dangerous compound dissolved and was washed out of the kernels. The result was a strong-tasting, mealy product, quite high in starch, protein and fat (B.F. Leach 2006:238). Maori did not need to try these foods out on dogs, or slaves, given their existing knowledge of detoxification of tropical plants.

The palatability of other tree fruits, like that of the tawa (*Beilschmiedia tawa*), was improved by removal of the exterior pulp and then cooking of the kernel for twelve to forty-eight hours. The product could then be stored for long periods and when required, reheated and pounded into a mealy paste in a heavy wooden bowl (Leach 1986:134). In the case of the hinau (*Elaeocarpus dentatus*), it was the hard stone that had to be removed, usually by long soaking before the oily flesh was turned into a storable meal or pre-cooked cakes. These cakes were sometimes placed under water to undergo anaerobic fermentation. The acid formed in this step contributed to their preservation.

I have left the most important source of carbohydrate for last. It was not recognised as toxic, but it exacted a massive toll on the dental health of Maori nevertheless. This plant was the bracken fern (*Pteridium esculentum*). We now know that its fiddleheads can be poisonous in some regions of the country, but the Maori were chiefly interested in bracken's underground rhizomes (Leach 2001; McGlone et al. 2005). There was no tropical fern that provided a guide for this practice. The Maori name *aruhe* was borrowed from an inedible fern in tropical Polynesia that springs up like bracken after forest is burned (Leach 2003b:150–52). The discovery that the Maori *aruhe* accumulates starch in its underground parts was made here, along with the basic techniques for processing it. The bracken transfers starch into its root system as the days shorten and the foliage dies down. If the dead fronds are burned in spring, the new shoots guide harvesters to the plant's energy stores beneath the surface. Maori dried the fernroot before it was consumed. Cooking the rhizomes was not difficult. They were dipped in water then briefly roasted in a scoop hearth, before being placed on an anvil stone and beaten with a light wooden implement. After being kneaded with the fingers, the mass of starch and fibre was chewed to dissolve the starch. At this stage the grit that wore down Maori teeth may have been already present on the dried roots, or else it stuck to them as they roasted in the hearth. After chewing, each diner spat out unwanted fibre into a basket. For a special occasion, the starch was extracted by soaking the roasted roots in water in a bowl and decanting the liquid. The gelatinous result was formed into a cake or pudding, just as arrowroot starch had been processed in tropical Polynesia. It was as close as Maori would come to refined carbohydrates until they encountered Pakeha cereals.

As archaeologists have quantified the animal remains left in Maori sites throughout Aotearoa, and examined the trends in consumption from the thirteenth to the eighteenth centuries, a picture of significant dietary change has emerged (Smith 2004). Early Maori settlers had obtained much of their energy from animal sources, especially sea mammals and birds. But in the north, a growing human population increased the effects of predation and accelerated habitat change. Moa became extinct and seal colonies retreated to inaccessible coasts. Fishing provided a substitute source of protein, but few fish could equal birds or seals as a source of high-energy fats. Carbohydrates were now even more important to balance the diet and restore the *kai-kinaki* division of the meal. Gardens were a critical investment in *kai*, along with the storage structures that protected crops over winter. But the food stores themselves needed protection – not just from the weather, but also from enemies. In the fortified pa built in many North Island regions, pits outnumber the house terraces. People could slip away from an attack under cover of darkness, but several tonnes of kumara were not so easily moved. Iwi who lost their crops or access to land suitable for intensive gardening became even more dependent on fernroot and other wild plants of swamps, scrubland and forests.

The Polynesian culinary tradition had provided the early Maori with a broad guide to what might be edible in Aotearoa, and of techniques for making them so. In this respect the tradition equipped them with skills vital for their survival. At the same time, it emphasised a food classification system that was to prove very hard to follow in a colder climate. Undoubtedly Maori determination to grow tropical root crops in a temperate landmass was linked to their concept of a proper meal, based on the *kai* of their ancestors. The pudding survived for the same reason, though in a barely recognisable form. That same culinary tradition ensured that the rules of hospitality applied even when food was seasonally scarce. It encouraged the accumulation of supplies of preserved food, and forward planning. Nowhere are these principles better demonstrated than in the *pepeha* or sayings of the Maori that elevated the role of a food producer over that of a warrior, praised hard work and condemned gluttony. I will finish with a *pepeha* recorded a century ago that is still sound advice:

Kai atu, whakairi atu ki te paataka
Eat heartily and hang some away in the storehouse
(Mead and Grove 2001:157)

2

Cookery in the Colonial Era (1769–1899)

Helen M. Leach

The year 1769 saw the first encounters between English culture and that of the Maori. Just over a hundred British men and boys on Cook's ship *Endeavour* interacted with groups of Maori people living at various settlements on the northeastern coasts of New Zealand. Though there were occasions when the old phrase, 'the clash of cultures', was an apt description of what occurred, for much of the time curiosity and conjecture prevailed on both sides. One Maori eyewitness from Whitianga described the speculation among his elders as to whether the white-skinned visitors were supernatural beings called *tipua*. When rowing they appeared to have eyes at the back of their heads, but like normal people they ate kumara, fish and cockles given to them by the Maori women and children (Salmond 1991:87). The food habits of the Maori were of equal interest to the British scientists and crew. They speculated whether the Maori camping at nearby Purangi River were eating roasted fernroot, fish and shellfish because they had been defeated in war and lost their provisions. Eighteenth-century Englishmen did not classify their related bracken species as edible, though the fiddleheads were known to have served as famine food in rural areas (Leach 2001:31–2). Both sides engaged in intense cross-cultural observations, with food and eating the centre of attention. At the same time the records of their contact that have been passed down as oral tradition or documents also reveal a great deal about their own attitudes to food.

In the first chapter I introduced the concept of a culinary tradition, that part of a culture that guides what we choose to eat, how we prepare it, how we compose our meals and think about them. Just apply Joe Bennett's no frills definition of culture in what he calls 'the true sense of the word' to its component food habits and you will understand the role of a culinary tradition: it's 'what people do because it's what people do, stuff that they do unconsciously' (Bennett 2008:23). The way we classify and rank foods – though seldom a topic of conversation around the table – is an integral part of every culinary tradition, helping to maintain its identity over the centuries. Previously I described how nearly all Polynesian cultures, including the Maori, used the term *kai* to refer to the essential starch basis of their meals. *Kai* might be breadfruit, bananas, taro, yams or kumara, but what each supplied was carbohydrate, an essential component in all human diets. In the eighteenth century, English-speaking peoples used a different classificatory system that ranked meat the highest, but regarded bread as the staple. So important was bread at all levels of society that its name came to stand for food in general. In the Lord's Prayer, 'Give us today our daily bread' has always stood for more than a loaf of bread.

In this chapter I will outline how, following first contact, the Maori added a new set of energy-rich plants to their traditional *kai* and how, until the middle of the nineteenth century, Maori entrepreneurs played a major role in the supply of food to Pakeha. Maori adopted European cooking technology, at the same time maintaining ancient Polynesian cooking methods. While they were numerically dominant, their culinary tradition was strengthened and enriched by contact with Europeans. In contrast, early Pakeha settlers had to revert to the cooking technology and practices of their great-grandparents. Gentlewomen had to learn how to bake bread and cakes, and preserve fruit. Supplies of basic commodities often ran low. To cope, these pioneers became rather more receptive to the culinary traditions of other colonial peoples than to those of their homeland. As the two populations drew level in size during the 1850s, the Maori gains turned into losses. Pakeha settlers began to catch up with their British cousins and with respect to the price and quality of produce, to move ahead. But how far would they go in culinary terms towards making New Zealand the Britain of the south?

EIGHTEENTH-CENTURY ATTITUDES TO 'BREAD'

My story begins with bread. There are two passages in the journals from Cook's first two voyages that provide a memorable if repulsive view of British and Maori attitudes to 'bread'. In the first, Sir Joseph Banks shows us that good science can override disgust. The bread that was taken on board the *Endeavour* to supply the ship's company had been pre-baked up to four times, and packed into casks. It took the form of ship's biscuits and better-quality cabin biscuits for officers.

Unfortunately what Banks referred to as 'vermin' infested the total supply during the voyage. He wrote: 'I have seen hundreds nay thousands shaken out of a single bisket'. In the Great Cabin where he had his quarters, there was an oven, where applying a low heat encouraged the vermin to 'walk off' the biscuits. But passengers elsewhere on the ship had to put up with the strong taste of the insects, which Banks likened to mustard or hartshorn. As a true scientist, Banks identified five culprits and made observations concerning their preferences for different types of biscuit (Salmond 1991:102–3; Leach 2007:59). Biologists think that four were actual flour-eating tenebrionid and Ptinidae beetles, while the fifth, a pseudoscorpion, was eating the beetles (Beaglehole 1962:393 fn.2). The dentition of most eighteenth-century sailors was not sound enough for crunching on hard tack, as these biscuits were called. Instead they were pre-soaked or broken up to add to stews, sea pies and gruels. This treatment killed the wild life though left their remains for consumption.

On the second voyage, the ship's biscuit suffered from an additional problem. Because it had been packed into newly made 'green' casks, it became mouldy and began to rot (Forster 2000:271). When this serious state of affairs was discovered, a portable copper oven was taken on shore in Queen Charlotte Sound and the biscuits were re-baked. But some were too far gone. Even the ship's pigs would not touch them. In the words of the botanist, George Forster (2000:282), 'the natives immediately repaired to the beach which we had left, and finding there a heap of bread-dust which had been rejected as unfit for use … they fell to, and consumed it all.' There was clearly some speculation as to why, but the scientists ruled out hunger because the local Maori had plenty of fish. Perhaps the attraction was novelty? Only later would nutrition science discover that people forced to adopt a diet with few available carbohydrates can develop a craving for starch. To Maori, the biscuit dust was a gift of *kai*, a pile of concentrated carbohydrate.

NEW CROPS, NEW *KAI*

These eighteenth-century records reveal the value placed on starchy foods in our two main culinary traditions, as well as the difficulties of interpreting other cultures' tastes and food habits. The story does not stop there. European maritime explorers commonly distributed the seeds or tubers of potential food crops to native peoples, either as gifts to chiefs, or by making model gardens to demonstrate how the plants should be grown. Their objectives were to improve the resources of the islands, both for the natives and future European visitors (Leach 1983). Starchy crops predominated. In 1769, the French explorer de Surville tried to introduce wheat, peas and rice to Doubtless Bay, almost at the same time as Captain Cook was handing over potatoes to a chief in Mercury Bay. Within two years, Marion du Fresne had planted a model garden in the Bay of Islands, with wheat, maize, potatoes and various nuts. On Cook's second voyage, model gardens were cleared and planted in five locations in Queen Charlotte Sound, and one in Dusky Sound. An even greater range of plants was introduced, including wheat. Cook was wise enough to inform local Maori that the potatoes were a sort of kumara, and there are grounds to believe that both his potato introductions succeeded. Of the other vegetables, the cabbage and the turnips self-sowed and reverted to wild forms which then spread rapidly without further human assistance. The wheat failed, probably because Maori had no familiarity with growing a small-seeded cereal and were initially unaware that it was the source of flour, the key ingredient of bread.

Records show that by 1801 there were fields of potatoes near Thames and by 1810, on the shores of Foveaux Strait. By 1806 we know that Bay of Islands Maori were trading potatoes to European ships. Maize was growing in their gardens by 1815, along with turnips, cabbages and the traditional crops of kumara, taro, yams and gourds. One mixed garden reported by Marsden was 40 acres (or 16 hectares) in extent (Leach 1984:101).

At this stage the Maori economy was benefiting from the new crops, and they were being integrated into the Maori culinary tradition in ingenious ways. Cabbages provided leaf wrappers for Maori cooks and were initially called *puka* after the large-leafed native tree (Savage 1807:60). Turnips were dried and preserved in exactly the same way as young kumara tubers were converted into the delicacy *kao* (Thomson 1859 I:159). Vegetable marrows were treated like gourds and turned into containers (Polack 1838 I:291). Cobs of maize were already pre-wrapped, so could be roasted in the ashes while still green. This technique was not suited to mature corn cobs, so another traditional method was adapted from the process applied to hinau and karaka fruit: anaerobic fermentation under water. When required the softened cobs were baked, made up into cakes, or boiled into gruel, named *kanga pirau* (Leach 1999:133). Europeans found the smell disgusting, but Maori valued this food highly, and it is made to the present day.

Maori still ranked kumara highest, and taro was also esteemed where the climate was warm enough for it to grow. At the same time as Maori were adopting new crops, they acquired new varieties of kumara and taro from around the Pacific. Potatoes being much hardier and more sought after by Pakeha were economically important, but seem not to have been considered as good to eat as the traditional crops. There were occasions where fernroot may have been consumed in preference to potatoes, though the explanation could be that while your last potatoes could be sold to Pakeha, they would not consume dried fernroot (Leach 2001:37–8). In some parts of New Zealand, Maori continued to use bracken until the late nineteenth century, during lean seasons and when traveling. It weighed much less than potatoes.

COOKING TECHNOLOGY: PAKEHA LOSSES, MAORI GAINS

The culinary tradition of the first missionary settlers in the Bay of Islands was English. Before their arrival Maori sampled a naval version of this tradition, dominated by salted foods cooked in large copper boilers. They showed no liking for either the salted beef or the seamen's alcoholic beverages (Leach 2007:57). Only flour-based foods like ship's biscuit appealed. When the domestic version of the English tradition was introduced by the missionary wives, it was a pale reflection of that of Regency London. By the 1820s, England's industrial revolution had reached the kitchens of the middle classes; they could purchase iron ranges, improved ovens, and had ample coal supplies to run them. Until the new technology and its infrastructure could be introduced to New Zealand, all migrants had to return to the more primitive cookery formerly practised by their ancestors, or still used by remote communities along Britain's western fringe. This technological regression occurred throughout New Zealand and in some rural areas lasted many decades. It meant that the first settlers could not install built-in spit-roasting devices, nor iron ranges. Until they had solid chimneys, New Zealand's pioneer settlers reverted to hearth cookery, using three-legged cauldrons and camp ovens. Once they had brick or masonry chimneys, they installed chimney cranes, hooks and chains, more typical of eighteenth-century rural Britain than Regency England. Even the Otago settlers who arrived in 1848 had to revert to hearth cookery during their first decade in the new township of Dunedin. Fiona Crawford's (2006) study of imports to the port of Otago documented the arrival of hundreds of camp ovens during the 1850s, a figure that increased as soon as gold was discovered in 1861. However as more permanent houses were built, with brick or stone chimneys, those who could afford to imported iron ranges from America, Australia and Britain until local production began in the 1870s.

To make life even more difficult for the pioneering women, they had to learn how to make their own bread. Most English towns had baker's shops that not only supplied bread, but would also cook dishes such as cakes and pies for people who lacked a suitable oven at home. The missionary wives had to learn how to keep yeast alive between bakings, how to knead, rest, and shape loaves and convert their cooking pots into ovens (Leach 2007:63). Marianne Williams reported in 1823 that she had 'been taking lessons … in making bread from leaven' (by which she meant a piece of dough saved from an earlier batch), and she regretted not having brought a bottle of yeast with her from Australia (Fitzgerald 2004:59). Five years later she had her own yeast barm, started with some brewing yeast and fed with flour and sugar. By that stage Marianne had a bread oven, but her Maori servant Fanny used an upturned iron pot on a hot hearth to bake her bread, just as Marianne had done as a new arrival. Marianne would not eat Maori bread, and made the revealing comment: 'We cannot fancy their fingers in our bread or they might save us much time and trouble' (Fitzgerald 2004:146). As an alternative to a brick oven, when there were no bricks, some settlers carved out bread ovens in clay banks (Porter 1974:93; [Pratt] 1877:196).

The uneven development of towns meant that many New Zealanders continued to bake their own bread during the nineteenth century. The simplest form of bread was unleavened damper, probably of Australian origin, which could be cooked in embers or in a traveler's frypan. Yeasted bread symbolised settling down, and when New Zealand newspapers began publication, instructions for making bread and keeping a yeast culture alive were provided both by correspondents and the newspapers themselves. Writing to the *Nelson Examiner* in October, 1850, W.T.L.T. [William Travers] stated that 'families residing at a distance from Nelson are frequently put to great inconvenience by the want of barm, and that in the Wairau bread is rather a luxury than an article of general consumption.' He then offered advice on feeding and storing barm, and creating a substitute from beer (*Nelson Examiner and New Zealand Chronicle* 9(452):140). Flour shortages and bakers' prices encouraged the addition of mashed potatoes to bread dough (as recommended by 'A Bakers' Terror' in the *Tuapeka Times* 2(93):3), in November 1869).

The missionaries had discovered that even though initial Maori attempts to grow wheat had failed, and though they lacked the equipment to mill it, this in no way diminished Maori taste for flour. In 1828, rations of second-grade flour from Sydney were offered as an incentive for Maori to stay at Paihia mission station in the Bay of Islands, where they were receiving religious and practical education. Iron pots were still relatively rare in Maori ownership, and it is possible that the thin paste in which this flour ration was eaten was uncooked. By the 1830s, Maori had acquired more pots, often in part payment for land, and this meant that boiled flour and water paste became an esteemed dish, especially with added sugar. It was quicker and easier to prepare than bread. The trader Joel Polack (1838 II:64) recorded both Maori and Pakeha names for this dish: 'stirabout or kororidori'.

Outdoor cookery was still the norm at the Maori settlement of Te Punaomaru, Waitaki (sketched here by Walter Mantell in October 1848), although the utensils were of European manufacture.
With permission of the Alexander Turnbull Library, Wellington, New Zealand, Ref. No. C–103–078.

Kororirori, the Maori name, refers to the stirring of the dish. Like many Polynesian puddings, it acquired its name from the action involved in preparation (Williams 1844:50). Its ceremonial importance suggests it was no mere imitation of a seaman's stirabout, but regarded as the latest in a long line of Polynesian puddings, taking advantage of two ingredients, flour and sugar, from which someone else had removed the fibre, rendering them homogeneous. The Pakeha name, stirabout, may have originated in Ireland, Scotland or America – but it was not an English term. My pick would be America, because of the regular arrival of American ships in the Bay of Islands. Intriguingly, Marianne Williams' recipe for a Pound Ginger Cake (Fitzgerald 2004:252) contained two ingredients, molasses and saleratus (an early raising agent), which point to an American source in the 1830s. In Britain, molasses was invariably termed treacle.

For Maori who participated in seasonal movements around their tribal land, the camp oven was a versatile device. Like the cauldron, it could stand securely on its three feet over hot embers, or be hung by its lugs from a chain on a tripod. It could be transported on canoes or carried on a back frame. Large iron pots served as ovens for bread, and boilers for pork and potatoes, and puddings. They did not replace

P.J. Hogan del. Colonial Hospital. Scotch Church. St. Paul's Church. Barracks

VIEW

the *umu*, or earth oven, but added another method for cooking everyday meals that may have been more economical on fuel than a hangi. While Pakeha invested in built-in ovens to improve their bread supply, Maori perfected the art of baking bread in camp ovens. They worked with a variety of yeast starters and improvers including unsalted potatoes, shredded flax, and ale. We enjoy the legacy of their experiments to the present day in the form of Maori bread (Fuller 1978:25–6).

INCREASING SELF-SUFFICIENCY

Importation of flour from American or Australian ports was essential for many decades, and when it ran out between shipments there was great distress for the colonists (Drummond and Drummond 1967:47; Petrie 2006:82–3). Potatoes were not an adequate substitute, though, as I have shown, they could eke out dwindling flour supplies. A Nelson settler, W.T. Pratt, found that he could not sustain himself on an exclusive potato diet for more than a fortnight before physical weakness set

Wesleyan Chapel.   St Matthew's School.   R.C.Church.   Ford & West Imp.

KLAND.

Maori supplied large quantities of food to Auckland settlers by canoe and sailing vessel during the 1840s and 1850s. From William Swainson, *Auckland, the Capital of New Zealand* ... (1853), frontispiece.

in ([Pratt] 1877:105). The sacrifice of a pig cured the symptoms on one occasion, but Pratt craved flour.

As missionaries struggled with wheat crops, cumbersome hand-mills and home baking, their techniques were closely observed by Maori. The erection of a water-powered mill at Waimate North in 1834 provided the final lesson in the production of a desirable and essential commodity. Maori were already supplying large quantities of food to Europeans, both settlers and visiting ships. From this trade in pigs, potatoes and other vegetables, along with dressed flax, they progressively acquired muskets and tools, pots and blankets, coastal vessels and eventually cash. This allowed them to invest in the necessary technology for their water-powered mills. In the 1840s and early 1850s many North Island Maori became wheat growers, flour millers and bread bakers, feeding their own people, and with the surplus enhancing their economic independence (Petrie 2006).

The foods that Maori supplied to European centres like Auckland and Wellington also eased the strain on the Pakeha economy, making it less dependent on imported items. The vegetables and fruits that were brought to Auckland were of species first introduced to the missionary gardens of the Bay of Islands, or brought in by whalers. Filtered through the Maori culinary and horticultural traditions, they reappeared in canoe loads on the Auckland foreshore in the 1840s (Hursthouse 1861:125; Petrie 2006:170, 226). Notable amongst the fruits were melons, watermelons and pumpkins. To Maori growers these were larger and sweeter cousins of bottle gourd. Peaches, apples and cape gooseberries were traded to Pakeha, fruits that at that time grew without difficulty as they had arrived before their pests. Maize was now a successful crop, and its green cobs were also sold to the settlers. Maori gardeners were skilled horticulturalists (Leach 1997), a fact recognised by Sir Joseph Banks in the eighteenth century but ignored by the missionaries who saw Maori as primitive agriculturalists requiring instruction. Maori gardening techniques were already attuned to the New Zealand climates and soil types, while Pakeha were still struggling to learn the new seasons (Leach 1984:114).

Judging by the shipping lists of the 1850s, Maori became successful and versatile farmers as well as gardeners. As an example I can cite the eighteen-ton vessel *Kaikahu* that arrived at the Port of Auckland from Opotiki on 2 December 1858 under its Maori master Penengapua. On board were 32 bushels of wheat, 13 bushels of corn, 2 tons of potatoes, 6 hundredweight of flax and 12 baskets of sweet potatoes, along with two Maori passengers (*Daily Southern Cross* 15(1193):2). Accounts of Maori feasts, such as that given for Governor Grey in 1849, or the one that cemented peace between two central North Island tribes in 1846, are evidence of an exceptional ability of Maori to assemble food supplies for their own purposes. At the 1846 feast, it was reported that there were 8000 baskets of potatoes and kumara for four thousand participants, plus half a million eels, 900 pigs, tobacco and clothing. In true Polynesian style, these items were formed into a pile, 200 feet long, 8 feet wide and 5 feet high (*New Zealander* 2(57):2). Though not as high as earlier *hakari* or feast displays, it was a true descendant.

Under the strain of moving to a new environment, the British culinary tradition began to admit new foods grown by Maori, notably pumpkins, squash and maize, and unfamiliar varieties of old foods such as purple-fleshed potatoes. Contemporary English cookbooks had no recipes for the new foods and so recourse was made to American sources. Pakeha had no interest in adopting the Maori cooking methods as well as the foods, so they looked to the former British colony where the inhabitants had in turn acquired these foods from the indigenous peoples and absorbed them into their culinary tradition. When recipes first appeared in New Zealand newspapers they were for maize meal, also known as Indian corn. In 1846, as the potato crops failed in the British Isles, a search for substitutes became urgent. The Wellington newspaper (*New Zealand Spectator and Cook Strait Guardian* 3(124):3) reprinted from an English paper American recipes for mush, slap-jack, Johnny cakes, hoe cakes, hominy and corn-bread. This was not because the potato blight was affecting New Zealand, but because maize was widely grown in the North Island and supplied by Maori to Pakeha settlers. The latter needed recipes to use it. Similar recipes reappeared in a later Wellington paper (*New Zealander* 7(546):4). On this occasion there were more corn puddings than breakfast cakes, which may have made them more attractive since puddings were an essential element in British dinners.

SEPARATION OF THE TRADITIONS

A turning point was reached by 1860. Wheat prices had fallen in 1856, leading to debt and loss of land for some Maori communities (Petrie 2006:218). Europeans now outnumbered Maori, and the discovery of gold increased immigration, especially to the South Island. Illegal land purchases over previous decades led to the outbreak of the New Zealand Wars. In turn, they led to further loss of land through confiscations. The two peoples pulled apart, and the level of contact that town-dwelling Pakeha had with Maori was far less than in the 1840s and 1850s. For the rest of the nineteenth century, as European migrants poured in, the Maori population decreased as a result of poverty and disease (King 2003).

What effect did this have on the two culinary traditions that I have been tracking? That of Maori became invisible in mainstream publications. After Lady Martin (1869) produced her handbook of recipes for medicine and foods in 1869, written in Maori for Maori readers (Beaton 2007:136–42), there are few accounts that recognised the existence of a separate Maori culinary tradition. Only Pakeha who participated in formal gatherings or travelled in the remote Urewera ranges or King Country recorded the wide range of traditional Maori foods still in use. For most European New Zealanders, Maori cookery was a quaint survival from a prehistoric era. Instead of buying vegetables and fruit from Maori growers as they had in the 1850s, town dwellers now obtained supplies from the first generation of Chinese market gardeners ([William] 1883:24).

CATCHING UP WITH 'HOME'

In the Pakeha kitchen, there was a rapid improvement in technology after 1860. After Lady Barker arrived in the Canterbury settlement in 1865, the kitchen of her new house near Whitecliffs was fitted with a large coal range, known as a Leamington kitchener. Her neighbours used what she called American stoves, which demanded constant attention. Also known as colonial ovens (Soper 1978:46, Plate IX), these took the form of an iron box, fitted neatly into the chimney. As an oven, it could be heated by lighting a fire underneath, but most of the time, the fire was set on top of the colonial oven. A gridiron was often positioned above the box, with trivets for supporting a kettle, and a galvanised iron boiler might be fitted beside the grate to provide hot water ([William] 1883:18). In 1880, the total cost of oven, grate and boiler was about £3, whereas the smallest 'Leamington kitchener' or coal range, was £10. Colonial ovens were standard in most cottages, but as they wore out, they were replaced by affordable locally made coal ranges. By the end of the century, the New Zealand kitchen had finally caught up.

Was this the right time for New Zealanders to reaffirm their identity, and realign their culinary tradition with that of England? Certain English gentlewomen, like Lady Barker, who wrote stirring and somewhat patronising accounts of their New Zealand experiences, were very conscious that the established settlers had acquired new practical skills. They had learned to cook, milk cows and make butter, they did their own household washing, and were no longer reliant on servants. Wrote Lady Barker: 'I often find myself wondering whether the ladies here are at all like what our great grandmothers were' (Barker 1956:21). She decided that they were, because in addition to their practical knowledge, they still knew how to 'surround themselves, according to their means and opportunities, with the refinements and elegancies of life'. I suspect Lady Barker would have approved if New Zealanders had recreated the highly stratified society that characterised their homeland. 'Bachelorising' or having a 'picnic life', as doing-without-servants was called by these ladies, was all very well for a short time. Significantly, Lady Barker went home to take charge of the National School of Cookery in London, an institution whose mission was to teach girls to cook, and become competent servants.

A Mrs William, who returned to Kent after two years in Canterbury in the early 1880s, noticed some other differences. New Zealand women participated in what she called 'gift auctions'. Produce was donated for these fund-raising events, including cheeses, butter, sides of bacon and piles of fruit. She remarked 'A tea-table … is a centre of attraction for all thirsty souls, and a "power of eating" goes on at them … and, certainly, New Zealand ladies can turn out a table, heavily laden with a variety of cakes and sweets, quite astonishing to behold' ([William] 1883:66). As a newcomer, she found the competition taxing. Do we need to look further for the origin of the New Zealand afternoon tea spread?

AMERICAN AND AUSTRALIAN INFLUENCES

From the 1870s, New Zealand newspapers kept local readers informed about the latest dress fashions from Paris and London, and the activities of the aristocracy. What about the latest dishes from European dinner tables? They made little impact. Recipes began to appear regularly in local newspapers from the late 1860s, initially one or two at a time, then from 1870 in greater numbers. Auckland's *Daily Southern Cross* was one of the first. From the start it is clear that a few of its recipes, like New England Mince Pies (*DSC* 26(4033):4) and Green Corn Pudding (*DSC* 27(4193):6) were American. What has only recently become apparent is that others such as Brown Betty (*DSC* 26(4033):4) and Cocoa-nut Cakes (*DSC* 26(4046):4) were also of American origin. On the whole, however, the *Daily Southern Cross* published recipes that could have slipped out between the covers of the latest Mrs Beeton or Mary Jewry cookbook from London, recipes without French names or expensive ingredients.

When the *Daily Southern Cross* cookery columns ceased late in 1873, the weekly *Otago Witness* took over. I had a close look at the first six months. From mid-August 1874 to mid-February 1875, a total of 211 recipes were published, of which twenty per cent (42) were American. Searchable databases have even located the exact sources. When the *Otago Witness* started up the Household Hints column in August 1874, the lady editor had in front of her the July issue (volume 35) of *Frank Leslie's Ladies' Magazine*, published in New York just six weeks before. She copied eleven recipes into three editions of the *Otago Witness*. When the January 1875 issue of the magazine arrived, she took two recipes from it. Two months before, in November 1874, she opened her copy of Eliza Leslie's *The Lady's Receipt Book*, published in Philadelphia in 1847 and copied out sixteen recipes, which she spread over five editions of the newspaper. This discovery adds to the significance of the remark made by Mrs William in 1883 about Canterbury settlers: 'It is astonishing how largely the public patronise American machines in New Zealand! Look to it, ye English manufacturers!' ([William] 1883:14). Even as they caught up with and in some respects surpassed the standard of living of their British cousins, Pakeha showed an openness to American technology and American recipes that was not apparent in Britain.

There were good reasons behind this permeability of their inherited culinary tradition. When Mrs William made her remark, the latest edition of Mrs Beeton was advising urban housewives not to bother making jam or pickles because commercial manufacturers could make a better product at a competitive price. In contrast, New Zealanders had larger gardens and seasonal gluts of tomatoes, currants and raspberries. In the north they had sub-tropical fruits that had never been grown in England. They turned to other English-speaking countries for the necessary recipes, and especially to America. They also needed recipes for the pumpkins, pie melons, citron melons, and squash that were producing abundantly in their back gardens. Formerly they had purchased these from Maori gardeners, who had in turn acquired them from American whalers and Australian-based missionaries.

It was not just newspapers that were receptive to non-British recipes. *Brett's Colonists' Guide*, produced by Auckland's Thompson Leys in 1883, drew on dietetic tracts published on both sides of the Atlantic (Leys 1883). His section on bread-making was acknowledged to an unnamed American authoress. Cornmeal recipes were included, such as Virginia Corn Bread. From an 1855 issue of *Godey's Magazine*, he copied a recipe for Indian Huckleberry Pudding, and from an 1868 issue of the same magazine, Cabbage Jelly. There were also recipes for Maryland Biscuit, Buckwheat Cakes, Gumbo, Hominy, Popcorn and Pea-nut Candy. The recipes for Ginger Crackers, Ginger Nuts and Ginger Snaps all called for molasses. These must have come from an American source for in Britain similar recipes used the term treacle.

Compared to *Brett's Colonists' Guide*, the recipes published in Isobel Broad's *New Zealand Exhibition Cookery Book* in 1889 were more consciously national (Broad 1889). She emphasised the diversity of fish species available here, even providing her own recipe for a local bouillabaisse. Game recipes included several for pukeko, wood pigeon and kaka, in addition to the introduced hare, rabbit, pheasant, Californian quail, and venison. Her recipes appear to be tailored to the tastes of the gentlemen members of the Nelson Club. There were no obvious American borrowings.

A contemporary book from Dunedin, the *Technical Classes Association Cookery Book* of 1890, gives a clearer picture of influences on the culinary tradition of Otago residents (Miller 1890). It was the work of Mrs Elizabeth Brown Miller, who taught cookery classes to girls and women of all levels of society, from the 1880s to the first decade of the twentieth century. She was a prolific writer, whom researcher Raelene Inglis (2007) has shown to be a major player in the transmission of cookery knowledge. Mrs Miller understood that a culinary tradition contains

Mrs Elizabeth Brown Miller, a leading Dunedin cookery teacher of the 1890s, provided cookery classes for school pupils, married women, and in this case, working girls. From *Elementary Cookery*, [c.1903], opp. p. 48, H. Leach Collection.

both traditional dishes, intimately connected with the maintenance of identity, and new dishes, adapted to changed conditions; together they give continuity to a tradition while keeping it viable in a new era. In recognition of Dunedin's Scottish heritage, Mrs Miller acknowledged five recipes from Christian Johnstone (who wrote under the pseudonym Meg Dods): Cock-a-Leekie soup, Hotch Potch, Potted Head, Scotch Haggis and Fairy Butter. Another five Scottish recipes were provided including the Scottish equivalent of Christmas Cake, known as Black Bun. She included some German recipes from an unknown source, possibly one of Dunedin's Jewish families. But the greatest surprise was Mrs Miller's use of an American source, which she did not identify, nor give any indication that the nine recipes she drew from it were American. The book was *Miss Parloa's New Cook Book*, published in New York in 1882, and the recipes included one that would go on to become a popular entrée in twentieth-century New Zealand: Little Pigs in Blanket[s] (Parloa 1882). These are fat oysters rolled inside bacon rashers and grilled.

Mrs Miller also played a pivotal roll in the introduction of the quick breads known as 'gems'. The earliest-known New Zealand recipes appear in newspaper columns from the 1880s. One published in the *Otago Witness* in 1890 was copied from Henry Scammell's 1885 American *Cyclopedia of Valuable Receipts* (Scammell 1885). In April 1892 Mrs Miller included gems in her class on bread- and scone-making, taught at Otago Girls High School. She modified her recipe several times over the next decade but the concept appeared in all of her cookbooks. Her pupils passed her recipes on, and gems became a popular baked item in New Zealand until the 1960s. In their country of origin, the United States, gems were swallowed up in the 1920s by the emergence of the muffin. New Zealand cooks made gems their own, while Americans forgot them, and their British cousins showed no interest in adopting them (Leach 2006).

Australia was much closer to New Zealand than was America. If the extent of borrowing of recipes is inversely proportional to distance, then we should expect our newspapers and local cookbooks to have a significant number of Australian recipes. Without recipe-by-recipe comparison, it is very hard to demonstrate borrowing when two traditions have a shared origin. For many years we have wondered who compiled the first edition of Whitcombe and Tomb's long-running series, *Colonial Everyday Cookery*, published in 1901 (Anon [1901]). Comparison with contemporary New Zealand cookbooks revealed that a few jam recipes were derived from Mrs Miller's books, but no other matches were made – until recently. I found that the compiler of *Colonial Everyday Cookery* had an early edition of *The Cookery Book of Good and Tried Receipts* issued by the New South Wales Presbyterian Women's Missionary Association. From it, at least forty-seven recipes were extracted and altered in subtle ways, perhaps to obscure the extent of the borrowing. These recipes include fifteen for meat dishes and entrées, twelve for preserving, seven for confectionery and drinks, nine for desserts, and three for cakes. My guess is that the unknown compiler, reputed to be a leading caterer (*NZ Tablet* 29:20), already had his own collection of baking and pudding recipes and saw no need to borrow more than a few from Australia.

This is not an isolated case. Certain recipes for using sub-tropical fruits and vegetables are acknowledged to other Australian sources. For example, in 1897 the *Otago Witness* provided two Australian recipes for using bananas derived from the new book by Australian cooking lecturer Mrs Wicken (*Otago Witness* 8 April 1897:45).

Readers of the *Otago Witness* may have been living far from the hubs of fashion, but they were certainly not out of touch. In an 1891 advertisement for magazines and newspapers obtainable in Dunedin, six Australian publications were listed, along with four American, and twenty-one from Britain (*Otago Witness* 1 January 1891:1). New waves of British migrants had poured into the country in the

Top: The first edition of Whitcombe and Tombs' *Colonial Everyday Cookery* (1901) drew heavily on a fundraising cookbook issued by the New South Wales Presbyterian Women's Missionary Association, but did not acknowledge this Australian input. *Bottom:* Dunedin cookery teacher and writer Mrs Miller copied nine recipes from this 1883 American cookery book by Maria Parloa.

H. Leach Collection.

previous decade, doubtless reinforcing the British character of the New Zealand culinary tradition. But at the same time, ideas about foods and recipes for new dishes were arriving as unaccompanied cultural baggage from other parts of the world, and especially from the New World. Though Britain was still 'home', the emigrants had left it for good reasons. In reproducing new recipes from America and Australia, they expressed a kinship with fellow colonists. In the next century, imported ideas would play an even greater role than actual migrants in shaping our culinary traditions.

3

Culinary Traditions in Twentieth-Century New Zealand

Helen M. Leach

The year is 1905, the place, Wellington. Miss L.E. Brandon and Miss Christine Smith have assembled recipes from leading ladies of their acquaintance and produced a cookbook in support of the Home for the Incurables Bazaar, held in July. Entitled '*Ukneadit*', this is one of New Zealand's earliest fundraising cookbooks. The idea for such books arose in America in the 1860s and spread to other English-speaking nations (Longone 1997). Charitable or community cookbooks, as they are often called, provided home-based women with an opportunity to advance community projects of particular concern to women. They were an acceptable and respectable commercial enterprise for women whom society normally expected to remain financially dependent on their husbands after marriage.

PAKEHA ATTITUDES TO MAORI COOKERY

'*Ukneadit*' begins with a recipe from Victoria Plunket, wife of Lord Plunket, the Governor General. Later in the book, readers find a short section called Bachelors' Corner in which most of the contributions are well-intentioned instructions for simple dishes that bachelors might need to cook, like eggs on toast. But then the tone changes. Mr S. Nathan has contributed a recipe for an explosive Military Cake and Mr W. Brown likens the Boer War to an omelette, in verse. Then follow three 'ancient Maori Recipes' said by their contributor, Mr W.D. Lyon, to have been discovered in an old Maori oven, torn out of an 'ancient Maori cookery book'. Mr Lyon was a prominent figure in Wellington, a lodge master and leading light in the Wellington Operatic and Amateur Dramatic Society. He claims to have had the recipes translated by an eminent Maori scholar. Their titles are 'Baked Warrior (also called "Long Pig")', 'Pakeha a la Tohunga (an entree)' and an incomplete recipe for 'Pickled Picaninnies' (Brandon and Smith 1905:104).

Ancient Maori Recipes.

. enclose a translation of an ancient document recently discovered ı old Maori oven in the North Island, and which evidently was a torn out of an ancient Maori cookery book. It has been carefully anslated by an eminent Maori scholar, and reads as follows :—

BAKED WARRIOR (also called " Long Pig.")

Select a well-tattooed warrior—the tattoo signifying rank, and, as all cases when cooking game, the higher the rank the better—lay him, with a plentiful supply of green leaves, in the oven; cover over with arth, &c. Bake for six hours. Then serve quickly, garnished with ax leaves and raupo sticks. Seasonable after a battle. Sufficient for whole tribe.

PAKEHA A LA TOHUNGA (an entree).

This is a favourite dish round about mission stations.

Ingredients: Pakeha Steaks, Dried Shark (well matured), Kumaras, Pork Fat, Mutton Fish, and Karaka Berries.

Trim the steaks, and, with a bit of flax, tie each one round a piece of full-flavoured shark. Skewer these all together with a sharply-pointed stick of manuka, place in the oven, and bake till tender. Have ready a hot sauce made of mutton fish (from last year's stock) chopped very fine, pork fat, and sea water. Pour this over at time of serving, surround the fish with baked kumaras, and garnish with karaka berries. This makes a dish fit for a rangitira.

PICKLED PICANINNIES.

Picaninnies from neighbouring tribes may be preserved for winter following——

unfortunately the leaf ends, but if you think the fragment of ent interest to publish you are at liberty to do so.

Mr. W. D. Lyon.

Australian Damper.

Pick good hard ground for your fire, which may be as big as you like. Box-wood is best in Australia, ti-tree in New Zealand. While the fire is burning down pour your flour out on the piece of bark, tin, or calico that constitutes your cooking board. If you have salt put some in. If you have baking powder use it, but the result won't be damper. Damper is flour and salt and water—nothing more. The more you knead the more damper you need. Having decided on the architecture of the masterpiece, scrape fire to one side and rest the raw loaf on the hot ground, carefully pushing the embers, which must not flame, entirely over it. Bake your pipe for an hour. If it is windy the damper will be burnt; if eaten, it's all right provided you're hungry. Fastidious bushmen frequently put wood-ashes in the water the day previous to mixing a damper. The potash acts as baking powder would, only don't put the acs in the bread.

Mr. C. L. Jewell.

104.

Miss L.E. Brandon and Miss Christine Smith, the compilers of *'Ukneadit'* (1905), a cookbook raising money for the Home for the Incurables in Wellington, included three spoof 'ancient Maori' recipes (p. 104) but no contemporary Maori dishes. Courtesy of Mrs Beverley Shore Bennett.

The recipes contain seemingly authentic details in the form of accompaniments like dried shark and karaka, and the methods of cooking. No doubt they were considered amusing and clever by the compilers.

What is most disturbing about these mock-Maori recipes is that the knowledge of Maori food traditions that underlies them should have extended to an appreciation of the offence they could cause to Maori. We do not know whether that offence was intended. Sadly, these three recipes are the only ones in the entire cookbook that acknowledge the existence of Maori people in New Zealand. They portray Maori cookery as uncivilised and alien in its own homeland.

Was such blatant racism a mark of other cookbooks at this time? Most recipe books simply ignored Maori ways of cooking, and seem unaware of the Maori contribution to the Pakeha diet in the mid-nineteenth century. '*Ukneadit*' offered no recipes for toheroa, pipi or any other shellfish besides oysters. Not a single recipe used kumara, and that was true of most other recipe books published in the first two decades of the twentieth century.

MAORI RECIPES FOR PAKEHA READERS

Only one recipe book stands out for its genuine attempt to incorporate a taste of Maori cookery. The book is called *300 Choice Recipes. A Souvenir of the All Nations Fair, Gisborne* and was published in 1908 (Anon 1908). It was printed by Te Rau Press at Te Rau Kahikatea College, where Anglican clergy were trained for Maori ministry. This explains the input of Mrs Keita (Kate) Kohere, wife of the Reverend Reweti Kohere, a tutor at the college for thirteen years.

Mrs Kohere's recipes explain in much detail how to process kina, make a hangi, prepare huahua, or preserved pigeons, and use puha or sow thistle (Anon 1908:6, 11, 13, 25). Her audience was not Maori, but Pakeha, and she was introducing them to Maori foodways. She wrote 'once prejudice is overcome Kina will be found juicy, tasty, and wholesome; a fit dish for epicures'. 'When Puha becomes popular', she noted, 'it will be like the once despised potato, a national boon'. Both traditional and current methods of making a hangi were described. A 'modern' hangi could be 'built more simply by throwing a large dish over it and piling earth only around the rim'. She believed that 'Only those having partaken of haangi food can appreciate the sweet flavour that makes every item most appetizing. It is not too much to hope' she concluded, 'that some day Haangi parties will become fashionable' (Anon 1908:6, 11, 25).

One hundred years have passed and Mrs Kohere's hopes have not been fulfilled. Between 1908 and 1975, New Zealand cookbooks that I have examined give the impression that if a Maori culinary tradition still existed, it had embraced the recipes and techniques of the European majority. For the compilers of national cookbooks like the series put out by the Women's Division of the Farmers Union and the New Zealand Women's Institutes, there was no suggestion that their Maori members should not be represented. But the prevailing view seems to have been that they cooked the same dishes as Pakeha women.

COOKBOOKS AND THE MAORI RENAISSANCE

It wasn't until the 1970s Maori Renaissance movement that Maori women began to publish their own recipes in printed cookbooks for Maori readers (Beaton 2007:73). These books did more than disseminate cookery instructions – they simultaneously asserted *mana Maori* and Maori identity. Sophia Beaton argues in her recent Master's thesis on the Maori culinary tradition, that it was not a case of reinventing a Maori cuisine, but reaffirming an ongoing continuous tradition, up till that time transmitted orally or in manuscript form. She found that the recipes in the new Maori cookbooks are not relics of the past but fully contemporary. Only a small percentage are for traditional foods processed by traditional techniques. The majority combine European and Maori food items and take advantage of modern kitchen technology. In these books, Maori breads are prominent and camp ovens are the appliance of choice in which to bake them. Shellfish are still dried, in the sun if possible, otherwise in the warming drawer of an electric stove (Anon 1975:44). Pork is preserved in fat just as muttonbirds were. Several types of steamed and boiled pudding have been adapted for hangi cooking and for catering for large numbers on the marae (Beaton 2007:84). There are even recipes which simulate hangi conditions in a covered roasting dish (Anon 1975:10; Beaton 2007:86).

Going beyond the actual recipes and kitchen technology, we need to remember that culinary traditions incorporate rules of conduct, systems of food classification, values and beliefs. Beaton found that in these components, there was absolutely no doubt of the continuation of the Maori culinary tradition from its Polynesian origins to the present day. Underlying current rules, such as washing tea towels and tablecloths separately from clothes, is the timeless binary principle of *tapu* and *noa*, which prohibits the contamination of clothes that come into contact with the human body by items that have a close association with food (Beaton 2007:119, 127). Many other guiding principles of Maori cookery and eating practices can be traced back in an unbroken line to the prehistoric era. No case can be made for assimilation and disappearance of Maori foodways under the blanket of the dominant Pakeha culture. Instead, the evidence points to assimilation of Pakeha ingredients and technology into the Maori culinary tradition.

INFLUENCES ON THE PAKEHA CULINARY TRADITION

This borrowing was not reciprocated. In the second chapter I showed that British migrants made use of Maori-grown produce in the mid-nineteenth century, but did not adopt or even adapt Maori methods of cookery. This is as true for the twentieth century as it was for the late nineteenth. Where then should we look for the ideas that fed the Pakeha culinary tradition? I have already provided evidence of a steady stream of recipes from America during the second half of the nineteenth century, along with some significant borrowings from Australia. Large numbers of British migrants who arrived in the 1870s and 1880s no doubt introduced new dishes, though they are much harder to identify against the shared British-New Zealand background. I will show that in the twentieth century it was not so much the movement of people that stimulated change, but the influx of ideas. Furthermore, I hope to explain why some aspects of the culinary tradition were more resistant to change than others.

Sources

We should first look at the printed sources of cookery information. A 1905 advertisement for cookbooks from Braithwaite's Book Arcade in Dunedin is swamped by British titles (Leach 2003:15). Two of them, *Warne's Model Cookery and Housekeeping Book* (consisting of 728 pages) and Beeton's *The Book of Household Management* (a 1644-page tome) were already classic titles into their fifth decade of publication (Jewry 1893; Beeton 1899). The most up-to-date and expensive in the list was Mary Ronald's *The Century Cook Book* (a mere 587 pages) published in 1895 (Ronald 1895). But this British dominance in cookbooks for sale in local shops does not mean that their influence was paramount. At the same time as cooks studied Mrs Beeton, newspapers were tapping sources that were much less conservative. A prime example of this alternative influence is provided by the Australian lamington. Within ten weeks of its first publication in Queensland, in January 1902, a Lamington recipe was printed in the *Otago Witness*, and repeated later that year. New Zealanders have continued to make them ever since (Leach 2008a:1).

Recipes published in newspapers and magazines were more widely distributed than those in expensive imported volumes like Mrs Beeton's. But did they last as long? How quickly were they replaced by newer and more fashionable recipes?

In 1905, the first edition of Dunedin's *St Andrew's Cookery Book* (p. 15) carried an advertisement from Braithwaite's Book Arcade, dominated by British-published cookbooks. H. Leach Collection.

Another mechanism helped to preserve the best of the newspaper and hand-written recipes that were circulating in the community. This was the fundraising cookbook, usually compiled by a committee of women. These collections often survived until the covers were lost and the index detached, simply because of their strong local and family associations. Several thousand fundraising cookbooks may have been produced in New Zealand during the twentieth century, and they are still published in the twenty-first. For a food historian they are treasures. They do not tell us what our ancestors ate, but what foods they had access to. Above all, they show us the repertoire of complex dishes of a particular group of cooks at a particular period. They contain the recipes that people wanted to be remembered for – in other words their signature dishes. Plain cookery was seldom included, but that can be found in another useful category of cookbook, the manuals produced by local cookery teachers and demonstrators.

The main course

It is important to distinguish between various categories of dish when commenting on the development of our culinary tradition in the twentieth century. These categories relate to their position within the meal structure. If you look at the main course of family dinners, there is very little change between 1900 and 1960. The content belongs firmly within the British tradition. Cooking teacher Mrs Elizabeth Miller spelled out the nature of this course about 1903 (Miller c.1903:105): 'A joint of beef or mutton; Potatoes always; Suitable vegetables'. In a longer work, she provided daily menus for a month, 'suitable for a family of moderate means numbering from eight to ten members' (families were larger in those days) (Miller c.1917:322). Contrary to the image of colonial New Zealanders as consumers of mutton, it was beef and veal that dominated the dinners, appearing in 44 per cent of them. Mutton or lamb constituted 25 per cent, poultry 14 per cent, pork and rabbit or hare each 8 per cent. The beef was eaten roasted, baked, or grilled; it was also boiled as corned beef, and made into beef olives, and steak-and-kidney pudding. The mutton or lamb might be roasted, boiled, baked or braised, or stuffed as Colonial Goose. The pork and poultry were eaten as roasts, and the rabbits and hares were roasted or baked. When I compare Mrs Miller's menus with the dinners I experienced growing up in the 1950s, I can say that every one of these meats was served in our home, and cooked in much the same way. The only significant difference between Mrs Miller's roasts and my mother's was that in Edwardian times a roast might still be rotated on a spit in front of the glowing coals of the fire grate, with a reflector behind it and pan to catch the dripping underneath. In the stoves of the 1950s, so-called 'roasts' were actually baked in a closed oven.

Potatoes were standard accompaniments to all these meat dishes. They can be confidently referred to as New Zealanders' second main staple food for most of the nineteenth and twentieth centuries, alongside wheat. One or two other vegetables were served besides potatoes, but in our home they were not, as David Burton (1992:21) has colourfully expressed it, 'systematically murdered' by overcooking. Like many New Zealanders of the 1950s we grew most of our own fruit and vegetables and appreciated their freshness.

From the 1960s, the main course of the New Zealand family dinner began to change. The time spent cooking meat for weekday meals diminished as more New Zealand women joined the paid workforce during the 1960s. There was a significant shift away from roasts and offal towards the use of beef mince and, from the late 1960s, factory-raised chicken. Small goods like sausages that had formed part of cooked breakfasts in the first half of the twentieth century could now be served at dinner. Casseroles with exotic names replaced mundane family stews, especially for entertaining.

The stranglehold of potatoes as the staple on our dinner plates was finally broken by rice, and later by pasta. The process had taken several centuries. Where staple foods are concerned, people can be extremely conservative. Rice had been available in Britain from medieval times. When it became affordable for middle-class tables in the seventeenth century it did not compete with potatoes – they were yet to be accepted – but with wheat flour in boiled or baked puddings. While rice puddings became very popular in the eighteenth century, rice could only extend its influence as an ingredient of a pilau (Leach 2008b) or accompaniment to a curry. Curry and rice became a standard Victorian entrée, but to our great-grandparents it was structurally unthinkable that a dinner party entrée could turn into a main (Leach 1993). As for pasta, it too had been an ingredient in certain eighteenth-century English puddings. In the Victorian era, macaroni cheese became one of the standard dishes served in the cheese course at the end of dinner. With the decline of that course to our present-day cheese and biscuits, macaroni cheese moved to family lunches, along with spaghetti in tomato sauce. Elevating a lunch dish to a main posed further structural difficulties. It took a decline in cooked lunches and the replacement of the eight-course formal dinner by new conventions of entertaining before a hostess could tell her guests confidently that the main dish was casseroled pork with rice, or beef stroganoff with noodles.

These trends should not be interpreted as a final move away from the British culinary tradition, in some sort of post-colonial rejection. If you look at contemporary British cookbooks you will see a similar range of dishes gaining popularity: curries, spaghetti bolognaise, chow mein and chop suey. The phenomenon occurred in many countries and is often linked to globalisation. That term raises a serious question that I will return to later: does globalisation lead to the obliteration of local culinary traditions?

The soup course

First we need to ask whether other dinner courses show the same trajectory as the main. In the eighteenth and nineteenth centuries, soup was the most common starter of a formal meal. Today few family dinners begin with soup, and even in the early 1900s it was optional. In Mrs Miller's month of menus, soup was served with lunch in the middle of the day, a more modern arrangement that allowed the breadwinner to have dinner after business hours. Most of her soups continued in use throughout the twentieth century and had themselves been formulated decades (if not centuries) before in Britain. Pea soups made from green or dried split peas are ancient types, along with mutton broth, oyster soup and the family of white soups. Other types, such as oxtail, kidney, potato and mulligatawny were standard Victorian dishes. Tomato soup was the newcomer, perhaps the only Edwardian soup that could be described as 'fashionable'. Lentil soup was also relatively new, promoted by the international health food movement but I suspect it was more virtuous than fashionable (Leach 2006).

Over the next five decades little changed in this essentially British repertoire of soups. The depression helped to popularise pumpkin soup, toheroa and mock-toheroa soup, the latter made from freely available pipi and cockles. It was not until the 1950s that cooks began to break away from bland cream-of-vegetable soups. One of the markers of rebellion was borsch, also circulating under the name 'Russian soup' (Anon 1955:11). Minestrone, portrayed as Italy's national soup, appeared in some up-market fundraising cookbooks of the 1950s, along with soups whose vegetable ingredients had been finely chopped in a 'vitamizer', as blenders were first called. At this time the number of community cookbooks with a dedicated soup section had begun a sharp decline, from 91 per cent in the 1940s to 34 per cent in the 1980s. Had it not been for the arrival of these international soups, we might have dropped the category completely.

The 1960s brought fresh interest in 'entertaining' at home. A suite of new soups was essential, including for the first time chilled soups like gazpacho and vichyssoise. The classic Greek egg-and-lemon soup avgolemono began to circulate in the 1970s. Their exotic names were no coincidence. To the hostess, they served as a passport to social success and their names hinted at international experience. In the 1970s, the American-style chowders based on seafoods or sweet corn were finally adopted. Several earlier introductions of the chowder had faded. The 1980s saw the rise of curried vegetable soups based on pumpkin, parsnip, apple, kumara and even swede. I believe these played a different role from the elegant iced soups of the dinner parties. Their appearance on café menus suggests that they are part of the recent return of lunch to the category of a 'proper' meal.

Puddings, sweets and desserts

I have shown how soups and mains adhered to the traditional British pattern until New Zealanders opened their kitchens to the world from the 1950s. Were puddings similarly affected? Their British origins are undisputed, with an antiquity stretching back to medieval times. Initially they were boiled in gut casings, with black pudding being the last survivor of this type. Then the name was transferred to the filling itself, which combined a fat, a starch product, and sometimes eggs, spices and dried fruits. By the eighteenth century, puddings were either boiled in cloth bags, or baked. During the nineteenth century, in the transition from open-hearth cookery to solid-topped ranges, it became easier to boil puddings in a covered bowl inside a cast-iron pot. Then, as stove-tops shrank with the introduction of gas, pudding bowls were often placed in a steamer above boiling water (Leach 2008c).

To assess the degree of similarity between British and New Zealand puddings, I recently compared two matched pairs of fundraising cookbooks. From around 1930 I chose church-produced books from Harlesden, London (Anon 1929) and Hastings, New Zealand (Anon 1932), and from around 1960 I compared cookbooks produced by the Scottish Women's Rural Institutes (Anon 1960) and the New Zealand Country Women's Institutes (Anon 1962). Steamed puddings make up more than half the pudding recipes in both of the earlier cookbooks. Suet was used in 40 per cent of these recipes, even though suet puddings take two or more hours to cook, compared to steamed puddings based on butter and eggs that are often ready in one to two hours. Baked puddings are even quicker to cook, but are not as sustaining. Most used eggs and milk in a custard or sponge-type dish. Meringue toppings were fashionable in both Harlesden and Hastings.

Were their cold puddings also similar? Dishes called trifles, creams and snows have been popular in Britain from the seventeenth century. The commercial production of gelatine in the Victorian era shortened their preparation time and

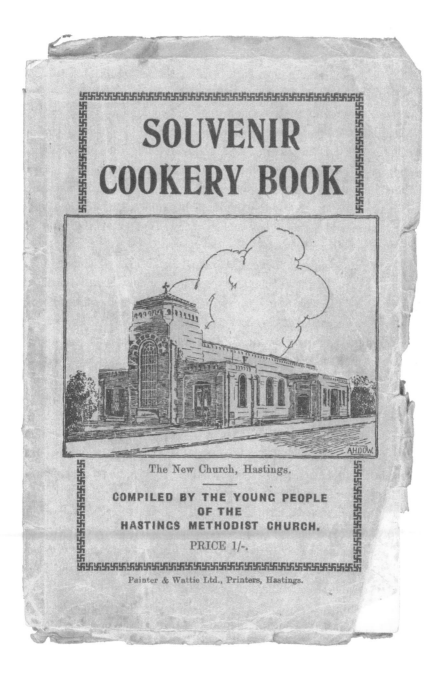

SOUVENIR COOKERY BOOK

The New Church, Hastings.

COMPILED BY THE YOUNG PEOPLE OF THE HASTINGS METHODIST CHURCH.

PRICE 1/-.

Painter & Wattie Ltd., Printers, Hastings.

Boiled or steamed puddings were common in this cookbook compiled in 1932 by the 'young people' of the Hastings Methodist Church, as part of the fundraising effort to replace their old church destroyed by the 1931 Napier Earthquake. H. Leach Collection.

costs. In fundraising cookbooks like these, simple jellies are rare. Their gelatine dishes are dressed up with egg custards and whipped egg whites, as in Spanish Cream. The New Zealand recipes of this type used more eggs than their British counterparts; however the recipe types are the same.

Moving forward to 1960, I found some clear differences. While steamed puddings still formed more than half (54 per cent) of the hot pudding recipes in Scotland, they had fallen to 34 per cent in New Zealand, as the balance shifted towards baked puddings. Suet still dominated Scottish steamed puddings, but had been limited to just the Christmas pudding in the New Zealand collection. However, cold sweets were still very similar, with gelatine a common component in the usual array of creams, snows, soufflés, mousses and fluffs. Trifles were well represented in both books.

The divergence apparent in the New Zealand decline in suet puddings can be explained as an internal shift. Subsidised butter made it our preferred cooking fat after World War II, while Scottish housewives had to choose between suet and margarine. A surge in paid employment of New Zealand women outside the home made baked puddings more practicable than steamed. However there is another factor apparent in the New Zealand cookbook that points to external influence – the adoption of new desserts from America. Most were placed in a section entitled 'Sweets for Special Occasions'. They include Baked Alaska, Heavenly Pie (an American cousin of the pavlova), Knickerbocker Glory, Banana Cheese Cake (in a biscuit-crumb base), and Lemon Chiffon Pie. These recipes were the advance guard. During the 'entertaining' boom of the 1970s, American-style desserts, together with European dessert cakes filtered through American publications, had a much higher profile and status than traditional English puddings.

American influence on puddings is evident in a higher-level battle involving not individual recipes but the category names used for these dishes. Victorians, whether in Britain or New Zealand, called hot sweet dishes 'puddings'. Opinion was divided about cold sweet dishes, some seeing them as 'puddings' and others placing them under the heading 'creams, jellies &c'. Towards the end of the nineteenth century, a new term became popular in Britain – 'sweets', not to be confused with confectionery. This word was seldom applied to hot dishes, but in New Zealand gained some popularity in the mid-twentieth century for describing cold sweet dishes. In the 1930s, a handful of commercial cookbooks in New Zealand began to use the word 'dessert'. This had been an old name for the final fruit, nut and sweetmeat course in British menus, but when course names and meal service rules were reformed in the late nineteenth century, only the Americans transferred the course name 'dessert' to cover puddings of all types. If you ask the question 'what's for dessert?' you are using an American food classification term, borrowed and expanded from its British ancestor. By the 1990s, the writers and compilers of New Zealand cookbooks routinely placed cold sweet puddings into sections entitled 'desserts', and 80 per cent of them treated hot puddings the same way. In England there has been conscious resistance against this American usage, in an effort to save the indigenous British pudding.

Baked goods

We should not see the history of New Zealand culinary traditions as limited to passive inheritance and active borrowing. So far, I have shown New Zealand cooks to be receptive to American and Australian ideas since first Pakeha settlement, and I don't need to spell out our interest over the last two decades in the culinary traditions of Asia and the Mediterranean. Now I need to balance this picture of external borrowing with the remarkable evidence of internal innovation and experimentation in baking that goes back to the nineteenth century and dominated our baking repertoire throughout the twentieth century. Kiwi cooks chose to express their identity in an area of cooking that is normally omitted from menus. You will remember how impressed British visitors were with the quality and quantity of cakes and other dainties served at community afternoon teas held in Canterbury in the 1880s. They commented on the competitive atmosphere at these occasions, and as we all know, competition inspires innovation. As fund-raising cookbooks proliferated during World War I, we start to see distinctive recipes found nowhere else but in New Zealand and Australia. I won't call them inventions or creations, because all have recognisable forerunners.

Anzac biscuits provide a good example. The technology for making rolled oats reached New Zealand around 1892. By 1915, we find published recipes for Rolled Oats Biscuits or Crispies. By 1919, these had been renamed in honour of the Anzac landing four years before, one of several quite different food items to be given this name in both Australia and New Zealand (Leach 2008d:164). During the 1920s, the process of experimentation and innovation gained momentum and we see the first appearance of classics such as Afghans, Tangoes, and Louise Cakes (for a full list see Symons 2008: Appendix 2). Michael Symons (2008) calls the period from 1890 to 1940 the 'Golden Age of Antipodean Baking'.

The most controversial development was the pavlova. The name was first used in Australia by Davis Gelatine in 1926, the year of Anna Pavlova's visit to Australasia. It was given to a four-layered moulded jelly. Then it was independently applied

61

to little coffee-flavoured walnut meringues in Dunedin in 1928. A year later the name was attached to the meringue cake, then highly fashionable in Sydney, San Francisco and London. The first pavlova cake recipe was printed in the *New Zealand Dairy Exporter* in October 1929. Over twenty pavlova recipes were published in New Zealand books and magazines before the first one appeared in print in Australia in 1940. As I explain in my book, *The Pavlova Story* (Leach 2008d), there never was a single pavlova recipe from which all others were descended. Instead there was a concept that encompassed a great deal of variation. A highly symbolic name became attached to this concept. From 1929 to the present day, many pavlova recipes have been tested and continuously adapted, and the name has even been applied to other categories of dish like marshmallow puddings and tortes. Pavlovas were developed for times when eggs were scarce and expensive, or for cooking in electric frying pans or later in microwave ovens, and even for diabetics. And yes, we borrowed at least one variant from Australia, the pavlina or pavlova roll. By 1960, the pavlova was a national symbol and from the 1970s a contested national icon. Although standardised recipes emerged for certain variants, many of the pavlova recipes to be found in fundraising cookbooks are unique. It is an important characteristic of home cooks that they never feel constrained to follow a recipe exactly. Just as with evolution, they introduce variations, some of which make the recipe better adapted to the changing conditions of our kitchens and household economy (Leach 2008d:158–62).

GLOBALISATION AND CULINARY TRADITIONS

Pavlovas are now popular in many parts of the world, and consumers are generally aware that they originated in New Zealand or Australia. In fact our 'pavlova wars' cause great amusement overseas. The spread and acceptance of pavlovas is a good example of globalisation, specifically what is called culinary globalisation. For two decades social scientists, historians and journalists have been debating the nature of this phenomenon. It has proved hard to define, and it is sometimes easier to explain it with examples. The worldwide appearance of restaurants such as McDonalds and Pizza Hut is often cited as a manifestation of globalisation linked to American political domination and the rise of multinational 'cult-like corporations' as Michael Symons (2000:307) describes them. Terms like 'Coca-Colanization' and 'McDonaldization' have been coined, drawing attention to their capacity for homogenising local cookery traditions and creating a single world cuisine (Wu 2002:57; Goody 1982). The extent to which they are imposing American fast food tastes in New Zealand worries nutritionists, but we should remember that New Zealanders have been receptive to American dishes for longer than the multinationals have been in existence.

Giant food corporations are not the only face of globalisation; immigration has been a significant factor in the process for several centuries. The estimated one hundred million migrants who crossed the seas in the nineteenth century all played a part in introducing foreign ingredients, tastes and styles of cookery to their new homes (Mintz 2000:176 fn). While some appear to have merged their culinary traditions with those of the dominant group, others like Italian, Mexican and Chinese migrants to America, or Indian migrants to Britain succeeded in introducing their cooking to the host nation. Initially their cafés and restaurants created acceptance of foreign dishes, often modified to suit local tastes. Then, it is argued, cooks began to copy particular dishes in their own home or buy commercially prepared versions to eat at home (Panayi 2008). Chop suey is a classic American example. There is an urban myth that it was invented in America by a Chinese cook who was required to prepare a meal when all that remained in the kitchen were the day's scraps. Authorities now agree that it was a genuine Cantonese term for miscellaneous leftovers. In California it was adapted to American tastes with oil, flour and canned vegetables (Anderson 2005:133).

Immigration seems to have played a relatively minor part in the globalisation of New Zealand cookery in the twentieth century, though it is set to have long-term effects in the twenty-first, judging from the multicultural composition of our largest city. Our adoption of stir-fried wok cookery in the 1980s may not stem from our exposure to long-established Cantonese restaurants in our cities so much as to the television programmes and cookbooks of international celebrities like Ken Hom. We did not start drinking wine in the 1960s because of any influx of French migrants. Nor did we adopt Hungarian goulash as a result of the arrival of Hungarian refugees! Instead we became more willing than ever before to embrace products and ideas from the outside world. This phenomenon is sometimes called internationalisation, and is seen as an early stage of globalisation (Cwiertka 2001:9; Panayi 2008:206). What is of particular interest is that it is internally motivated, not driven by immigration or multinational corporations.

Internationalisation in the 1960s brought some very striking changes to the culinary repertoire in New Zealand and Australia. Michael Symons (2006) refers to the events as a 'revolution', while Tony Simpson (1999:165) describes 'a sudden chasm' separating New Zealand's current food culture from the British-based food tradition of earlier generations. Britain and many other European countries showed remarkably similar trends. The Internet may not have existed, but magazines, newspapers and books ensured a rapid dissemination of recipes for international dishes. We were not the only cooks to discover almost simultaneously the excitement of making 'pizza pie', ratatouille, moussaka, chow mein, and chop suey. Authenticity was not a high priority, and we were sometimes vague about the country of origin.

A good example of a supposedly international dish is 'kai si ming', which I have been unable to trace any further than Australia. Such was our difficulty with foreign terms that it occurs under several different names and many spellings – including 'ming ling', 'ming sing', 'chong wong san', 'kisseime', 'Susie Wong', and 'Mrs Ming'. For those who couldn't handle these names it was 'easy Chinese mince', 'easy Chinese tea dish', or 'easy mince chow mein'. One contributor called it 'Lebanese chow mein'. My earliest example is from *Carefree Cooking*, a fundraising book put out by Feilding Free Kindergarten in 1965. Kai si ming is unquestionably tasty – it contains curry powder, onion and one or two packets of chicken noodle soup. It is also easy to make because the rice and vegetables are added to the mince mixture, making this a true one-pot meal. The concept cannot be Chinese, given the curry powder, yet the original name may have been suggested by a speaker of Mandarin, for *gai* means 'to cover over' and *meng* means 'to simmer over a low heat', which is precisely how this dish is cooked. I have long suspected, without proof as yet, that the recipe was named by a Chinese employee of a multinational corporation promoting their line of chicken noodle soup. Whatever its origin, it was taken into New Zealand homes, modified, passed on repeatedly, and more than forty years later is still part of the Kiwi repertoire. In the light of fusion cuisine developed by some leading chefs in the 1990s, kai si ming does not seem so bizarre.

Carefree Cooking (Anon 1965) shows no sign of being swamped by recipes from other culinary traditions. Like many other community cookbooks from this era, it has its own section for 'International Dishes'. There beside kai si ming you will find stroganoff, Hungarian goulash, pasta dishes, Turkish shish kebabs, coq au vin, nasi goreng, and pizza pie. It is as though their country of origin was unimportant. Instead of homogenisation of local cuisines, as feared by some commentators on globalisation, internationalisation added new variety to our culinary traditions. From the outset, the dishes we borrowed were translated into our language of cookery. We altered their ingredients, proportions and cooking methods, and have continued to do so. We even changed their names, as I showed in the case of kai si ming. Was this so different from the borrowings of the nineteenth and earlier twentieth century? The answer is, only in scale. More new dishes appear as mains

Carefree Cooking (1965) contained the earliest known recipe for the mysterious Kai Si Ming. Despite its name, it is known only in New Zealand and Australia. H. Leach Collection.

INTERNATIONAL DISHES
Meats

BEEF STROGANOFF

Mrs. A. L. Brown

1 lb thick flank steak
1 tabsp. flour
1 teasp. salt and pepper
1 tabsp. vegetable oil
2 onions
1 garlic clove
1 lb tomatoes
1 pkt. mushroom soup
½ pint water
1 destsp. vinegar
½ cup unsweetened milk or cream

Cut steak into fingers and roll in flour, salt and pepper, lightly fry steak and onions in oil, add garlic, cubed tomatoes or puree, muchroom soup blended with water and simmer 1½ hours. Add vinegar and milk before serving. Serve with rice.

SPANISH BEEF

FOR FOUR SERVINGS:

4 sirloin or porterhouse steaks
¼ cup chopped onions
½ lb mushrooms
3 tabsp. red wine
Salt and pepper

Place each steak on a large piece of silver foil. Cook onions gently in butter, add mushrooms and cook a little. Remove from fire and add wine. Portion this out over meat and wrap up individual parcels being careful to seal in juices. Bake 1 hour in flat dish. Add salt and pepper when cooked.

HUNGARIAN GOULASH

1 chopped onion
1 chopped clove garlic
¼ cup butter
1 lb beef
1 lb pork
1 lb veal
1 cup water
1 tabsp. paprika mixed in
¼ cup water
1 destsp. salt
¼ teasp. pepper
1 can sauerkraut
¼ pint sour cream

Crush garlic and sprinkle with salt then saute in butter with onion. Add meat cut into cubes and brown. Add water and seasonings, simmer slowly two hours. Just before serving add sauerkraut rinsed in cold water and drained and sour cream.

Serve on 1 lb Siam rice hot and fluffy, or 1 lb buttered egg noodles.

55

Like many cookbooks from the 1960s, *Carefree Cooking* issued by the Feilding Free Kindergarten Committee in 1965 included many recipes that readers considered to be 'international' (p. 55). In this fundraiser, such recipes had their own section. H. Leach Collection.

in the 1960s than in any other decade. In contrast, desserts and baking show greater continuity.

Other factors for change need to be considered, albeit very briefly. These include new technology and socio-economic trends. Jam making and bottling went into a sharp decline in the 1960s as more women joined the paid workforce. Deep freezers offered an easy alternative to bottling. Section sizes diminished, and with them the seasonal garden surpluses that had stimulated much home jam making and preserving in the days of 'waste not want not'. But there are limits to the power of new technology to alter a culinary tradition. When the space-age microwave landed in our kitchens in the early 1980s, we did not adopt a new set of dishes to make in it. Apart from a few oil-based cakes of American origin, most of our microwave recipes were for classic Kiwi dishes. Much local experimentation went into the microwaved pavlova, ginger crunch and 'lazy lasagne' (see Teal, Chapter 4), to name just a few adaptations. Similarly, when gas and electric stoves were first introduced, there was little change in repertoire, just in cooking instructions for already familiar dishes.

CONCLUSIONS

Overall, I have argued that our two main culinary traditions are remarkably resilient. Despite the dramatic downturn in Maori numbers and fortunes after 1860, their culinary tradition survived, to reappear in the 1970s, still recognisably Maori and well adapted to contemporary needs. The Pakeha tradition also had to adapt to colonial conditions. Although Pakeha cooks obtained supplies from Maori, they looked elsewhere for recipes, in particular to Australia and America. Structural rules for composing the traditional British dinner exerted a conservative effect upon menus until the 1960s. However, in baking, Kiwi cooks were freer to express their skills and fascination with novelty. As the range of cakes, biscuits, squares, fingers, scones and gems increased, the types of meat considered edible were reduced. Sweetbreads, heads, brains and tongues disappeared from dinner menus. This reduction in variety was concealed by cooking the remaining meat cuts with new herbs and spices, and adding new vegetables to the dinner plate. More obviously, we appropriated classic dishes from countries that we had borrowed little from in earlier decades, in order to show we were truly international players.

As far as can be judged from the cookbooks, the net gain from the inter-nationalisation of our outlook surpassed the losses of traditional British dishes. The internationalisation of the 1960s was followed by increasing global interconnectedness involving ideas, commodities and people – what we now recognise as full globalisation. We have not returned to the old British meal structures, preferring a more flexible pattern of starters, mains and desserts. Only those who habitually eat at fast-food outlets and restaurants have other cuisines' structures imposed upon them. For the rest of us who still prepare food at home, there is little danger of us sinking into a homogenised 'world cuisine' (Goody 1982). But what is critical to the future survival of all our culinary traditions, whether Maori, Pakeha, Pasifika, old Cantonese, new Hong Kong, South African, or Cambodian, is that we remain in control of the kitchen. That is the only location where we can adapt new ingredients and technologies to our tastes, and embed them in our culinary traditions. I will finish with a brand-new 'saying' to express this message: 'Lose your identity in the supermarket. Preserve it in the kitchen.'

PART II

Cookbooks and Culinary History in New Zealand

4

Changing Kitchen Technology

F. Jane Teal

Although most nineteenth-century European colonists came to New Zealand from homelands with well-established heavy industry, it was not a case of simply re-installing their cooking technology, such as open-fire cast iron ranges and chimney cranes, and resuming their traditional cookery. As Leach has shown (Chapter 2), many early colonists had to revert to the cooking devices used by their seventeenth- and eighteenth-century ancestors. Colonial kitchens display very uneven development in technology, depending on household resources and distance from population centres. This variation persisted into the twentieth century. The idea of a unilinear and evenly spread progression from camp oven to microwave is therefore too simplistic. Instead, we should examine changing technology as a series of themes.

As source material, use has been made of written records from early settlers, surviving kitchen artefacts, the records of appliance manufacturers, and the cookbooks that introduced new technology to the community. From the outset it is important to stress that changes in kitchen technology always affected kitchen practices and generally brought about changes in the dishes that characterised our culinary traditions. This chapter will concentrate on the history of the most common types of cooking apparatus used in New Zealand from the colonial era – specifically those fuelled by wood and coal, coal gas, and electricity. It will finish with two case studies that show how recipes are modified as new technologies are adopted.

TEMPORARY SOLUTIONS

Once the colonists had landed, they had few alternatives for cooking before settling into their accommodation, provided that it was actually built. In Nelson, the Stanton family of seven which arrived on the *Clifford* in May 1842 were initially housed in the building which was to be the hospital, and then moved to a partially built house in 'Bolton Square'. Their eldest son, William Moses, remembered the changes they experienced:

> The cooking oven convenience in front of the door (or rather doorway) or
> entrance, formed, gypsy-like, with forked sticks, supporting a transverse
> bearer for hanging, by chain and hook the pots and kettles for our frugal
> unsophisticated fare which comprised ship's provisions of stale brown
> Biscuit, 'Irish pork', and 'Indian Beef', in salt[petre?] with homemade
> bread, of mysterious 'Leaven', with barrelled American flour, generally sour,
> and frequently found in hard compressed lumps, which had to be hard
> crushed, for use, and rolled into or repulverized with with a round bottle,
> in order to being [sic] converted into damper or scones, or more frequently,
> pancakes. In due time, ovens were found practicable, constructed, or built,
> with stones from the river bed, and clay mortar—or the 'Loaves' (of bread)
> were baked, in the three legged iron pot, known as a 'go a shore' until
> the introduction of the now familiar, and scarcely superior 'Camp oven'.
> (Stanton ms:7)

In these new surroundings it would have taken some time for the family to work out how to control the cooking temperatures. The placement of cooking utensils at different distances and heights from the fire, as well as collecting wood that combusted at different speeds, would have made for an all-day task. Charlotte Godley writing home to her family confirmed that Lyttelton in 1850–51 was no better than Nelson. Fires were lit in holes just outside the doors just as Jane Williams had observed them in Poverty Bay in 1840 (Godley 1951:160; Porter 1974:93). In Christchurch, cooking was 'carried on outside to the great edification of passers-by' (Godley 1951:177). Charlotte Godley also experienced the risks associated with cooking indoors while staying at Riccarton with the Deans:

> I heard a great scream from Powles and when I ran out she showed me
> a little bit, on fire, in the wall, as it seemed, of the kitchen chimney, but
> so close to the raupo walls that my hair was all set on ends in an instant.
> Powles ran off for water, about twenty yards, and I burned my hands in
> trying to get the spout of the kettle into the fiery hole, which was between
> the outer and the inner thatching, and must have caught fire from some
> spark lodging in a hole of the sod chimney, and gradually getting through
> that to the very inflammable stuff about, when it made quick work.
> (Godley 1951:178)

The resulting 'heap of black ashes' was replaced with another raupo house, without a chimney. The Godley's house in Lyttelton had other problems. It let in the rain and had 'a somewhat wilful stove' from Sydney. Charlotte claimed it was not 'half so good as many that the Colonials, rich and poor, have brought out with them' (Godley 1951:184).

What was brought to New Zealand in the holds of the sailing ships varied enormously, depending on the information which immigrants received before they left. It was common practice to publish letters in local journals and while one settler suggested taking 'a stock of cooking utensils', another recommended 'a couple of pots [and] a small camp oven' (Hargreaves and Hearn 1978:32, 38). New Zealand benefited more than other countries from the fact that the major sources of supply, England, Canada, America and Australia, all had previous experience of being both coloniser and colonised and therefore the exporters could judge what was appropriate and useful in similar circumstances.

Crawford's (2006) case study of the outfitting of colonial kitchens in Dunedin from 1848–60 indicates that with detailed research in a specific location it is possible to begin to understand the initial importation of cooking equipment. Later arrivals could always purchase goods second-hand. On the same day that H. Parkes advertised a meeting to plan the celebrations for the fifth anniversary of the arrival of the Canterbury Pilgrims, Messrs F. Campbell Noble were selling 'kitchen utensils' on behalf of Captain Simeon, and Longden was selling 'kitchen utensils in great variety' for Conway Rose. An advertisement for the auction of J.C. Watts-Russell's household effects at Ilam on 1–2 January 1856 listed 'kitchen utensils of all descriptions, Soyer's Magic Stove, fender and fire irons' as going under the hammer. F. Mason's Colonial Store in Norwich Quay had iron boilers, tea kettles, saucepans, frying pans, camp ovens of all sizes, while C.W. Bishop at Market Square listed dutch ovens, milk double saucepans, tart pans, oval boilers and saucepans of all sizes, and enamelled saucepans and preserving pans (*Canterbury Standard* 22 November 1855:2–3). The building of more substantial houses with exterior chimneys of corrugated iron or brick meant that this cooking equipment was increasingly used indoors in open hearths.

CAST IRON COOKING RANGES

In the *Daily Southern Cross* of 24 January 1866, Robert Peace advertised that he was going to apply 'to the Governor in Council for LETTERS PATENT for a new and improved COKKING STOVE and RANGE [sic], not heretofore made in this or any other country'. It may be the same three-ring model as the cast iron stove which can be found in the Auckland Museum which has 'Robt Peace Auckland Rise New Zealand' embossed on the carcass and a dove carrying an olive branch with 'Peace' written above it on the door to the firebox. The flue of sheet

This fireplace with its original bread oven has been modified to accommodate a Shacklock Orion coal range. It has also retained space for a pot to be hung directly over an open fire. Challies Kitchen Range, c.1920. The Nelson Provincial Museum, Ellis Dudgeon Collection 252687/7.

metal with its double-skinned cylindrical oven and baking tray were later rebuilt from plans. Its ancestry is obviously the three-legged American woodstoves that arrived in quantity in New Zealand as flat packs ready to be assembled (Auckland Museum Col 9.1-17 ID 55101; Antiquestoves.com).

The New Zealand Eclipse Cottage Stove at Ewelme Cottage, Parnell may be the only surviving example from Herbert Henry Smith's Auckland Iron Works that was established in 1870 and manufactured 'Eclipse Economist Mistress Ranges' as well as 'Portable, Side and Colonial Ovens' (Murdoch 1888). According to Lush family tradition, it was installed in 1871, replacing an earlier one that was delivered in February 1864. Made of wrought iron, it consists of an oven and a water tank. The firebox is brick-lined with a metal grill and the flue has a metal lever that acts as a damper (Webster 1987; New Zealand Historic Places Trust Chattels Form XEC: 972). These New Zealand-built stoves appear to have used wood as their main source of fuel, requiring continuous feeding to maintain a consistent temperature, whereas the American and British imports were designed for the more fiercely burning bituminous coals. Only a few of New Zealand's coal fields are bituminous (Waikato, Taranaki, Northland, Ohai), with the majority being sub-bituminous (thirteen fields from Greymouth to Seddonville, Ohai), or consisting of lignite (Kaitangata, Central Otago, Eastern Southland) (Sherwood and Phillips 2008).

It was probably the lignite from Kaitangata (Kai Point Coal), with its high moisture content, that led H.E. Shacklock of Dunedin to cast a wide and shallow firebox with flues which encouraged the flames to travel further (Angus 1973:8; Anon 1905). From the time of its conception in 1876, the coal range that Shacklock created and named after the constellation Orion, but did not patent until 1882, retained its basic ease of installation and consistent visual appeal (Hocken Collections AG-175 and AG-175-17+). It was this type of range that was fondly remembered as the heart of the home. Gordon Parry recalled,

> In the winter there was a soup pot permanently planted towards the back of the range. And it was usual to make porridge in a large pot just above the firebox. The coal scuttle and shovel stood by the hearth. There was no thermometer on the range. In those days it was a matter of judgment to decide when the oven was ready for the scones or sponges. (Parry 2005:17)

Shacklock knew that it was more than just a matter of judgment. He urged his customers to

> Study the working of the range and see that all doors and the flue rake are in proper order. The damper should be open just wide enough to give the requisite draught. With a newly made fire it should be opened wide, and after the flame is fairly going, close it a little. When the work is done, leave it just a little open, so as to preserve the fire for future use and keep the range warm. Proper attention to the damper will help give a regularity of heat, and effect a great saving of coal. (Miller 1898:6)

It was only after these skills were mastered and the cook applied them to each individual stove that the well-known stories about gauging oven heat by touching the oven door knob, putting a hand in the oven, or watching how long brown paper or a scatter of flour on an oven tray took to change colour, actually gave consistent results.

The Shacklock stove at Highwic in Auckland provides another clue about New Zealand stove makers. On one of the twin chimneys there is a name plate for J. Broady, City Ironworks, Auckland. John Broady set up his own business in 1885, specialising in coal ranges, having previously been employed by Hyauiason's

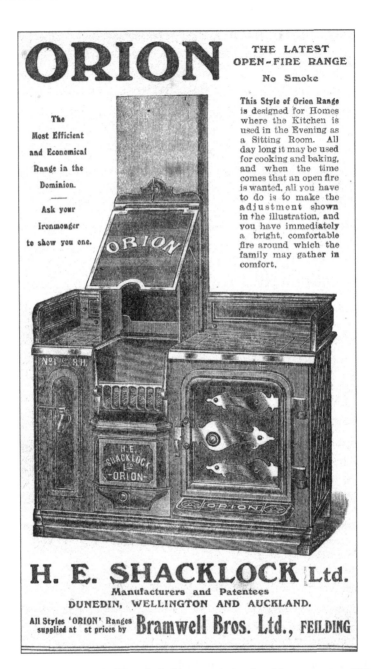

ORION

THE LATEST OPEN-FIRE RANGE

No Smoke

The Most Efficient and Economical Range in the Dominion.

Ask your Ironmonger to show you one.

This Style of Orion Range is designed for Homes where the Kitchen is used in the Evening as a Sitting Room. All day long it may be used for cooking and baking, and when the time comes that an open fire is wanted, all you have to do is to make the adjustment shown in the illustration, and you have immediately a bright, comfortable fire around which the family may gather in comfort.

H. E. SHACKLOCK Ltd.

Manufacturers and Patentees

DUNEDIN, WELLINGTON AND AUCKLAND.

All Styles 'ORION' Ranges supplied at st prices by **Bramwell Bros. Ltd., FEILDING**

Although H.E. Shacklock Ltd of Dunedin had been producing closed-fire ranges since 1875, this illustration from *Our Boys' Cookery Book* published in Wellington in 1915 indicates that as well as being used for cooking, ranges also heated water and aired clothes. The open fire modification in which flames were visible drew the family together in the evening. H. Leach Collection.

range makers and locksmiths following his emigration from Cheshire in 1879 (Anon 1902:367–8). It was to Doug Broady that the stove at Ewelme Cottage was sent for repairs in about 1970 (Webster 1987). John Broady's two partners Charles Allan and Alfred Martin had previously worked for other Auckland stove manufacturers. Allan was apprenticed to H.H. Smith and Martin was employed by Reuben Nicholls, the 'Manufacturer of the celebrated and Unbreakable Steel-Top Cooking Ranges'. Established in Upper Queen Street in 1873, this firm patented the 'Orb' cast iron stove (Anon 1902:373). Charles Handley of Elliot Street, Auckland, also served his apprenticeship with H.H. Smith, and subsequently worked for Hyauiason and Broady & Co. By 1903, Handley was manufacturing stoves of wrought iron with steel tops, marketing them not only for domestic use, but also for ships (Anon 1902:371). In Wellington, S. Luke and Co. Ltd purchased the existing company of Gilchrist and Waters. Although their specialty was marine engineering and dairying utensils, they also held a patent for cooking ranges and were awarded a gold medal in the 1906–07 Christchurch Exhibition (Anon 1897; Cowan 1910:408).

Shacklock's greatest rival was the firm of Scott Bros of Christchurch. George and John Lee Scott purchased the Railway Foundry in 1872, ten years after its founding by Henry Barnes. It included casting, turning, pattern and copper-making shops and a smithy (Starky 2007; Anon 1903:311). These provided the equipment for the development of their first coal range in 1878. Models were known over the years as 'Atlas', 'New Atlas', 'Record', 'New Record', 'Victor', 'Peerless', 'Unique' and 'Camp' (Anon nd c). Another competitor was Brinsley & Co., of Dunedin. In the 1906–07 Christchurch Exhibition, Shacklock and Brinsley were awarded a gold and silver medal respectively for their coal ranges (Cowan 1910:408).

Shacklock and Brinsley & Co. were also awarded medals at the Dunedin and South Seas Exhibition 1925–6. Shacklock's 'Large Island Coal Range', with two fireboxes and four ovens which weighed four tons, was given a first prize, while one of his unspecified 'Domestic Coal Ranges' was awarded a second. Brinsley & Co. gained a first award for their 'Coal Ranges and Combined Range and Open Fire'. Exhibitions of this kind brought appliances to public notice in a very prominent way as the average daily attendance over the twenty-four weeks was 22,538 (Thompson nd:137, 164). Although Barningham & Co. of the Dunedin Victoria Foundry did not begin manufacturing until after Shacklock, the 'Zealandia' patent coal range was well known and the firm had additional outlets in Wellington and Auckland. *Wise's New Zealand Post Office Directories* (see Table 1) provide the

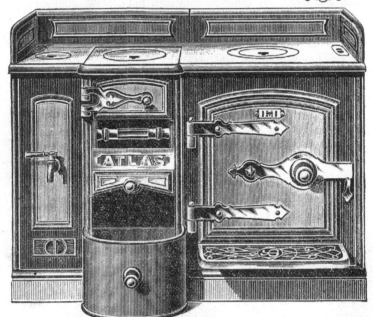

☞ HOW TO COOK!

Use an Atlas Range

AS MANUFACTURED BY

SCOTT BROS. Ltd., CHRISTCHURCH.

These Ranges have secured the **Highest Awards** wherever exhibited, and are guaranteed to give the utmost satisfaction.

The Peerless, Victor & Record Ranges

ARE ALSO MANUFACTURED BY

SCOTT BROS. Ltd.,

Scott Bros of Christchurch produced the 'Atlas' closed-fire range under a number of different names. These models were made of steel plate and could be purchased in different sizes to suit each individual kitchen. From *Colonial Everyday Cookery*, 1st edition [1901] H. Leach Collection.

Table 1. New Zealand stove and range manufacturers, extracted from *Wise's New Zealand Post Office Directories* 1883–1955.

Name of Manufacturer	Location/Outlet	Date
Allan, C F F	Auckland	1906
Atkinson & Son	Christchurch	1883–1931
Baden, James	Wellington	1902–1904
Barningham & Co	Auckland	1926–1951
Barningham & Co	Dunedin	1883–1951
Barningham & Co	Wellington	1930–1951
Bell, Hodgson	Wellington	1904
Brinsley & Co (see Radiation)	Dunedin	1898–1931
British General Electric Co Ltd	Wellington	1936–1946
Broady, J	Auckland	1894–1940
Brown, J	Auckland	1883
Crompton & Co/ Crown Iron Works & Co	Christchurch	1890–1928
Davies, Richard	Wellington	1910
Derby, C R	Newton	1890–1900
Don Electric Range Co	Wellington	1930–1931
Eclipse Foundry Ltd	Wellington	1946–1955
Electric Ranges Ltd	Wellington	1942–1951
Ferris & Co/Ferris & Cresswell	Wellington	1906–1910
Froggatt, B	Christchurch	1885–1893
Hay, J	Invercargill	1885
Hepburn & Sons	Christchurch	1902–1928
Hern, J	Christchurch	1883
Hosking & Sons/C Hoskings/Woolcock & Hoskings	Palmerston North	1896–1904
Hyauiason & Sons/D Hyauiason	Auckland	1883–1931
Judd Electric Stove Co Ltd	Wellington	1933–1936
King, Albert John	Dunedin	1914
Langmuir & Co Ltd	Invercargill	1916
Luke & Sons	Wellington	1896–1931
McIntyre, Douglas/Keats & McIntyre	Auckland	1900–1908
New Scott Range Co	Christchurch	1930–1934
Newman George	Auckland	1892–1904
Nicholls Bros	Auckland	1894–1931
Nicholls, G	Christchurch	1890–1893
Nicholls, R	Auckland	1883–1906
Osborne Stove Co Ltd	Christchurch	1936–1955
Payne, C W	Auckland	1938–1940
Pryer & Sons	Wellington	1938–1951

Continued ...

Name of Manufacturer	Location/Outlet	Date
Radiation (see Brinsley & Co)	Dunedin	1933–1955
Rae, Charles E	Auckland	1920–1938
Reid, John W	Wellington	1920–1936
Roberts Iron Steel & Oven Works	Wellington	1918–1931
Scott Bros	Auckland	1918–1955
Scott Bros	Christchurch	1885–1955
Scott Bros	Timaru	1912–1922
Shacklock, H E	Christchurch	1926–1938
Shacklock, H E	Wellington	1930–1938
Shacklock, H E	Auckland	1930–1938
Shacklock, H E	Dunedin	1883–1955
Smith & Co/Smith & Veale	Auckland	1912–1914
Smith, H H	Auckland	1890–1899
Stokes Cookers Ltd	New Plymouth	1938
Stones & White	Auckland	1904–1920
Storrier & Co	Timaru	1900–1910
Thornicroft, A J	Dunedin	1894–1900
Tonkin, J	Auckland	1883
Tripex Patent Grate Co NZ Ltd	Christchurch	1926–1931
Walker & Son	Invercargill	1902–1912
Watters, T J	Christchurch	1883–1920
Whyte, F	Auckland	1936–1938

names of many firms who claimed to be stove or range manufacturers but it is very difficult to determine just how many of them were agents or manufacturers, and how many made alterations to imported stoves, or simply repaired them. It is also apparent from newspaper advertisements and advertisements within community cookbooks that not all firms (e.g. NEECO) were represented in this source.

As far as it is known, none of the New Zealand coal range manufacturers published or distributed a recipe book specific to their product. Cooks had to use their own manuscript collections and printed volumes that they brought with them or purchased from a local bookseller. Signatures and dates on the flyleaf or title page are an invaluable source of information about the ownership of recipe books. It is from sources like this that we know that Marianne Williams purchased her 7/6d copy of the 1818 edition of *A New System of Domestic Cookery; Framed up on the Principles of Economy and Adapted to the use of Private Families by a Lady* (Mrs Rundell) in 1819, when she was training to be a maternity nurse and teacher as well as taking cooking lessons, prior to her departure for New Zealand

(Fitzgerald 2004:opp. p.78; Booth 1996:465). Manufacturers and suppliers also advertised in cookbooks. In 1888, T. & S. Morrin & Co of Auckland advertised a large stock of kitchen ranges and cooking stoves and J. & J. Dickey of Auckland were supplying Atlas ranges (Murdoch 1888), while the 1925 edition of the long-running St Andrew's series of cookbooks contains an advertisement for both Shacklock's Orion coal range and for the technology which was to succeed it, a Moffat electrical range (Anon 1925:122, back cover).

GAS STOVES

The earliest recorded use of gas for cooking in England is 1802, but it was not until 1826 that James Sharp, the Assistant Manager of the Northampton Gas Company, installed an experimental stove in his own home. Encouraged by his patron, Earl Spencer, he gradually began to produce them commercially (Glendinning 2008:58). They were still unusual in England in the 1880s but some immigrants would have experienced them prior to their arrival in New Zealand. In Dunedin, the first recorded use of gas stoves was in a trial held at the Town Hall in 1884 (Anon nd k:17), but widespread adoption depended on the availability of a continuous gas supply. Many city and borough councils built their own gas works for supplying public utilities, especially lighting, but the laying of pipes for consumers was sometimes a long and drawn-out process. Some locations were never included.

Initially there was no way of gauging the heat in a gas oven, although

> the temperature may be roughly estimated by hand. To do this, open the oven door gently, place the hand in the centre of the oven and count slowly. If it becomes uncomfortably hot after counting three, the oven is Very Hot; after counting five, Hot; after counting ten, Moderately Hot, if it feels just comfortably hot and not unbearable, Moderate, if just warm, Slow. (Good Housekeeping Institute 1950:42)

It was to advertise this type of stove that the second and enlarged edition of *The New Zealand International Exhibition Cookery Book*, compiled by Mrs Patrick Gill (c.1905), was sponsored by the Christchurch Gas, Coal and Coke Company Ltd. Not only did they use the covers for advertising, but they also arranged for a series of repeating advertisement lines extolling the virtues of gas stoves and gas cooking to be added under every recipe. Like their English counterparts (Glendinning 2008:59), they offered the opportunity to either purchase or hire (at 5/- or 2/- per week respectively). As well as enthusing about 'No Soot, Dust or Dirt' the Gas Company Showrooms drew on the comments of Dr Stevenson Macadam, a teacher of chemistry and consulting analytical chemist of Edinburgh. He was quoted as saying that meat cooked in gas stoves 'would be found to be *more juicy and more palatable* ... [and] more *easily digested*'. The 'two best Gas Cooking Ranges' advertised for this purpose were the 'Waterheat' and the 'Perfection'. The latter had won the Gas Company a gold medal at the 1906–07 Christchurch Exhibition (Cowan 1910:408), but their manufacturer is not clear.

From 1923 onwards, the regulation of heat in gas stoves was achieved through the Regulo. Invented by John Wright and Co. who were later incorporated into the English firm Radiation,* it is a simple device that is based on the principle that some metals expand more that others when heated. The control knob did not have the actual temperatures on it, but rather a series of numbers that had to be compared with the Fahrenheit temperatures for the particular model that was being used. Different makes of stove were not comparable for temperature (Chatterton nd:18; Good Housekeeping Institute 1950:41), so a change in the make of a gas stove could require the testing and modification of familiar recipes. The Parkinson Stove Co. Ltd of Birmingham instructed cooks to 'Follow the instructions and put your faith in the "Adjusto"' (Hughes nd:5). Like the Regulo it was operated by a valve, but Parkinson took the precaution of letting users know that it did 'not begin to act till the oven is really hot, so the flame will not go down until then' (Hughes nd:5). Stoves like the 'Newpark' and 'Minette' came both with and without this feature while the 'Reknown' and 'Crest' were supplied with it as a matter of course.

Radiation gained a major foothold in New Zealand when it took over Brinsley & Co. in 1933. They were the manufacturers of coal ranges as well as the 'Champion' gas stove. Their gas stove entry in the Dunedin and South Seas Exhibition gained them a first ahead of the overseas firms of The Falkirk Iron Co. Ltd of Scotland and City Iron and Ovens from Long Beach in the United States (Thompson nd:164). The oven was originally produced with burners at the sides. Later they were replaced by one along the base of the back wall, and with the addition of the Regulo and the use of a browning sheet as required, this ensured a more even heat. It would seem that E.N. (Neige) Todhunter's *'Champion' Cook Book* series (c.1933, c.1940, c.1945) was a direct result of this change in management. The recipes in them were 'carefully selected to be representative of the cooking of different types of food and dishes' (Todhunter c.1933:1). She was also most enthusiastic about

---

* The firms which constituted Radiation were Arden Hill & Co., The Richmond Gas Stove and Meter Co. Ltd, The David Gas Stove Co. Ltd., Fletcher, Russell and Co. Ltd, Wilsons and Mathiesons Ltd, John Wright & Co.

"CHAMPION" COOK BOOK

FOR
"CHAMPION"
OVEN REGULATED
Gas Cookers

Prepared by
E. N. TODHUNTER
M. H. Sc.
Cookery Medallist
City and Guilds Institute
London

Radiation New Zealand Limited
MANUFACTURERS OF
"CHAMPION" Products
BRINSLEY WORKS
JUTLAND ST., DUNEDIN

Radiation New Zealand Limited highlighted not only the oven regulator, but also the ease with which women could prepare meals while dressed to receive guests. H. Leach Collection.

Gas and electric stoves gradually became more compact and the colours that could be produced by enamelling influenced and were influenced by kitchen design. This cabinet gas cooker is from the eighth edition of Isabella Finlay's *Gas Cookery* (c.1939). H. Leach Collection.

'Whole Meal Oven Cooking'. This had been promoted by Radiation since at least 1930, following the introduction of the 'New World' cookers, and 'the saving in time and attention which this procedure renders possible will be appreciated by all housewives and cooks' (Anon 1930:144). Copies of English Radiation recipe books may have been given away by stockists, as a copy in the Canterbury Museum is stamped 'Timaru Gas Coal Company' (Peel nd). The Dunedin City Gas Department's many editions of their *Cookery Book*, compiled by Isabella Finlay, had links with Brinsley & Co. and Radiation, with baking instructions for the various 'Champion' and 'New World' Series cookers included in the fold-out baking charts at the back of each edition.

By the late 1930s, gas and electric stoves were competing for the same consumer. Increasingly, comparisons were made about the costs and, in an attempt to woo customers, the Christchurch Gas Coal and Coke Company introduced the 'All Gas' tariff, which paid for overheads while at the same time reducing the overall annual costs to the householder (Anon c.1933). They also regularly advertised demonstrations at the company's showroom (Teal 2006:92–3). In Dunedin, it was proved that it was possible to cook a dinner for twelve in two hours for 2 ½d in an Osborne 4A Combination Gas Cooker (Finlay c.1933). By the beginning of the 1980s only two gasworks remained in the country. In 1982 the Christchurch works closed (Pollard 1987) and then in June 1987 the Dunedin works, 'the first and the last place in New Zealand where coal gas was manufactured' (Anon nd k:2), was also closed.

ELECTRIC STOVES

The availability of electric appliances in New Zealand homes was again dependent entirely on the development of infrastructure. Although electricity had been generated here since 1888, it was mainly used for industry and lighting and was reliant on private power plants and generators. The first all-electric house was built in Tauranga in 1915 (Rennie 1989:84), but it was not until the development of large-scale projects like Waipori (1903–7), Lake Coleridge (1911–14) and Horahora (1910–13), with their associated transmission lines, that it became possible for towns to be lit and new industries to develop.

The electric stove as it was first developed was 'a stoutly constructed metal framework containing the electric wiring and heating elements all carefully and thoroughly insulated, controlled by their respective switches and protected by a set of neat circular cut-outs each containing a fuse' (MED c.1938:28). Once more H.E. Shacklock Ltd and Scott Bros were leaders in the manufacturing field. Shacklock's

'Orion No 52' began production in 1926. It was initiated by J.B. Shacklock who was, coincidentally, one of the main forces behind the Waipori Hydro Electric Power Scheme (Angus 1973:54). The electric stoves produced by Shacklock were cast iron like the coal ranges, with nickel-plated tops, enamelled door panels and twin elements. The electricity in both the oven and the top rings was controlled by three-heat switches, also known as reciprocating switches. Temperature control in the oven was achieved by switching on the top and bottom elements to high until the required temperature was registered by the 'Heat Indicator' on the oven door. Many cake and biscuit recipes then required both switches to be turned to low, while others recommended that they should both be turned off and the items baked using the heat which was stored in the oven.

The spread of knowledge about the benefit of electric stoves can be attributed to two main sources: demonstrators and recipe books. Shacklock employed Elizabeth Warburton (later Mrs Sonntag) to demonstrate their appliances at exhibitions throughout the country and to testify to the advantages of the 'perfect servant' (Anon 1947:back cover), 'white coal' (Angus 1973:54), and the importance of patronising 'New Zealand made goods' (Porteous nd:1; Warburton 1929:7). Their salesmanship was such that by 1929 there were 20,254 electric ranges in New Zealand, an increase of 28.4 per cent from 1928 (Reilly 2008:71). The 1929 *Instruction and Recipe Book for Users of Orion Electric Ranges* that Warburton wrote, provides illustrations of the three most popular models at that time (No's 62, 72, and 74), with their box-like shape perched on cabriole legs. The firm also introduced the table type (No 75) with its additional warming oven, porcellained high covings and shelf. The inclusion of testimonials from New Plymouth to Mataura to their efficiency, economy and cleanliness as well as ease of use was all part of the marketing strategy.

Scott Bros produced fourteen editions of the *Atlas Cookery Book* from 1949–69 and at least one edition (1952) was printed in Braille (Woods-Dalloway, pers. com. 2006). The current edition was given to all those who purchased one of their electric stoves. The introduction briefly covered the history of the firm and then, depending on the edition, detailed the procedure that was necessary to obtain the correct heat. In their earlier models, the instructions referred to the three-heat switch and fuse that controlled the two oven elements, with the heat indicated by a thermometer on the oven door. Even with the introduction of the thermostat that controlled the maximum temperature, and then the single thermostatic temperature selector switch, the recipes were not altered except through the placement of a label stuck on the outside of the book stating:

> IMPORTANT This range is fitted with a selector switch and where a recipe
> in this book states 'set the oven control switch to high bake or a number'
> the preselector switch knob should be set to 'bake' after preheating the
> oven. (Anon 1963:front cover)

Throughout they were very aware that

> the cooking temperature and time given on the chart are a guide only.
> Individual thermometers vary slightly and individual methods of cooking
> vary greatly. By trial vary the temperature 50 degrees or more as required to
> obtain good results and correct the figures given on the chart. (Anon 1951:4)

The National Electric and Engineering Co. Ltd (NEECO) was another Dunedin-established firm. Founded in 1906, it was involved in the supply of electrical equipment for various electrification projects. It moved to Kaiwharawhara, Wellington in 1935 and began making ranges, not by casting and enamelling, but from pressed steel, the first in the country to do so (Rennie 1989:87). Their *700 Recommended Recipes* and *700 Neeco Tested Recipes* (Anon nd a; Anon nd b) appeared under two titles but maintained the same stove illustration, recipes and cooking instructions throughout.

The retail store of Turnbull and Jones had been agents for Moffat stoves from Weston-Ontario in Canada since 1921 and the stove's Gold Medal award in 'Group 20, Heating' at the New Zealand and South Seas Exhibition, held in Dunedin in 1925–6, indicated that at least in the eyes of the judges their product was better than the Hotpoint Electric Range which was entered by Edison Electric Appliances Co., Inc., of Chicago (Thompson nd:164). The medal was proudly displayed on the front and back covers of an edition of their cookbook published about 1927 that was given to those who purchased their stoves (Anon c.1927a). Moffat's Gold Medal Electric Ranges logo also ran across each page of Catalogue No 103 (Anon c.1927b). The back page of this catalogue invited owners of Moffat stoves who did not possess one of their cookbooks to write to Canada to obtain one. It is through international sources like this that recipes can be added to the culinary repertoire. On the other hand, the McClary Manufacturing Co. of Canada, whose electric stoves and furnaces were displayed in the Canadian Court at the Christchurch International Exhibition in 1906 (Cowan 1910:256), later had their recipe book – with New Zealand recipes – published in New Zealand (Sinclair 1929).

Turnbull and Jones had at various times investigated business arrangements with both NEECO and Westinghouse. With the increasing market share that was being obtained by Scott Bros, and the damage that was happening to the stoves in transit, they negotiated with Moffat about the possibility of manufacturing in

New Zealand. It was necessary to obtain an import licence to manufacture in New Zealand and so there was discussion with both NEECO and Radiation about a joint manufacturing company. Despite misgivings, it was with Osborne* that Moffat began manufacturing cast-iron electric stoves as a joint venture.

The change to thermostatic control caused cooks some consternation. The previous system of top and bottom elements in the oven with their separate three-heat switches (high, medium and low) had provided cooks with a considerable amount of individual flexibility. When this was changed to a single switch that controlled both elements, 'pandemonium hit the market' – many housewives complained that their baking burnt on the bottom, yet Moffat claimed that the Home Science graduates who had advised them had not had any trouble. This next step took away all discretion from the cook – a single thermostat knob which 'supplied the proportion of heat for each element in a manner pre-determined by the stove' (Boyles 1988:85, 86).

A new model from Moffat, the '1054 Spacemaster' which came from Canada, reached the New Zealand market in 1955, and was 'streets ahead of anything made in New Zealand' (Boyles 1988:86). However, marketing stoves when there was competition from five other manufacturers was a difficult business. It was believed that the sale of about 3000 stoves annually was necessary to make a reasonable profit. Even when Moffat changed from a Canadian-tooled stove to one that was completely New Zealand-designed (the 'Calypso'), it was recognised that Shacklock's American-influenced models 'had a level of presentation and sophistication well ahead of anything else on the market' (Boyles 1988:116).

Radiation New Zealand Ltd moved from making gas stoves to electric ones, but continued to use the 'Champion' brand name. They teamed up with the Robertshaw-Fulton Controls Company of Pennsylvania and produced the New Zealand-printed *Robertshaw Measured Heat Cook Book*, which included advertisements for the Champion 'Cadet', 'Ensign', 'Ensign A', 'DL2H' and 'DL3H' electric stoves, all with a Robertshaw thermostat. The book was 'to aid you in cooking the food you buy to best advantage … in full flavour, texture, tenderness and appetizing wholesomeness' (Anon nd i:1).

---

* This firm began as the New Scott Range Company and operated under that name from about 1925–34. It was set up by three members of the second generation of the Scott family (Percy Randal Scott, Ernest Herbert Scott and Annie Lucy Scott). From 1936–55 it was the Osborne Gas Stove Ltd. In 1955 R.H. England became the manager and it began to manufacture Moffat Electric Ranges. The Moffat warehouse still operates from Osborne St, Christchurch.

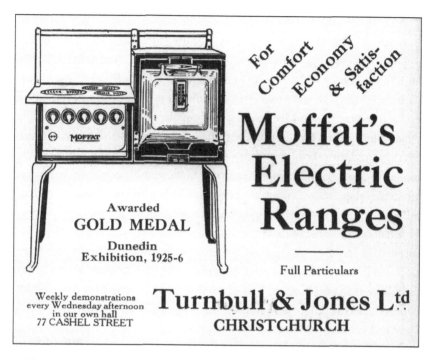

Moffat and Co. Ltd of Canada were awarded a gold medal at the Dunedin and South Seas Exhibition with this E31-K model electric range illustrated in the Christchurch Branch of the Plunket Society's *Violet Day Cook Book* in 1928. Turnbull and Jones used them extensively in their weekly demonstrations to encourage even unskilled cooks to make a commitment and purchase one for their own use from one of their many outlets throughout the country. H. Leach Collection.

Cookbooks were also provided by electric power boards and municipal authorities, as part of their marketing to promote their wares, and to provide service and costing information. In Dunedin, the City Council issued *Electricity in the Home* 'with the object of assisting with the better use of Electrical Current' (Porteous nd:front cover). In it are mentioned products from GEC (Magnet), Atlas, Orion, NEECO, and Moffat, which were all available locally. Scott Bros in Christchurch also advertised, and for those still cooking with coal The Bruce Coal Co. Ltd delivered daily. The Heathcote Council Council issued Technical Publications' *Electric Cookery*, with its advertisement for Moffat (Anon nd d). The Hawke's Bay Electric Power Board produced *Cooking by Electricity* (Anon 1947), which included information about both top and bottom switches and thermostatic control, while the Springs-Ellesmere Electric Power Board gave away Mrs E. Barrington's *Centennial Recipe Book* (1940).

A series of cookbooks that shows considerable continuity was issued to consumers by the Municipal Electricity Department (MED) of Christchurch. Originally published by Whitcombe and Tombs, the first three editions can be dated from c.1927 to c.1938 (MED c.1927; MED c.1935; MED c.1938). Even when the printing was taken over by H.W. Bullivant in 1951 (MED 1951) and the recipes tested by Marion McCrostie, certain popular recipes remained, including Lemon Buns, Kisses, Ginger Biscuits, Coffee Chocolate Cake and Cherry Cake. It is the introductory information that shows the greatest longevity. Although the number of pages expanded with the increase in the number of electric appliances that could be purchased, the basic information about services, reading meters, don'ts for the users of electricity and electric cooking remained essentially the same for about twenty years. In the 1951 version an automatic oven control chart was provided for those who might find it useful. Whitcombe and Tombs also made much use of this same introductory information in their *Modern Home Cookery and Electrical Guide* (Anon nd l) and included the same long-lived recipes. Like gas stoves, electric ranges were available on a time-purchase system (*Otago Daily Times* 18 December 1926).

New Zealand cooks source their recipes from a wide range of cookbooks including community fundraisers, books promoting commercial products and appliances, and family scrapbooks. Published books were not only written at specific times but also during periods of overlapping technologies. In order for them to be useful the cook needed to have a working knowledge of what went before or how to obtain that knowledge.

During the transition from imperial to metric measurement and from Fahrenheit to Celsius temperatures, many community cookbooks provided conversion tables, but there is also ample evidence that recipes were annotated by the cook alongside the original information. A sample of thirty-two community cookbooks from Otago, Wellington and Taranaki, which were published from 1975–93, suggests that this personal adjustment is probably the most reliable method, especially when a transition from temperature descriptions in words rather than numerals is involved. Table 2 shows that a 'warm' oven might be interpreted as any temperature from 140 degrees to 200 degrees Celsius – such variation could result in costly mistakes.

The electric range, like the gas stove, changed the way in which the kitchen operated. The open hearth and then the built-in coal range tended to draw people to one room for both warmth and food. Gas and electric stoves were items in a

Table 2. Temperature ranges in dated community cookbooks from Otago, Taranaki and Wellington, 1975–93.

Descriptive Terms	Range of Temperatures °F	Range of Temperatures °C
Very hot	450–500	220–260
Hot	400–450	200–230
Moderate/Moderately Hot	325–375	160–190
Warm/Moderate	275–375	140–200
Slow	250–325	120–165
Cool	225–325	110–160
Very cool/Very slow	220–275	100–140

bevy of appliances which altered not only kitchen design but had the potential to separate the preparation of food from its eating, and sent people into other rooms in search of warmth.

MICROWAVE OVENS

In the same way that camp ovens, coal ranges, gas stoves and electric stoves have been used by cooks in parallel, so it is with the microwave. However, its addition to the kitchen has not been an integrated one. Although the most recent data from the Ministry of Economic Development (ITG 2003) indicates that 81.7 per cent of households have a microwave, anecdotal evidence suggests that its use, on the whole, does not extend much beyond defrosting, heating up leftovers and takeaways. One-person households tend to make better use of it by testing and adapting recipes.

These 'radar ranges' as they were first known, were claimed to cause blindness, sterility and impotency, and also to contribute to nutrient loss. Such myths were vigorously refuted (Electrical Development Association of New Zealand nd:2, 9). The basic principle of the microwave is that food contains moisture. When moisture molecules absorb the microwave energy entering the oven cavity from the magnetron, the friction from their vibrations produces heat energy that is conducted throughout the food. Good microwave cooking depends on appropriate containers and the placement of food within the oven. Ring containers, for example, allow the microwave energy to penetrate from the centre as well as from the sides.

The first commercially produced microwaves were marketed in the United States in 1947 but the best evidence puts the date of the arrival of the microwave in New Zealand as the early 1970s.* Initially, cooks had access to generic volumes of recipes produced by appliance manufacturers. Only a few microwave cookbooks were written for New Zealand conditions (for example Blake nd; Bilton 1984; Henry 1991; Holst 1987a, 1987b, 1991; Raffills 1988; Waterman 1985, 1987a, 1987b, 1988a, 1988b, 1989). There have also been television programmes, adult education classes, and evening classes held by retailers. Home Science teachers, too, have played their part in adapting the curriculum to include microwave cooking for all Year 7 and 8 students (Bennett et al. nd; Henderson et al. nd; Anon nd f).

When they first appeared in community cookbooks, microwave recipes were simple to find, as they were in a dedicated section. Since 2000, this isolation is less evident and they are now found throughout. It is now necessary to read the recipe text to find out which technology is being used. No microwave recipes have, to date, been found in community cookbooks before 1983, so there appears to be at least a ten-year lag between the arrival of the technology and the dissemination of recipes through this source.

Research shows that when microwave recipes did make their way into community cookbooks, they came from a range of sources. The most obvious are the operational manuals specific to each microwave and generic manufacturers' manuals. Essentially these are a teaching resource for a cook and contain basic recipes with an array of different names, so one of the major problems is to find a distinctive recipe to trace. The manuals were expected to last for a number of years, so many are not dated. This makes it difficult to construct a sequence of recipes. However, in a few cases we can trace the movement of recipes into the community – the Chocolate Swirl recipe from the *Genius National Microwave Oven Cookbook* (Waterman 1985) is one example. This recipe appears in *Everyday Recipes* produced by the New Brighton Plunket sub-branch in 1984 (Anon 1984:22). The contributor, Adele Stewardson, was a microwave consultant and one of the compilers of the Phillipstown Manual Training Centre *Home Economics Recipe Book* (1985). She must have obtained the recipe from an edition prior to Waterman's 1985 New Zealand volume. The North Otago Herb Society recipe book (Anon c.1996: 28), and two volumes published as the result of radio

---

* This date is taken from Waterman's comment on p. 2 in *New Zealand Microwave Cooking* (1988a). This approximate date was confirmed by Alison Holst at the 2nd New Zealand Food History Conference, November 2007, held in Dunedin.

Microwave

APPLE DELIGHT

1 tablespoon lemon/orange juice
3 tablespoon brown sugar   2 tablespoon butter (soft)
¾ cup plain sweet biscuits (crushed)
360g apples (cooking, sliced finely)

Place apples evenly on the base of a pie or flan dish, spoon juice over apple, mix together sugar, butter and biscuits and spread over apples. Microwave on HIGH for 5-7 minutes. Serve with custard or ice-cream.

BOILED FRUIT CAKE

450g tin pineapple and juice   500g mixed fruit
1 tablespoon sherry   1 cup brown sugar
1 teaspoon liquid gravy browning   125g butter
1 cup plain flour   1 cup self raising flour
1 teaspoon mixed spice   1 teaspoon baking soda

Combine pineapple, fruit, sherry, sugar, gravy browning and butter in a 2 litre casserole dish. Microwave on HIGH 4-6 minutes. Stand till cool. Fold in flour, spice, baking soda and beaten eggs. Place batter in a 24cm round ring dish. Decorate with almonds and cherries if desired. Microwave on MEDIUM 14-16 minutes, elevated. Cover loosely with plastic wrap and leave to cool.

From 1983, fundraising cookbooks, such as *Watcha Got Cookin'*, produced by the South Otago Rebekah District Lodge c.1986, began to introduce sections devoted to microwave recipes.

H. Leach Collection.

competitions in Nelson and Marlborough indicate the adoption of the recipe (Anon nd g; Anon nd h:52).

The recipe for Lazy Lasagna suggests additional transmission within community cookbooks themselves. Alison Holst publicly claims to have devised it in 1998 (Holst and Holst 1998), but the first published appearance of it was in 1986 when optional microwave and conventional cooking methods were provided (Holst 1986). It clearly had its origin in the 1974 Lasagne in *More Food Without Fuss* (Holst 1974:66). As a microwave recipe, it has undergone a little transformation over the years: garlic has been chopped and crushed, the packet of soup has varied between a half and a whole, cheese in the latest version is specified as tasty, tomato concentrate is now tomato paste, beef stock has been instant or granules, and the varieties of lasagna now available are acknowledged. The methodology is similar throughout its history, but now takes into account the fact that the topping does not always set in the microwave and may need grilling to finish it off (Holst 1987a; 1987b; 1991; 2007).

These minute changes provide the means of tracing the recipe's adoption and movement within community cookbooks. The 1986 version appears in the Orana Park cookbook (Anon 1993:71–2), and those from St Martin's Spreydon (Anon 1995a:53) and the Manukau Polytechnic (Anon nd e:[43]), whereas the 1987 version which could have come from either Alison Holst's *New Microwave Cookbook* or *New Toshiba Microwave Cookbook* can be found in cookbooks produced by CFC Netball Club (Anon 1990a:60), the Burnside PTA (Anon 1990b:51), Temuka Rata Kindergarten (Anon 1998:28), and St Ninian's Presbyterian Church (Anon 1995b:20–21). In the late 1990s, it was contributed to the St Joseph's Papanui *Recipe Book* as a 'Family Lasagna' (Anon c.1998:97). In the *St John's Scouts Celebrity Cook Book* Warren Lees lays claim to it (Anon nd j:[49]), as have many others over the years. The tomato paste is left out of versions from Whakatane (Anon 1992:87), St Andrew's in South Canterbury (Galletly 1994:120) and Pleasant Point (Anon 1996:45). Canterbury University has created a budget version for students, which uses a can or jar of already mixed pasta sauce (Anon 2001:38). The 'One Step Lasagne' from Woodbury reverts to the past with instructions for both microwave and conventional oven while requiring a can of tomato soup and purée, but halves the amount of mince required (Anon 2006:81). Intermediate school and technology centres have also added it to their repertoire (Boyd [c.1994]:14; Bennett et al. nd:41; Anon nd f:[4]). Some of these recipes also include a modified methodology and adaptation to the characteristics and wattage of their particular microwave.

Table 3. Perceived advantages and disadvantages of various cooking technologies used in New Zealand, drawn from advertisements and experience.

Coal Range

Advantages	Disadvantages
Hot water supply from built-in tank or wet back	Daily ash removal
Variety of heats available in oven	Weekly cleaning of flues
Large range top offering a gradient of heats	Blackleading to prevent rust
Heats kitchen and house	Overheated kitchen in hot weather
Plate warming rack and clothes drying	Variability in quality of fuel

Gas Stove

Advantages	Disadvantages
Portable	Gas supply can be disrupted
Instant heat on ignition	No hot water supply
Controllable oven temperatures with Regulo/ Adjusto	New pots might be required – e.g. enamel unsuitable for heating milk or sauces
Economical	Costs for installation of pipes and meter
Warming oven on some models	Smell and risk of gas leaks
Whole oven cooking	Smaller cooking surface area on top
Griller and toaster	Inconsistent temperature regions within oven
Cooler kitchen	Affected by draughts
	Burners need regular cleaning

Electric Stove

Advantages	Disadvantages
Portable	Electricity supply may be disrupted
Control of heat by switches	Solid elements slow to heat up
Absence of fumes	Electricity initially expensive
Thermostatic control of oven on later models	New equipment needed (importance of flat bottomed pots)
Insulated oven, even temperature	Oven can overheat and destroy thermometer
Clean	Connections and heavy duty wiring required
Griller	No hot water supply
Warming oven on some models	

Microwave

Advantages	Disadvantages
Programmable cooking times, memory	Little room for error in cooking times
Saves time	Browning requires special dish or conventional oven
Appliance stays cool	Doesn't fry or grill without browning dish
Energy and cost saving	New cooking containers required
Dishes straight to the table	Power levels vary between appliances
Quick reheating and thawing	Foaming and boiling over with some foods
Retains nutrients and flavour	Electricity supply may be disrupted
No need for heavy wiring	
Smaller quantities of liquid required	

CONCLUSIONS

As Table 3 demonstrates, adoption of new technology inevitably involved comparisons with older technologies, and advertising accentuated both the perceived advantages of the new and the disadvantages of the old.

The twentieth century saw dramatic shifts in energy sources used in cooking. Many urban households probably moved from wood and coal, to coal gas, and then to electricity, all within the first fifty years. More recently, some of those households replaced electric ranges with models that run on bottled gas, as well as adding numerous small electric appliances to the kitchen inventory. At the same time that stove technology has become more robust, more reliable, and more widely available, it has also become increasingly complex. The cook is now reliant on the automatic nature of cooking technology and expects it to work well, and work well instantly. At the same time there has been continuity and conservatism within the dishes of our culinary traditions. Community cookbooks bear witness to the repetition of recipes over time, sometimes with well-entrenched local variations. New Zealand's inherited culinary traditions have responded to new technology by changes in kitchen practice and spatial layout of appliances, but the actual dishes prepared show only minor modifications. The arrival of the first gas stoves from Britain or microwaves from America did not result in the wholesale adoption of new recipes. Instead, cooks used these new appliances to cook New Zealand dishes in improved ways.

5

The Uptake of Nutritional Advice in the Twentieth Century

Janet Mitchell

In their ingredient lists, cookbooks record what foods are available, and in their recipe instructions they record common procedures. Sometimes they record notes on healthy eating. Hence an examination of their contents alongside official nutrition messages promulgated to the community can help us assess the uptake and application of such nutritional information and its potential influence on our culinary traditions.

Helen Leach (Chapter 1) has suggested that our culinary tradition is the part of our culture that guides what we choose to eat, how we prepare it, how we compose our meals and how we think about them. This chapter aims to document the influence of nutritional thinking on domestic culinary traditions in twentieth-century New Zealand by examining a selection of cookbooks from the University of Otago Library and Leach's collection. To trace the transmission and uptake of nutrition advice through cookbooks, certain markers in the texts were noted: formal nutrition notes where included, recipes containing ingredients with special nutritive properties, such as oat bran, which was known to reduce serum cholesterol, and methods of cooking that were topical in current nutritional thinking.

The study period will be examined in three parts. The first period ends in 1940, when the supply of food was limited because of the war, the second period ends in 1970, after which major changes occurred in the lifestyle and food supply of New Zealanders. Cookbooks selected for examination from the first period were primarily fundraising cookbooks. These were usually compiled by committees of women and while they do not tell us exactly what each community ate at that time, they indicate what foods they had access to, and the recipes contributors might want to be remembered for. They also indicate food fashions of the era. Other cookbooks used at this time were manuals prepared by cooking teachers, and commercial cookbooks that promoted a new product or demonstrated the use of a new piece of cooking equipment, such as a gas or electric stove. Authored cookbooks, on the other hand, are characterised by the selection of their recipes by the author and by the arrangement and style of presentation.

In her own cookbook collection, Leach noted that authored cookbooks increased during the war years (Leach and Inglis 2006:74). Fewer organisations published fundraising cookbooks, and nutritional information that had previously been included in community cookbooks was distributed as leaflets by authorities such as the Department of Health. This trend towards authored cookbooks continued after the war years, when cookbooks based on television cooking programmes, ethnic cookbooks and special-interest cookbooks on topics such as vegetarianism, diet and health increased. However, cookbooks published by well-established commercial organisations promoting their own products, such as Edmonds (later Bluebird Foods), continued to appeal to the public as they were reprinted and updated regularly to respond to new food trends and nutritional ideas. Community cookbooks continued to be produced locally and often reflected food trends from authored cookbooks and magazines.

NUTRITION AND COOKBOOKS 1900–1939

At the end of the nineteenth century, nutritional knowledge was mostly disseminated to the community in a trickle-down process. Knowledge of food and diet was often embedded in the physician and translated to the ill patient, as a curative measure. For example, the following nutrition advice by Dr. H. Simpson, a London physician, was included in *Brett's Colonists' Guide and Cyclopaedia of Useful Knowledge* (1883) for New Zealand colonists:

> As the body consists of mineral constituents, of water, and saline matter
> and of organic matter both nitrogenous and non nitrogenous ... in order
> to supply the requirements of the body our food must consist of the same
> ingredients, or of substances that can be easily changed into them when
> submitted to the process of digestion. (Leys [1883]:570)

Nitrogenous compounds, 'flesh-formers', were known to be available from animal foods as well as peas, beans and lentils. This knowledge meant legumes could be substituted for meat in the diet. Consequently the Women's Christian Temperance Union (WCTU), who believed meat increased the craving for alcohol in men, could now recommend a vegetarian diet that provided appropriate nutrients and would help solve the problem. Mrs E.B. Miller's *Improved Economic Cookery Book* (1901), originally based on cooking lessons given by WCTU members in Dunedin, included this information. Vegetarian recipes began to appear in other New Zealand cookbooks as well; the fifth edition of *Colonial Everyday Cookery* (Anon 1907), for example, introduced a new vegetarian section.

In 1911, the sources of nutritional knowledge in the community expanded with the establishment of the first chair in Domestic Science (later Home Science) at the University of Otago. The early Home Science curriculum included chemical characteristics of proteins, fats and carbohydrates, processes of cookery studied in relation to their fundamental principles, mechanics of cooking and preparation of meat, fish, etc. (Anon 1913). In 1921, the curriculum was expanded to include the essentials of a healthy diet, based on the nutritive properties of food materials and application of these to the feeding of the individual throughout infancy, childhood, adolescence and old age. Lectures on the importance of vitamins were also part of the new curriculum (Anon 1922).

Information about vitamins was conveyed to the public in various cookbooks. For example, Mélanie Primmer, the author of *The Up-to-date Housewife*, noted vitamins were 'a most important factor in life especially for children ... [they] are found in greenstuff, certain fruits as oranges, lemons, milk, egg-yolk, tomatoes, etc.' (Primmer 1926:18). The New Zealand Plunket Society (established 1907) also provided nutrition advice on feeding children in fundraising cookbooks (Millar 1928; Cameron 1929).

Goitre was another health concern for the New Zealand population in the 1920s. A survey in 1920 found a high incidence in areas where iodine was lacking in the soil. As a result, iodine was added to table salt in 1925, but it was not added in sufficient amounts to control the disease until 1941 (Bell 1962). Meanwhile, cookbooks such as *New Zealand's Leading Recipe Book* suggested a remedy for the problem through the use of agar agar as a setting agent in desserts (Harvey c.1936).

The years of the Great Depression 1930–35 brought economic hardship but the nutritional state of the population was never at a seriously low level (Bell 1952). Nevertheless, in 1935 the Department of Health realised adequate nutrition on a low income was a problem and published *Hints on Health* that included the section 'Dietaries for low incomes'. It emphasised milk as important in the diet both for children and adults, also butter, as it was a good source of vitamins A and D and could not be wholly replaced by other fats. Cheaper meats were suggested

FIRST EDITION, APRIL, 1926.

"Now, Good Digestion wait on Appetite, and Health on both!"
Shakespeare

The Up-to-date Housewife

RECIPES
FOOD SUGGESTIONS
and
FAMILY HINTS
For all Occasions.

The Recommendations and Directions
of an Experienced Housewife.

Editress:
MÉLANIE S. PRIMMER, B.A.

Printed and Published by
COULLS SOMERVILLE WILKIE, Ltd., Dunedin and Wellington.
Wholesale Distributing Agents:
Williamson Jeffery, Ltd., Dunedin, Wellington, Christchurch, Invercargill,

Mélanie Primmer's *The Up-to-date Housewife* (1926) provided modern recommendations on nutrition as well as recipes. H. Leach Collection.

for stewing, and steaming was recommended for fish and vegetables to prevent the loss of mineral salts (Anon 1935).

Cookbooks incorporated some of this advice. The Women's Division of the New Zealand Farmers' Union cookbook, *New Zealand Women's Household Guide,* suggested milk desserts should be used as a means of introducing the required amount of milk in the diet, particularly if there were children in the family. It advised against boiling fish but recommended either steaming or baking to make it more digestible, especially for invalids, and recommended salads, fruits and vegetables for their nutritive value, mineral salts, vitamins and cellulose. It also viewed the butter in cakes and puddings, and cakes filled with cream, as important sources of vitamins A and D (Anon c.1936:82, 131).

Similarly the *Home Cookery Book,* compiled by the New Zealand Women's Institute from recipes contributed by members, indicated current nutrition knowledge. A section on the nutrient value of foods was included as well as a section on vegetarian dishes, meatless dishes and use of wholemeal flour, while the concern for a healthy children's diet is reflected in instructions on feeding children, and suggestions for school lunches (Anon 1939).

Invalid diets and cookery

In the nineteenth century many sick and convalescent people were cared for at home on diets prescribed by their physician. For this group, it was particularly important to eat nitrogenous foods to form flesh and repair the body, but it was equally necessary that food should be easily digestible. Foods suggested for invalids in the *Improved Economic Cookery Book* (Miller 1901) and the first edition of the *St Andrew's Cookery Book* (Anon 1905) included light milk puddings, custards, boiled mutton and the undercut of beef. To be avoided were pastry, puddings, fried and all fatty food, pig meat and oysters (Leys [1883]:453). A popular recipe for invalids was beef tea, despite the fact its nutritional benefit was challenged as early as 1860 by scientists who declared it had no nutritive value but might be valuable as a stimulant and a nerve tonic (Kamminga 1995).

The nutritionist approach to requirements for a healthy diet changed during the period. At the beginning of the twentieth century, food was thought of as body-building, nitrogenous or non-nitrogenous or carbonaceous, heat and energy-producing. But when vitamins were acknowledged as necessary for a healthy diet in 1937 by the League of Nations Technical Commission, food was designated as either protective or supplementary energy giving (Gregory and Wilson 1952).

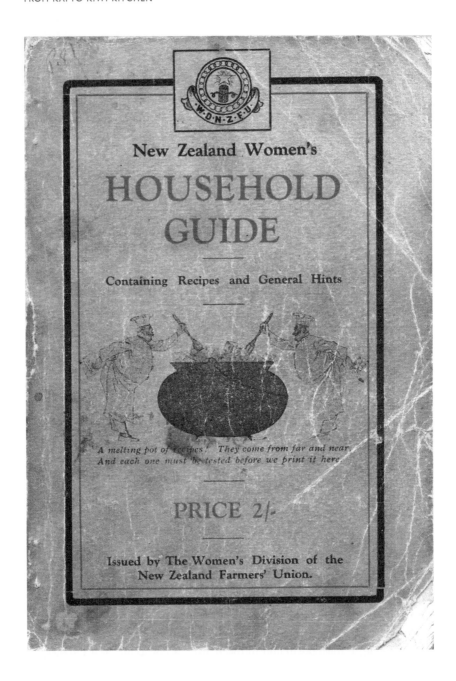

New Zealand Women's

HOUSEHOLD GUIDE

Containing Recipes and General Hints

A melting pot of recipes! They come from far and near,
And each one must be tested before we print it here.

PRICE 2/-

Issued by The Women's Division of the
New Zealand Farmers' Union.

From the first appearance of the *New Zealand Women's Household Guide* (c.1930), the editors provided more than just recipes to their rural readers, introducing each cookery section with advice on nutrition and household economy. H. Leach Collection.

GOOD AND TRIED RECIPES. 177

INVALID COOKERY

Caudle.

Mrs Duncan, St. Clair.

Half-pint gruel, 1 dessertspoon of sugar, 1 teaspoon of lemon juice, 1 yolk of egg, a little nutmeg. The gruel should be boiling hot, and not too thick. Take it to the side of the fire; mix the yolk with a little cold water and the lemon juice and nutmeg. Stir this all in, and when thoroughly mixed use hot. More sugar may be added if preferred.

Calf's Foot Jelly.

Mrs Wilson, Upper Walker street.

One quart of stock, the thin rind and juice of 3 lemons, ½lb of sugar, ½oz of isinglass, the shell and whites of 5 eggs. Boil the feet for 3 hours, then skim and let stand till cold; then remove all fat and sediment; whip the whites of the eggs to a stiff froth; put the stock into a saucepan, stir till it boils, put on one side to simmer for 20 minutes, add ½ glass of sherry or brandy, and strain through a jelly-bag.

Maltine.

Mrs A. Burn, Montpellier.

Put about 8lb of crushed malt into earthenware vessels, well cover with water just off the boil, mix well, and leave 12 or 16 hours; strain through cheese-cloth (squeezing well), and boil liquor in preserving pan for 5 or 6 hours until brown and as thick as golden syrup; bottle and cork at once.

Steamed Rice for Invalids.

Mrs Barnett, Stafford street.

One cup rice, 1 cup boiling water; soak for 1 hour, then add 1 cup cold milk; stand basin in saucepan of boiling water, and steam for 2 hours; let it stand a few minutes before turning out.

The 'Invalid Cookery' section of the first edition (1905) of Dunedin's long-running *St Andrew's Cookery Book* was typical of most in its choice of bland food and nourishing drinks. Such sections persisted until the 1960s. H. Leach Collection.

The sources of nutrition information also changed from being relayed to the community by the medical profession, predominantly male, to being disseminated mainly by women, such as lecturers and graduates of the School of Home Science. The latter became teachers, extension workers and homemakers who often contributed their knowledge to fundraising cookbooks (see Inglis, Chapter 7). The New Zealand Health Department also became involved in dispensing nutrition advice through its own publications, while the advent of the Plunket Society and awareness of the importance of good nutrition for all age groups meant that instructions for feeding children appeared in many community cookbooks.

It was also notable that some individuals and organisations in the community used nutrition information selectively to promote their own beliefs and faddist diets. The WCTU promoted a vegetarian diet to curb alcohol consumption, while the discovery of vitamins in wholemeal flour gave additional authority to groups who advocated wholemeal cereals and bread, such as the Bread Reform League (who were associated with the WCTU).

However, in this period the community response to nutritional information in cookbooks was limited: additions to cookbook contents were gradual and major changes to New Zealanders' culinary traditions were not apparent.

NUTRITION AND COOKBOOKS 1940–1970

At the beginning of the war years, the nutrition advice for New Zealanders issued by the Department of Health was based on the League of Nations Recommendations for Optimum Nutrition that took account of age groups and expectant and nursing mothers. Foods were divided into either protective foods or supplementary energy foods (Gregory and Wilson 1943:36). After 1941, the Department of Health used Recommended Dietary Allowances of the National Research Council of the United States of America as a reference (Gregory and Wilson 1943). Food restrictions introduced because of the war encouraged New Zealanders to adopt these recommendations, and as a result there was an improvement in the diet of most New Zealanders. The meat intake of the population was reduced, and rationing of butter, sugar and eggs meant the population reduced their cake and biscuit intake, while home production of vegetables by women and children meant the vitamin C content of the nation's diet was more than adequate. Later in the war years, an increase in the extraction rate of flour to 78 per cent, which retained more of the outer layers and germ of the wheat grain, improved the vitamin B content of the diet. In 1948, the Daily Dietary Pattern for New Zealanders was issued by the Department of

Health, based on a revision of the Recommended Dietary Allowances, with the allowances expressed as New Zealand foodstuffs. These guidelines became an important standard for advising New Zealanders on a healthy diet (Gregory and Wilson 1952:57).

Beyond 1940, shortages and rationing influenced recipes in cookbooks. The *War Economy Recipe Book* claimed 'all the recipes have been tried and tested and besides being economical they contain all the necessary vitamins' (Anon c.1943a:preface). The *Red Cross War-time Rationing Cookery Book* emphasised the importance of vitamin A in the diet to help the body resist infection and prevent night blindness, and suggested foods such as milk, cheese, eggs, liver, and green and yellow vegetables to compensate for butter rationing (Anon c.1943b:preface). *Stretching the Meat Ration in New Zealand* responded to the wartime rationing of meat. It explained how to make the most – 'nutritionally speaking' – of war-rationed meats at the lowest possible cost in coupons, and suggested substitutes for meat dishes such as cheese, macaroni and spaghetti dishes, while providing notes on a balanced diet (Anon 1944).

Members of the New Zealand Women's Food Value League, a community organisation established in 1937 to help New Zealanders get the best value from their food, also campaigned during the war years to educate women about the nutritional value of all foods. They were particularly vocal about the vitamin value of wholemeal bread and vegetables. *Rationing Without Tears,* their first cookbook, included recipes for the best use of meat. Offal dishes were prominent (eight of the eleven meat recipes used offal) and other recipes included substitutes for meat dishes such as peanut cutlets. The importance of milk and cheese in the diet as a source of vitamins A and D was stressed, and rosehips were promoted as a substitute for oranges because of their vitamin C content (Anon 1943). In 1947, the League published a second cookbook, *Calling all Cooks,* which included a chart of mineral and vitamin functions and the Daily Dietary Plan. Recipes suggested the use of wholemeal flour where possible, fish, and the addition of carrageen moss or other seaweed to stocks and soups to remedy the lack of iodine in the diet (Anon 1947:14, 31, 41).

After the war years, the Sanitarium Health Food Company published the *Sanitarium Recipe Book* to promote its own products and cater for members of the Seventh Day Adventist Church, who were largely vegetarians. It listed the values of various mineral salts in the diet, suggested carrageen and seameal dishes as a source of iodine, included protein replacements for meat and advocated a diet principally based on wholemeal products, bread, cheese, milk, green vegetables and fresh

These wartime cookery and advice booklets for New Zealand housewives appeared towards the end of World War II as rationing spread to major foods such as meat, eggs, butter and sugar, and became increasingly stringent. H. Leach Collection.

fruit (Anon c.1945). At the beginning of the 1950s, *New Zealand 'Truth's' Cookery Book* indicated the dietary issues of most concern to the population. It included a section on food values and vitamins, invalid, diabetic and health cookery and a new section on slimming (Anon 1950).

Nutrition advice from the Department of Health in the 1950s continued to include information about vitamins and age-group nutrition but overweight became a new issue as New Zealanders' incomes and food supply improved. Consequently the Department of Health, in its publication *Good Nutrition*, included a section entitled 'Advice to overweight adults', rules for sensible slimming and a sample menu (Gregory and Wilson 1952:60–61). A growing concern about the association of animal fats in the diet with coronary heart disease also emerged, although in the 1950s no firm connection could yet be drawn (Bell 1957).

Many of the nutrition issues facing New Zealanders in the 1950s were indicated in cookbooks. Slimming was featured in *Choosing and Cooking Meat* published by the Auckland Meat Company, which promoted meat in the diet because of its nutritional value and as a slimming food. It advised readers to 'Watch your figure. A meat diet can help you to reduce safely. Meat is not fattening' (Anon 1956:2). *The Family Cook's Book* issued by the New Zealand Family Planning Association also had notes on slimming, which included a list of foods to avoid, instructions to reduce all fatty and starchy foods, not drink with meals, not eat between meals and restrict the amount of fluid intake (Anon c.1958).

In the 1960s, weight continued to be a prominent nutrition issue. The Department of Health for example advised the public in an article to 'Leave your weight on your plate' (Anon 1965:8). Research also continued into the relationship between diet and heart disease. The public was advised that circumstantial evidence suggested diet, obesity, and exertion may be related (Hunter 1960:14).

Despite these concerns, dietary advice declined in cookbooks during the period, as Table 1 illustrates. The collection was examined to determine the proportions of cookbooks with recipes or section headings flagged as 'international' or for entertaining and parties. In addition, the proportion with overt references to 'healthy' food, diet and nutrition and cookbooks acknowledging rationing and food shortages were calculated.

The table shows nutrition information was most prominent in 1940s' cookbooks, when food shortages and rationing were in place. It also indicates nutrition information in cookbooks tended to decline as later cookbooks embraced international cookery or entertaining. Interestingly, the number of nutrition-related pamphlets issued by the Department of Health increased in the 1950s, and

Table 1. Percentage of New Zealand-published cookbooks from the 1940s–60s in Leach collection displaying nutrition awareness, responses to rationing, international recipes and recipes for entertaining.

Decade	1940s	1950s	1960s
Number of books	79	113	178
Per cent with diet or nutrition notes and recipes	30.4	14.2	6.2
Per cent with adjustments for rationing and/or shortages	13.9	5.3	0.0
Per cent with international recipes	1.2	7.9	21.9
Per cent with recipes for parties and/or entertaining	1.2	12.4	31.5

as nutrition education became more widely disseminated, it is possible there was less need for it to be included in cookbooks.

When nutrition information was included in cookbooks, it was usually incorporated as a special section or notes. Generally the focus was on eating a balanced diet, and many cookbooks included this information after the Daily Dietary Plan was introduced in 1948. But cookbooks did not recommend recipes to help achieve this plan. Most community cookbooks tended to focus on cake and biscuit recipes because knowing the correct proportion of ingredients and how to handle a mixture was critical to the recipe's success.

The importance of vitamins in the diet continued to be acknowledged, especially during the 1940s when food shortages made it more difficult to obtain the recommended amounts. Emphasis was placed on the association of vitamins A and D with milk and butter, vitamin B with meat, and vitamin C with fruit and vegetables. But it was noticeable that the focus on using wholemeal in recipes tended to decline when the 78 per cent extraction rate was introduced for flour in 1946.

Because of rationing of butter, sugar and eggs, the war years resulted in a reduction of cakes and biscuits in the New Zealand diet but post-rationing people returned to their preferred eating habits, which included large amounts of meat and baked products. In 1952, Gregory and Wilson listed the errors and deficiencies in the New Zealand diet as too much meat, too much sugar and confectionery, too much butter, fat and cream (Gregory and Wilson 1952). Cookbooks were no longer constrained by lack of ingredients, and the content emphasised serving food attractively rather than healthily – consequently dietary advice began to focus on slimming.

COOKBOOKS AND NUTRITIONAL KNOWLEDGE 1970–1999

During the 1970s dietary advice in New Zealand tended to focus on the rising prevalence of coronary heart disease (CHD); although no cure was known, several risk factors were identified. The National Heart Foundation (NHF) established in 1968 was foremost in fostering research into this area. In 1971, its scientific committee presented its dietary recommendations for the general population. It suggested the population should maintain a normal body weight, reduce fat consumption, and moderate high cholesterol foods.

Further recommendations as a result of a survey conducted in 1977 urged New Zealanders to increase complex carbohydrates, reduce total fat consumption, reduce saturated fats and balance them with polyunsaturated and monounsaturated fatty acids, reduce cholesterol intake, take steps against obesity by reducing fat and sucrose consumption, increase high-density foods and foods with fibre, and moderate alcohol intake (Birkbeck, 1977:19). The New Zealand Department of Health regularly issued new nutrition guidelines based on the four main food groups: milk and milk dishes, meat and alternatives, fruits and vegetables, and bread and cereals. They also published guidelines for the use of fats, sugar and salt in the diet.

One method of evaluating the transmission of nutrition knowledge to the community via cookbooks is to correlate changes in the guidelines with changes in recipes and ingredients. Two types of New Zealand cookbooks were chosen for such a study:

1. **Edmonds'** *The "Sure to Rise" Cookery Book.* This commercial cookbook had numerous editions that allowed changes to be monitored. It was first published in 1908 and its name evolved through many editions until it eventually became (from 1978) the *Edmonds Cookery Book*. In the period 1969–99 almost two million copies were printed. New versions issued between 1970–99 were examined, with particular attention paid to the sections that had traditionally called for high-energy foods.

2. **Fundraising community cookbooks from the Leach collection.** At the time of the study this collection had 1300 New Zealand cookbooks in its database. Because fundraising cookbooks seldom reappeared in revised form, cookbooks written by two different types of organisations were chosen for analysis:

(a) Country Women's Institutes;

(b) playcentres and kindergartens.

Changes in the Edmonds' cookbooks

In the 1960s, dietary recommendations for butter and fat were 1oz. of butter per day with lard, margarine or dripping suggested for cooking. In the 1970s, butter was restricted for those with a weight problem. By the 1990s, official advice was to prepare food with minimal fat, especially saturated fat (Bell 1960:16; Bell 1969:15; Gillies and Swindells 1986:16; Anon 1991:35). The recommendations for fat in the diet changed drastically over the period. Butter was previously recommended as a good source of fat-soluble vitamins A and D and was suggested for table use. It was rationed during and after the war years, therefore not linked to obesity until the 1950s when over-consumption became possible.

Obesity and fat consumption in the diet were previously linked to over-consumption of cakes and biscuits, dietary items popular with New Zealanders, as illustrated by the number of cake and biscuit recipes in cookbooks. *Edmonds Cookery Book* was published to promote baking powder, an essential ingredient in most cakes and biscuits; thus the cake and biscuit section was the cornerstone of the cookbook. The popularity of this section is illustrated by the fact that between 1969 and 1992, despite saturated fat in the diet being discouraged, the number of cake and biscuit recipes decreased by only ten, from one hundred and one to ninety-one. The only concession to healthy food choice in this section was the adoption of an oil-based carrot cake, which first appeared in 1988.

Fat was also associated in the New Zealand diet with our high meat intake: both as a component of the meat itself and as a medium for cooking it. A review of fat in meat recipes in *Edmonds Cookery Book* revealed that a change took place between 1970 and 1999. In the 1970s, all recipes used dripping or fat for browning but in the 1990s only oil was suggested for this purpose. Irish stew, a popular recipe in the 1970s that normally used neck of mutton or stewing chops, in the 1990s specified hogget shoulder chops with the fat removed. The increase in poultry recipes (poultry normally has less fat than other meats, especially if the skin is removed) also indicated an awareness of the need to reduce fat.

Sugar is mentioned many times in recommendations for healthy eating. It has always been an issue in the diet because of its effect on obesity and dental decay. The 1970 guidelines suggested sugar, honey, jam, etc. to satisfy appetite but also suggested bread in preference to biscuits, cakes, and ready-to-eat cereals, which may be sugar-coated. Because sugar is a key ingredient in cakes and biscuits, dietary advice has made little difference to cookbooks in terms of this ingredient. As is the case with unsaturated fat, sugar is not easily reduced in baked items and Edmonds' cookbooks continued to reflect popular demand for traditional cakes and biscuits.

Changes in community cookbooks

Cookbooks representing two different organisations in the community, Country Women's Institutes and playcentres and kindergartens, were chosen from the Leach collection and their nutrition messages examined. The names of the cookbooks published by the Country Women's Institutes in the following decades indicated the conservative nature of the contents and their likely audience: *A Real Gem. Tried and Tested Recipes* [Eastern Bay of Plenty Country Women's Institute] (Anon 1973), *Home and Country Cook Book* [New Zealand Country Women's Institutes] (Anon [1982–6]), and *Recipes from the Heartland* [The Country Women's Institutes of New Zealand] (Anon 1995a).

An analysis of these cookbooks revealed no strong trends associated with nutrition. Bran biscuits and bran muffins were included in the 1980s' cookbook. Oat bran carrot muffins were included in the 1990s' cookbook along with a vegetarian section, but the recipes in this section were for vegetable dishes only and did not include legumes, which are usually part of a vegetarian diet. Possibly the audience for these cookbooks preferred familiar recipes and did not rapidly adopt nutrition trends, although the use of oat bran in muffins suggested if ingredients have special properties they may be substituted for the normal ingredient.

Community cookbooks published by playcentre and kindergarten groups were also examined to see if a younger age group submitted recipes for cookbooks that indicated they were more aware of health messages. Three cookbooks were examined from the 1970s. *What's for Lunch?* (Anon 1971a) included ideas for school lunches, but the ideas were not necessarily associated with good nutrition. The recipes from two other cookbooks, *Kitchen Kapers* from the Stratford Methodist Young Wives' Group Committee (Anon 1971b) and *Favourite Recipes* (Christie 1971), did not indicate health messages influenced their recipe repertoire.

Seven cookbooks were examined from the 1980s. All showed some awareness of nutrition trends. One cookbook (issued by the Dunedin Parents Centre) included several bean and lentil recipes, another a bean salad, and three other cookbooks published recipes for muesli which included a variety of cereals (Anon [c.1980s], Anon 1980, Anon 1981a, Anon 1981c, Anon 1981d).

The vegetarian movement had grown rapidly in New Zealand in the 1980s. Specialised cookbooks for vegetarians were published and these may have influenced playcentre and kindergarten mothers, who were more likely to follow food fashions than older members of the Country Women's Institutes. *Dietary Goals for New Zealanders* (Anon 1981b) suggested eating more fibre, but wholegrain cereals had become popular with vegetarians before this date and had started to appear in community cookbooks. *Edmonds Cookery Book*, however, did not include a muesli recipe until 1992, when a special breakfast section was created to promote Flemings' products, notably oat bran, which had become a nutrition superfood through the evidence it reduced serum cholesterol (Anon 1992).

The 1990s witnessed a further incursion of ingredients with healthy reputations into recipes published in fundraising cookbooks by the younger group. Brown rice was popular, especially in salads, together with ingredients such as bean sprouts and sunflower seeds. Muesli and birdseed bars that included ingredients such as sesame seeds, wheatgerm, sunflower seeds and peanut butter were also popular recipes. A recipe for lentil patties published in the *The Playcentre Collective Vegetarian Recipes* (Anon 1995b) was lauded as 'famous' and *Jonathan Rhodes Kindergarten Recipe Book* included low-calorie self-crusting quiche, pavlova for diabetics, diabetic high-fibre chocolate cake, and 'hi' energy muffins (Anon c.1997:34, 45, 57, 68).

Compared with the Country Women's Institute members, it might be concluded that the playcentre and kindergarten group of mothers were more aware of food and dietary trends. Younger people are often more likely to be receptive to new ingredients and tastes, hence are more likely to try new recipes. Contemporary cookbooks by food writers such as Alison Holst may also have influenced their repertoire. For example, *The Best of Alison Holst* (Holst 1991) included sections entitled 'Peas Beans Lentils and Tofu' and 'Rice and other Grains'.

Coronary heart disease was a prominent diet-related disease during the period of the study and was correlated with the rise of obesity. Whereas from the 1940s to the 1960s emphasis in the diet was on protein and vitamins, the emphasis from 1970–99 was on obesity and reduction of fat in the diet and this guideline influenced food choice. It led to a reduction in meat eating (fat was correlated with protein) and an increase in fibre provided by cereals, fruit and vegetables. Fibre not only added bulk to the diet and gave a feeling of fullness but was also believed to protect against increased serum cholesterol levels.

This change of emphasis in foods considered good or bad was reflected to varying degrees in the cookbooks studied. Community cookbooks were sometimes slower to respond to newer eating fashions, partly because new recipes often found their way into these cookbooks after they had been published in authored cookbooks, magazines or newspapers. As well, inclusion in a community cookbook was dependent on the group sponsoring the cookbook and the audience it was intended for.

During the last study period, 1970–99, the number of organisations advising the public on what they should and should not eat increased. The New Zealand Heart Foundation, New Zealand Nutrition Foundation, and New Zealand Cancer Society all produced literature about healthy eating for the public as well as the Department of Health (Ministry of Health). Perhaps for this reason formal nutrition advice was not common in cookbooks during this era. At the same time, more cookbooks related to special diets were published. Cookbooks for vegetarians were produced – formerly only a few cookbooks included a vegetarian section – and cookbooks featuring low-fat recipes also made a debut. Changes and pressure for change in New Zealanders' food habits were also reflected in the new sections added to cookbooks. In 1992, *Edmonds Cookery Book* for the first time included a new section, 'Good Nutrition', which incorporated the Heart Foundation's Healthy Eating Pyramid. It also included a 'Pasta and Rice' section, suggesting dishes with less meat were becoming popular. Other cookbooks, for example *The Best of Alison Holst* (Holst 1991), included similar new sections that indicated that although the public may not consciously follow nutrition guidelines, if ingredients with nutritional significance are embraced and promoted by food manufacturers and high-profile food writers – fibre products and low-fat substitutes are examples – consumers might unconsciously follow dietary recommendations.

CONCLUSIONS

This study has revealed how cookbooks have transmitted nutritional knowledge to the population. But did the uptake of nutritional knowledge as portrayed in cookbooks really alter our culinary traditions in the twentieth century? The cookbooks suggested nutritional advice has changed our thinking about some ingredients and modified our meal structures, but while nutrition information may affect our knowledge of the biological dimensions of food, knowledge does not always mean application. As baking recipes reveal, social and traditional values related to food are often conservative. Cookbooks have shown there is a gap between nutritionally informed authored works and those serving the needs of the community. Within the fundraising category, nutritional awareness also varies according to age group and background. Where nutritional advice has been taken up, clearly it has been easier to accept it in relation to, for example, the cooking medium for meat and fish, where oil rather than dripping or butter is recommended, than to give up treasured recipes for home baking.

6

Putting Fish Back on the Menu

Duncan Galletly

Colonists from Britain had experience of a mature and long-established fishing industry, together with a repertoire of recipes for processing and cooking the wide range of freshwater and marine species available in British markets. During the nineteenth century, population growth in Britain had placed pressure on once-numerous and inexpensive species such as oysters, so the abundant seafood along New Zealand's extensive coastline (reported by visitors from the time of Captain Cook) should have provided a good incentive for intending migrants. But, once here, they had to secure reliable supplies and learn the best methods of cooking unfamiliar species. To what extent and for how long did they rely on the superior fishing knowledge of the Maori? When were fish markets established? Did the colonists and their descendants include recipes for particular species in their cookbooks?

This chapter addresses these questions through a comparative study of fish and seafood recipes in cookbooks, and the developments taking place in commercial fishing prior to 1950. It is based upon an analysis of a sample of 380 cookery books printed in New Zealand between 1887 and 1950.

FISHING BEFORE 1900

Early visitors and colonists recognised that Maori were sophisticated fishermen, with a range of techniques suited to individual and group harvesting of seafoods (Best 1929). Both freshwater and coastal species of fish, crustaceans and shellfish were harvested. Food preservation by drying was a vital response to seasonal variations in supply. This allowed Maori to extend the food source in times when weather was bad, or when travelling, and provided opportunities for coastal iwi to trade with inland Maori as well as European whalers and, later, European colonists. The new colonists ate either fresh fish as soon as it became available in coastal

115

centres, or fish that had been preserved in some manner. Most of the early colonial fish supply had been caught and traded by local Maori, usually after drying.

With the decline in the local whaling industry during the first half of the nineteenth century, alternative sources of income were explored, such as fish salting for export. As early as the 1830s, exports of dried or salted fish were being sent to Sydney. But, while the early colonists were used to locally salted and dried fish, they clearly preferred fish that was reminiscent of home and tended to buy imported canned, salted or dried varieties, with smoked kippers a favourite. Attempts were made to produce smoked fish at Stewart Island in 1862 and, slowly, local production began to compete with imports (Johnson 2004).

The national trade in oysters was well established by the 1860s, with problems of preservation largely solved by transporting the live oysters in their shell, strapped to the decks of ships where wave action would keep the sacks moist and cool. Unfortunately the early oyster trade was such that the productive dredge oyster beds at Dunedin were depleted and concerns as to the long-term viability of these resulted in New Zealand's first fisheries legislation, the Oyster Fisheries Act of 1866, with the stipulation of a closed season from November to March.

In 1868, the first experimental attempts at trawling were made from Port Chalmers, Dunedin. Under sail, the trawler *Redcliff* took small quantities of sole, trumpeter, ling and hapuka, as well as crayfish. Although not to continue, this trial was noted in Wellington, and in the same year Dr James Hector chaired the first commission into the potential of the New Zealand fishing industry (Hector 1872). In 1872, Hector produced his 'Notes on the edible fishes of New Zealand', printed in *Fishes of New Zealand* together with Hutton's 'Catalogue with diagnoses of the species' (Hutton 1872; Hector 1872). In its preface, Hector suggests an approximate annual fish consumption of thirty-five pounds per person of those close to fishing ports but notes that 'little attention was directed to the preparation of fish, either for sale in the interior or for export'.

European stocks of trout, carp and salmon were successfully introduced in rivers throughout the country from the 1860s, and over time they formed discrete geographic distributions, with brown trout and salmon to the south, and rainbow trout in the north (Sherrin 1886; Watkinson and Smith 1972). Introduction of other species, such as lobster, was not successful.

By the 1870s the main fish imports were canned fish, and although attempts were made to establish local canneries, the production of smoked and salted fish was already well established in Otago, and regularly supplied the market. Fresh fish supplies were extremely sporadic, however, and limited to coastal centres. As a consequence of this, as well as the lack of refrigeration, there were no permanent shops specialising in fresh fish. Most fresh fish was sold by street hawkers as it became available from the docks. Increasingly there were public complaints as to the need for a steady, predictable fresh fish supply. To meet this need, the Deep Sea Fishing Company was established in 1872 with the intention of providing a regular fresh fish supply that would be unloaded at Lyttelton and transported quickly by rail to be sold at the railway station in Christchurch. The venture was short-lived, however, with the main difficulty being to keep the fish fresh, as well as being able to catch and unload regular quantities.

In 1882, the first exports of oysters were made by steamship to Sydney, supplying the then-fashionable 'oyster saloons'. However, the continuing depletion of beds led to the revised Fisheries Conservation Bill and a closed season in 1884. By that time, exports had exceeded one million dozen per annum. Although the new legislation succeeded in reducing exports for several years, between 1888 and 1890 exports were in excess of 1.25 million dozen. Country-wide annual consumption by the population of 600,000 was said to be three million dozen. In 1892, the Oyster Fisheries Act was revised, export duties were imposed and pickers began to be licensed. Within a few years, the Act and other measures led to a fall in exports to 250,000 dozen per annum.

One of the earliest New Zealand oyster saloons was Sanderson's and West's in Bridge Street, Nelson, which advertised in the *Nelson Examiner and New Zealand Chronicle* on 21 August 1861. By the 1880s oyster saloons were common: Pownceby's in Wellington in 1880, George Smart's on Lambton Quay in Wellington in 1885 (Arnold 1994) and, in 1889, an oyster saloon in Christchurch opened as a room within F. Arenas' Café de Paris (Johnson 2004).

In 1882, attempts were being made to trawl using steam-powered boats, and a mullet cannery was established in the Bay of Islands. By then 45 per cent of canned imports were from the United States, mainly salmon and lobster. Another preservation method, freezing, offered further opportunities for export. Developments in refrigeration in the meat industry allowed the first exports of frozen flounder and mullet to London in 1883, and by the late 1880s the availability of refrigeration and regular ice supplies from freezing works encouraged the first specialist fish shops to open. In 1886, as fishing activity increased, Hector's original 'Notes on the Edible Fishes' (1872) was updated and expanded by Richard Sherrin (1886).

By the 1890s, larger fish markets had been established, trawling under steam was possible, and refrigeration, using refrigeration plants or ice, allowed the preservation of fresh fish. An expanding rail system provided means for the safe, rapid supply of the perishable commodity to inland centres. Specialist fish shops with fish displayed on blocks of ice were common. In theory, then, by the turn of the century, a fresh fish supply could be reasonably guaranteed. How did this new industry impact on cooks? Recipe books offer a previously untapped source capable of answering this question, linking the history of the industry with that of its consumers.

NINETEENTH-CENTURY COOKBOOKS

Although printed in England in 1864, and entitled *The English and Australian Cookery Book; For the Many as Well as the Upper Ten Thousand*, Australia's first cookbook, by 'aristologist' Edward Abbott, also contains a short section on New Zealand fish, and recognises the sophistication of Maori fishing knowledge.

> One hundred different species of fish have been described by naturalists as frequenting the coasts; and this list is apparently very imperfect, seeing that the natives have enumerated to me many more they are in the habit of eating (Abbott 1864:226).

Although Abbott gives no specific recipes for indigenous New Zealand fish, and some of his material is questionable, he provides an outline of common species and, for some, the manner in which they were prepared or preserved by Maori.

Abbott's book was, in large part, a collection of pieces taken directly from other sources, stitched together by his own personal opinion. He introduces the chapter on fish with a quote from Cooley's *Practical Receipts* on the place of fish in nutrition. After noting the ease with which fish is capable of putrefying, Cooley says that white flaky fish is easy on the digestion, while oily fish is more nutritious but may 'offend the stomach'. Salt fish are thought to be more wholesome than freshwater fish. Cooley adds the opinion that 'The frequent use of fish as an aliment is said to promote the sexual feelings, but not the increase in population, unless a sufficiency of other food is taken at the same time' (Abbott 1864:92).

The first recipes known to have been printed in New Zealand are believed to have been compiled, in Maori, by Lady Mary Ann Martin, and printed by Henry Hill at St Stephen's Press, Parnell in 1869. A small collection of culinary and non-culinary recipes/remedies, the little twenty-three-page booklet was used as a teaching resource for young Maori girls. There were no more than a handful of recipes and none related to fish.

As a comprehensive guide for recent colonists, *Brett's Colonists' Guide and Cyclopaedia of Useful Knowledge*, edited by Thomson Leys (1883) and published in Auckland, includes a section on cooking. Of uncertain authorship, (and including material from British, American and probably other sources), indigenous species are absent. The fish recipes are either for unspecified fresh or cooked leftover fish with techniques for kippering, potting, smoking and salting small species such as sprats and herrings, as well as recipes using crayfish, anchovies, oysters, mussels and eel.

Until 1887, all true cookery books were imported into New Zealand. The most common were British works such as those by Rundell, Soyer and Francatelli. These were comprehensive cookbooks with specific sections such as entrées, meat, puddings, and fish. The species of fresh fish recommended for each dish differed from those available to early New Zealand colonists; thus experimentation would have taken place to identify equivalent species and the most appropriate cooking methods. The English names given at that time to New Zealand varieties – such as 'cod' or 'haddock' – might have given clues as to their culinary characteristics.

The first known true cookbook published in New Zealand appeared in 1887. Written by Mrs F. Murdoch of Napier, priced at one shilling, and published by Dinwiddie and Walker, *Dainties: Or How to Please Our Lords and Masters* was an expansion of a previous printed compilation of recipes that has not as yet been located. Introduced in the conversational style of Soyer's (1849) *The Modern Housewife or Ménagère*, Mrs Murdoch provides recipes divided into sections according to food type. Each section is introduced by a conversation between an uncertain young wife, attempting to do her best for her 'lord and master' but hampered by the incompetence of her own cook, and a knowledgeable aunt – for example

> … Jack has invited a friend of his, who it appears, is a vegetarian, and so I am to try and teach cook to fry fish properly. By the bye Aunt did you ever hear of a vegetarian eating fish and eggs? (Murdoch 1887:14)

Murdoch's recipes are generally for unspecified fresh or previously cooked fish, with instructions such as 'Any kind of fish can be done this way', and 'Take any cold fish', as well as oysters, eel and tinned salmon. The only clearly indigenous seafood is kahawai, although when *Dainties* went into a slightly expanded second edition in 1888, kahawai became simply 'stewed fish', and 'cray fish' became 'crawfish'. As might be expected, there are no fish shop advertisements in either edition, although the J.C. Briden 'Celebrated Pie Shop' of Napier proclaims 'hot fish, grills, chops, and steaks … at any hour' (Murdoch 1888).

In Dunedin, the Women's Christian Temperance Union (WCTU) began providing lessons on cooking to young girls at Leavitt House during the winter of 1887 and 1888. The principal instructor was Elizabeth Brown Miller. At the end of 1888 Miller compiled a collection of these lessons, and the WCTU published these as *Economic Cooking Lessons* in December 1888 or January 1889; a second and third edition were published later in 1889. An 1889 edition of the WCTU *Economic Cooking Lessons* devoted almost 10 per cent of its recipes to seafood (Anon 1889). Mentioned specifically are 'cod', blue cod, red cod, and ling, as well as tinned salmon, sardines, lobster and oysters. Haddock is used to describe smoked cod. Given that the lessons were designed for the girls of lower socioeconomic families, the content of these lessons clearly suggests that cod and ling were reasonably cheap and readily available, as of course was the oyster during this boom period of the industry.

Published in the same year as the WCTU cookery lessons, Isobel Broad's *New Zealand Exhibition Cookery Book* (1889) was published by Bond, Finney and Co. of Nelson. Dedicated to Countess Onslow, this hardback book was priced at two shillings and gave the impression of being a book of some authority. Yet its author was only twenty-one years old, the daughter of a well-known local magistrate, Lowther Broad. Her father's interests in acclimatisation are apparent and she exhibits a notable degree of sophistication in her tastes. She says in her introduction

> This cookery book, by a New Zealand girl, does not profess to be entirely original. All the recipes have been carefully adapted to the materials available in the Colony ... some are original especially those dealing with the cookery of New Zealand fish and birds. (Broad 1889:1)

Devoting over 15 per cent of her book to seafood, the range of species she includes is extensive: crayfish, John Dory, moki, kahawai, snapper, hapuka, kingfish, groper, butter fish, grayling, frost fish, trumpeter, sole, flounder, garfish, mullet, fresh herrings, gurnet, hapuka roe, rock cod (blue cod), eels, whitebait, and smoked fish (using barracouta, snapper, rock cod and moki). At least twenty-one different varieties of seafood are cited. Unfortunately the grayling recipe is perhaps one of the last for a species (*Prototroctes oxyrhynchus*) that by the 1870s was already in decline and by 1930 extinct.

In many of her recipes Broad provides commentary from her own experience. At Westport, where whitebait is plentiful, they ate them 'boiled and served with melted butter flavoured with Tapp or Anchovy sauce'. For trout with cream, she notes that 'the remains of a lake Wakatipu trout are excellent cooked this way', and on travelling through the West Coast with friends, she had pickled grayling, 'that were simply delicious' at Stewart's Hotel, Kumara. She observed that 'The lobster put up in tins by Crosse and Blackwell answers very well for lobster sauce' and in Lobster Risotte, 'Crosse and Blackwell's is best'. However, she notes 'It is a pity the great fish-preserving firms cannot discover something better than tin in which to put up their condiments – many people will not touch tinned fish who would readily eat it if preserved in jars' (Broad 1889:28, 30, 35, 36, 63).

Broad devotes an entire chapter to the oyster:

> Tastes differ about the New Zealand Oysters. One person will prefer the Auckland Rock, another the Stewart Island, whilst a third will declare that the Queen Charlotte Sound oyster, in good condition, cannot be excelled for delicacy of flavour.

> The Auckland Rocks and Stewart Island oysters are plentiful, cheap, and delicious. The Queen Charlotte Sound beds, are wisely closed for a time. They are so far as known only of limited extent, and would soon be poached out of existence, but for the strict application of the Act. The Astrolabe oyster, found as its name implies at Astrolabe, near Nelson, is a fine large fat oyster when in good condition, but rather too coppery in flavour to be eaten *au naturel*; cooked however, it is excellent, and if kept for a time and fed, it loses much of the unpleasant metallic twang, and is considered very good by many people.

> Oysters can be prepared in many ways – and spoiled in all of them – if reasonable care and patience are wanting. With these, it is surprising how many delicious dishes can be made at small cost. I think the following recipes for preparing our New Zealand oysters will be found good, and by no means too expensive. (Broad 1889:37)

It is likely a reflection of the extensive oyster trade and the ease of transport that allowed Broad to combine both Auckland and Stewart Island oysters in a single recipe – Oyster soufflé (Broad 1889:43).

It was clearly Broad's intention to provide recipes for the range of common edible seafood and freshwater fish, but she also devotes much space to New Zealand meat and game. A similar intention can be found in *The New Zealand Cookery Book and Household Guide,* published by C.G. Carter of Tauranga in 1891. Probably a compilation of contributed recipes, the book has 10 per cent of its recipes devoted to aquatic species, with an extensive range of fish, molluscs and crustaceans: barracouta, conger eel, flatfish, frostfish, garfish, gurnard, hapuka,

John Dory, kahawai, kingfish, mackerel, mau mau, moki, mullet, snapper, yellow tail, trevally, terakihi, sprats, carp, salmon, trout, New Zealand trout, eel, whitebait, cockles, shrimp, crayfish, koura (freshwater crayfish), mussel, periwinkle, pipi and of course, the oyster. Carter's chapter on fish is the first in his book:

> We begin our cookery book with fish, as there is such a variety of this excellent article of diet in the numerous bays and harbours of New Zealand, we think it is entitled to first place. We of course have only touched upon those kinds of fish which are used by Europeans, but the natives make use of both the shark, stingray, &c. Fresh water fish, however, are not very varied, but the salmon, trout and carp have been introduced and are becoming plentiful. (Carter 1891:1)

Carter notes, however, that the New Zealand native trout (as with the grayling) was becoming scarce.

Of note, Carter's book provides the first recipe for a hangi in a cookery book:

> *Snapper, a la Kapera Maori.* – Make a shallow hole in the ground, put in a small piece of lighted ti-tree, and a number of stones about the size of an egg. When the stones are red hot remove all wood and arrange the stones neatly around the bottom and the sides of the hole, place on these a couple of layers of cabbage leaves or thistles, and put in an open work kit your fish, without removing the entrails. Cover with sacking, pour on the stones cold water by lifting the edges of the sacking, then close down and put something on the edges of the sacking to keep in the steam. This is the way the Maoris cook their fish, pork and potatoes, placing all together in the kit. Fish done this way have an excellent flavour, which cannot be obtained by cooking any other way. The entrails are easily removed after the cooking, which will take about an hour. (Carter 1891:4)

Prior to 1900, most cookery books were authored works or works compiled by a publisher. An exception was *Henry H. Tippler's Cookery Guide* (Tippler 1891), a grocer's give-away promoting products in his shop. Henry H. Tippler, 'Italian warehouseman' (the owner of what we might call today a delicatessen), had his shop at 191 Lambton Quay, the well-to-do end of the commercial centre of Wellington. His book devotes a significant 12 per cent to seafood recipes using unspecified fish, or to the fancy imported varieties which were sold in cans or jars: bloaters, lobster, prawns, salmon, as well as whiting and bream.

The pre-1900 cookery books, for the most part, set out to provide a balanced range of recipes, commonly dividing the text into sections such as soups, fish, meat, etc., but with no specific emphasis. In each of these books, the section on fish occupied 10 per cent or more of the recipe pages. Thus, although the fishing industry was in its infancy, the period between 1889 and 1891 must have been one in which there was sufficient availability and interest in fish for it to have a very significant place in cookbooks and menus.

THE FISHING INDUSTRY FROM 1900

The most important post-1900 refinements in commercial sea fishing were the introduction of oil-powered trawlers and refrigeration plants on fishing vessels. By 1917, twenty-nine steam trawlers and forty-one diesel-powered trawlers were in operation. Diesel power allowed fishing boats to remain at sea longer and travel further from their port of origin; however, they were less powerful than the larger steam trawlers, which continued to land most fish until after 1940. The introduction of refrigeration plants in trawlers further extended their range and duration (Makarios 1996, Johnson 2004).

Trawling was confined to the continental shelf and, in general, while the catch might include about forty species, most of these were in limited quantity; a small number of species made up the bulk of the catch. Common species might include snapper, terakihi, trevally and red gurnard, although different areas around New Zealand had different proportions of certain species. Thus snapper was common in the Hauraki Gulf, whereas sole and red cod were common on the east coast of the South Island.

The introduction of Danish seining at Auckland in 1923 was a significant refinement in fishing technique. Whereas the trawlers had dragged nets behind a moving vessel, the Danish seiners laid vertical nets, like a fence, around a shoal of fish and pulled it to a stationary vessel. The Danish seine was quicker, cheaper and used less fuel; large numbers of wooden seiners were built in the 1930s, especially in Auckland. From the 1930s, 70 per cent of the seine catch was snapper and certain fishing grounds were closed to the technique (Watkinson and Smith 1972).

Another new form of seining was the purse seine. In this method, a row of rings is attached to the lowermost part of the vertically hanging net. Through these rings a rope passes, and when the shoal is encircled, the rope is pulled and the net closes from below like a purse, preventing the fish diving below the nets. The purse seine was used in particular for pelagic fish that shoal, such as sardines, mackerel, anchovies, kahawai, pilchards, sprats and herring. Purse seining in New Zealand was done experimentally in the 1940s and therefore the contribution of the technique to the period prior to 1950 was minor (Watkinson and Smith 1972).

COOKBOOKS AFTER 1900

In the twentieth century, the number of new cookery books printed in New Zealand increased dramatically. Whereas prior to 1900 the total number of cookery books was about ten (or about twenty if different editions and New Zealand re-bindings are included), over the next fifty years over 300 different books had been published and over 200 were reprinted, or given new editions. The most prolific period was between 1930 and 1939, when over 200 discrete printings can be identified.

Despite the increasing number of new cookbooks, the number of authored works similar to those of Broad remained reasonably constant, therefore making up a smaller and smaller proportion of the total cookery book output. Thus, while authored books made up the majority of the pre-1900 publications, by the 1930s the proportion had fallen to less than 10 per cent.

An early, small, but important genre of cookery book was the unauthored publisher's cookbook. In 1893, Whitcombe and Tombs had published the unauthored *Practical Household Recipes; with Chapters on Garden Management and Legal Memoranda, Adapted to Colonial Requirements*. Culinary recipes made up almost one third of the total work, and of these about 5 per cent are related to seafood (including moki, eel, kahawai, snapper, trout, flounder, whitebait, crayfish and oysters) (Anon 1893). A decade later, Whitcombe and Tombs produced the *Colonial Everyday Cookery*, published in Christchurch in 1901 and possibly written by an unidentified local caterer (Anon [1901]). With many editions and reprintings, along with some title changes along the way, *Colonial Everyday Cookery* lasted until the 1960s. As with the pre-1900 books by Broad, Carter and Murdoch, and the books that had been imported from Britain in the nineteenth century, *Colonial Everyday Cookery* was a balanced compilation of recipes with sections for each food course. The fish section in the 1901 first edition was small (5 per cent of the work). The fresh sea fish recipes were mainly for unspecified fish, with cod the exception. Although there were recipes using crayfish, oysters, cockles, whitebait, fresh salmon and trout, as well as tinned salmon, sardines, anchovies and cockles, for a book of its size and given the increasing availability of aquatic foods, the fish content was notably small. Later editions (e.g. of 1912 and 1927) were largely similar to the first. It may be that the limited fish section reflected an annual New Zealand fish consumption in 1914 of only two kilograms per person (Makarios 1996:8). However, by about 1940 (when copies in print totalled 278,000) the book – now-titled *Whitcombe's Everyday Cookery* (Anon c.1940a) – saw an increase in the range of recipes to include butterfish, flounder, groper, flathead, kingfish, snapper, sole, tuna and whiting, although the proportion of fish recipes in the book remained at a low 5 per cent.

The tremendous increase in cookbook output from 1900 was the result of the introduction, over time, of several new genres of cookery book. In consequence, the total output of published works varied increasingly in intent, presentation and content. In turn, these changes influenced the number and proportion of fish recipes and the methods of cooking described. Fashion, the goals of the author, compiler or publisher, the audience, and the method of compilation were all critically important influences. Further complicating this dynamic, in terms of the effect that recipes would have had on culinary practice, as well as the dissemination of the works, were the varying edition numbers, print runs and distribution networks that were available.

The new twentieth-century cookery genres were: educational cookery books; local community cookery books; commercial cookery books produced either by food manufacturers, appliance manufacturers or commercial organisations with no direct association with food; power company cookery books; nutritional cookery books; books compiled by national organisations; a small number of military cookery books; and overseas books reprinted in New Zealand. We will now look at these categories in more detail.

Educational cookbooks

Following her experience with the WCTU in 1887–8, Elizabeth Brown Miller became a cooking instructor at the newly opened Dunedin Technical Classes Association as well as providing private cookery tuition. Through the 1890s and well into the next century, Miller authored a sequence of books taken from lessons she had given at the Dunedin New Zealand Exhibition in 1889, as well as the Technical Classes. Intended for a wide adult audience, her *Economic Technical Cookery* went into sixteen editions, the last in 1923. *Economic Technical Cookery* was a comprehensive collection of recipes, divided according to food type. The small fish section made up 5 per cent of the recipe pages, with a range of fish including sole, whiting, cod, red cod, kingfish (a species generally found around the North Island), ling and flounder. There are recipes for whitebait, lobster, crayfish and oysters as well as smoked haddock and smoked red cod. Miller also provides recipes for the use of pike and even seaweed (Miller 1906).

With her daughter J. Archer Miller (a Teacher of Cookery to the Otago Education Board), Miller co-authored an educational manual for use in schools and technical colleges, as well as for use by candidates for the Cookery Examination of the City and Guilds of London Institute – the *Elementary Cookery Book* published by Whitcombe and Tombs in c.1903. In this they describe fish as being a

> cheap, nourishing, and light food, easily digested, and particularly suited to those who have much brain work. Its greatest disadvantage is that it will not keep long. (Miller and Miller c.1903:22)

A small eight-page booklet, probably used at the Dunedin Technical School at the same time, and likely composed by Miller, notes, as did Abbott half a century before, that

> Whiting and sole have a white delicate flesh, free from fat, and are easily digested when boiled. Salmon and Herring are rich and oily, they are more sustaining, but require a stronger digestion. Fish is a less stimulating and sustaining food than meat. It requires to be eaten in larger quantities and at more frequent intervals if used in the place of the latter. (Anon c.1900s:2)

The nutritional properties of fish were therefore primarily seen as being sustenance, with its value as 'brain food' being a widely held belief. By then the earlier concerns of Edward Abbott regarding it being an aphrodisiac had presumably been forgotten.

An important effect of the national establishment of technical classes was the emergence in New Zealand of formal tuition in cookery for those girls intending to work as domestic cooks. In consequence, simple educational manuals, beginning with Miller's *Elementary Cookery Book,* began to appear from the turn of the century. These usually combined lessons in the cookery of simple dishes with tuition in nutrition and economy.

Gard'ner, in an early edition (c.1920s) of her *Recipes for Use in School Cookery Classes,* devotes 7 per cent to seafood; all for unspecified cooked or fresh species, as well as a single recipe using crayfish. Revised in later editions by Merle Blackmore, the recipes continued to provide no specificity as to species. Renwick's (1916) *Primary School Cookery Book* devotes 6 per cent of its recipes to seafood, again all for unspecified fish. Similarly, *Cookery Book Issued by The Auckland Gas Company for the use of students in Manual Training Schools* (Anon c.1935a) specifies only a single recipe for flounder out of eight species-unspecified fish recipes.

Two important consequences of the technical school development were the increasing number of young women who attended such classes and of women who had taught at them. A number of these teachers went on to author or contribute to many cookery books, or to be employed by companies and organisations to compile cookbooks. Thus, although the number of educational books was small, the potential influence of the school and technical class lessons on cooking, and in helping to define the food tastes of twentieth-century New Zealand, was enormous.

Community cookbooks

The genre to have the greatest influence in terms of numbers was the community cookbook. Derived from a fundraising idea originating in the United States, these made up the majority of all published cookery works between 1902 and 1920. They were books compiled from contributed recipes within local organisations. Frequently used as church fundraisers, and often associated with fêtes or bazaars, these books showed a strong bias towards baked products such as cakes and biscuits. The first was published in New Plymouth as the *Coronation Cookery Book* in 1902 (Anon 1904), but was rapidly followed by others from Papanui, Wellington and Dunedin. Although one occasionally finds token male contributors, the community cookery book was primarily the product of women, and with a focus on afternoon tea. Because of their altered focus the proportion of fish recipes was small, on average about 3 per cent, although some compiled books attempted to have some balance between sections. The Christchurch *Fendalton Cookery Book* (Anon c.1920) and the *St Andrew's Cookery Book* from Dunedin (Anon 1905) had fish sections of 10 per cent and 7 per cent. The Catholic emphasis on Lenten and Friday fish meals may explain why the later *St Saviour's Book of Recipes and Household Information* (Anon 1939a) had a relatively high 7 per cent fish content (and this may also help to explain Isobel Broad's earlier interest).

Most community books had small print runs and limited local distribution and therefore influence. There were exceptions however. By virtue of its duration of publication, the *St Andrew's Cookery Book*, with thirteen editions between 1905 and 1932, almost certainly had influence beyond Dunedin. Some achieved national distribution – the *St Saviour's Book of Recipes and Household Information* developed by the Catholic community in Christchurch was reprinted with different covers for sale in Wellington and Auckland.

Commercial cookbooks

From 1920, the dominant new genre of cookbook was commercial. Between 1920 and World War II, just under half of all cookbooks were produced by commercial companies either promoting their own food or appliances, promoting chains of food retail stores, or using recipes (and other 'useful' material) as a way of encouraging the housewife to read and perhaps keep what was primarily a piece of advertising. Many of the companies, for example dry cleaners and hire purchase moneylenders, had no association with food or cooking. An important influence that may have encouraged the production of these books was the Depression, which had a profound socioeconomic impact in the late 1920s and early 1930s.

First introduced in Wellington with the L.D. Nathan's *Defiance Cookery Recipes* (Anon c.1905), small commercial booklets promoting specific food products were initially relatively few, but with large-scale national distribution their print runs and influence could be large –150,000 for the first edition of Edmonds' *The "Sure to Rise" Cookery Book* (Anon 1908). By the 1920s, the commercial cookbook took over from the community cookbook as the dominant form and remained as such until at least 1950. As with the community books, we see in these commercial publications a skew in favour of specific products; most had little interest in fish, with only one third having a fish content of greater than 4 per cent. Thus the first edition of Edmonds' (Anon 1908) and the essence manufacturer *Stevens' 'Cathedral Brand' Essences Cookery Book* (Trent c.1920s) were almost entirely devoid of fish content. As might be expected, manufacturers of cereals and of course chocolate, sweets and fruit were equally uninterested in fish. Some manufacturers attempted to provide a more balanced range of recipes, presumably hoping that their books would become essential items of kitchen equipment; thus a manufacturer of condensed milk in the *Highlander Economical Cookery Book* (Anon 1914) devotes 8 per cent to fish in its 1914, 1922 and 1923 editions. The long-running *Edmonds "Sure to Rise" Cookery Book* introduced some fish in its later editions, but in the 1955 Economy Edition the proportion was still only 2 per cent (Anon 1955).

The first New Zealand cookbook on fish was produced by the Auckland-based fishing company Sanford's. Albert Sanford founded New Zealand's first large fishing company and opened a permanent fish market in 1894 (Titchener 1981; Makarios 1997). In 1927, the company produced their *Eat More Fish: Hints for the Housewife and Cook on the Proper Treatment of Fish as Food*. Priced at three pence and produced in an edition of 25,000, this unauthored booklet was the first New Zealand volume devoted solely to seafood and set out to provide the best methods of cooking each variety of fish. The health-giving benefits of fish are stated as 'There is no food richer for this body and brain stimulating protein than fish', and 'Fish is more easily digested than meats, and for this reason it is particularly adapted for those of feeble constitutions and sedentary occupations'

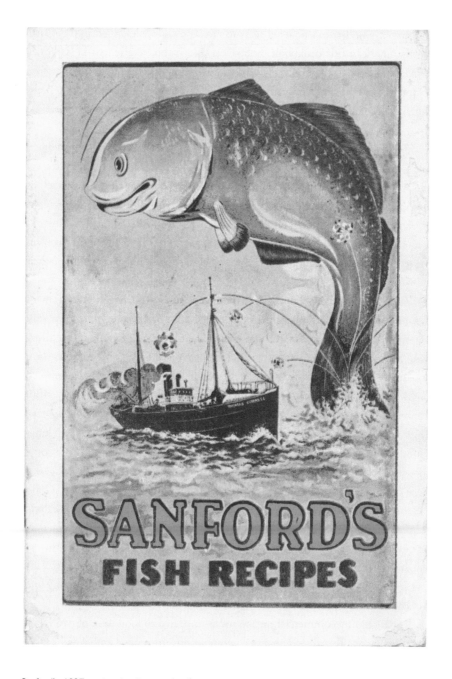

Sanford's 1927 recipe book was the first commercial publication devoted to New Zealand seafoods. H. Leach Collection.

(Anon 1927:2). These benefits of fish are similar to those described in the earlier North American fish cookbook by Spencer and Cobb, referred to in Sanford's booklet (Spencer and Cobb 1921). The health-giving benefits of fish are therefore portrayed, as they were by earlier authors, in terms of digestion and protein content, although advertisements in the Sanford's booklet also promote their 'Blue X-ray' oil for sufferers of rheumatism.

Specific recipes are given for dab, flounder, groper, hapuka, kingfish, snapper, sole and terakihi, as well as smoked terakihi and snapper, snapper roe, oyster, eel and whitebait. No mention is made of cod or the common tinned fish such as sardines or salmon, although tinned commodities are clearly visible in photographs of Sanford's Auckland retail shop in 1920 (Makarios 1997:10). In its nineteen recipe pages, at least twenty-two recipes are for unspecified previously cooked or fresh fish, and for many fish species. Only passing mention is made of their culinary properties.

From 1929, cookery books were produced that would be given away with ovens or other kitchen appliances. These tended to be balanced compilations with the emphasis on the use of the particular cooking device. The manufacturing companies commonly used instructors at the technical colleges to compile these books, and many were named as authors, presumably as the companies attempted to give credibility to their products by selecting a well-qualified authority. Thus Elizabeth Neige Todhunter compiled the *Champion Cook Book; for Champion Oven Regulated Gas Cookers* series (e.g. Todhunter c.1940), Isabella Finlay's long-running gas cookery book *Cookery* (Finlay c.1932) was re-bound for the Osborne cooker (c.1934), Florence Sinclair compiled the *McClary Electric Range Cookery Book* (1929), and E. Warburton compiled the *'Orion' Cookery Book; for 'Orion' Electric Ranges* (1929). Although the *Champion Cook Book* contains few seafood recipes (less than 2 per cent), Warburton's book contains 9 per cent, although only one recipe specifies a fish species. Finlay with 6 per cent seafood recipes provides the greatest variety: barracouta, flatfish, flounder, groper, kingfish, cod, trevally and sole, as well as whitebait, anchovies, smoked blue cod, smoked herring and tinned salmon.

Cookbooks by commercial organisations unrelated to food were of two types: either the company gathered together a group of advertisers and embedded recipes and other information around their advertisements (the advertising almanac), or the company would promote itself with its own advertising around the recipes – for example, the *Souvenir Book of Cookery Recipes; also the Romance and Facts of the Dry Cleaning Industry* (Anon 1934).

One of the earliest advertising almanacs was the *The Householders Annual Of Useful Information And Directory Of Selected Business Firms For Householders to do Business with. With which is incorporated The Household Annual Index and The Home Annual*, published in Wellington (Anon 1912). The most important example, however, is *Enquire Within*, produced annually between c.1940 and 1953, printed by Crawfords in Palmerston North, and mailed gratis to householders in the lower North Island and South Island. The total recipe section initially was small – three of sixty-four pages in the first edition (Anon c.1940b) – but increased in later editions to over 10 per cent. Content, both recipe and advertising, varied according to region. The seafood component varied enormously, most editions having less than 5 per cent but several of the later editions had over 20 per cent. Fresh fish species were invariably not specified, and although oysters and occasionally mussels are mentioned, the bulk of recipes were for tinned salmon and sardines.

Power authority cookbooks

Between 1927 and 1940, over fifty cookbooks were published by electricity or gas authorities, or were associated with the promotion of these energy sources. Booklets containing recipes were used as a means to demonstrate the controllability, safety and economy of each. As with commercial cookbooks associated with appliance manufacturers, respected cookery authors and demonstrators were used to promote gas or electricity (never both): Mildred Trent, Isabella Finlay, Sheila Porteous, Bee Powell, Betty Stewart and Hilda Connor. The majority of these publications had seafood content over 6 per cent, presumably as the authors attempted to demonstrate that the energy source was capable of cooking a wide variety of foods, rather than concentrating simply on baking or meat.

Nutritional cookbooks

Nutritional cookery books were a relatively small but important genre appearing during the Depression and through World War II. Commercial nutrition books largely promoted cereal products such as 'Proteena' (Anon c.1930s) and wheatmeal, although fish and seafood were also perceived as being important nutritional resources during the mid 1920s.

Up until that time fish had been viewed primarily as a protein 'brain food' that was, in the case of white flaky fish, easily digested. This interest in digestion, as well as bowel function, is a reasonably common theme in many recipe books of the period. Cod liver oil had been promoted for many years as a treatment for rheumatism (as in Sanford's booklet), and also rickets, long before its cause (vitamin

D deficiency) had been recognised. Other concerns regarding the nutritional status of New Zealanders emerged with the discovery of the relationship between goitre and low soil iodine in 1925. The work of Charles Hercus and Muriel Bell in Dunedin had a significant impact on the perception of the value of different foods, and initiated the addition of iodine to table salt. Coupled to an emerging understanding of 'vitamines', the work on iodine began to influence both cooking methods and the types of food that were being considered important to eat as part of a 'healthy' diet. It was almost certainly no coincidence that these interests in nutrition were also occurring as New Zealand was entering the Depression.

It was nutritional concern, as well as the need to extend food horizons during the Depression, that most likely influenced the publication of *Cooking of New Zealand Fish and Other Sea Foods* by Merle Blackmore (c.1929). Blackmore's book was considerably larger than Sanford's booklet two years earlier. With eighty-eight pages, she gave recipes for a large range of fish species as well as shellfish (one of the earliest for paua), seaweed and muttonbird. Her work detailed the nutritional benefits of fish, and in particular the effect of iodine on goitre and the high iodine content of seaweed and fish. Of note is her acknowledgement of help received from the University of Otago physiologist Professor John Malcolm, the supervisor of Muriel Bell's work on goitre. A re-printed 'Teachers edition' of Blackmore's book clearly indicates that it was intended as an educational resource.

Later, during World War II, Malcolm contributed to, and Muriel Bell edited, the Health Department's *Good Nutrition: Principles and Menus* in five editions between 1940 and 1956. Given Bell's interest in iodine, the number of fish recipes is surprisingly small (5 per cent) and the book includes recipes only for unspecified fish and cod (Gregory and Wilson 1940). Although few publications were printed by government departments, they were influential by virtue of their authority and national distribution.

In about 1930 the Dunedin company W. Gregg produced two small promotional editions of *Recipe Book for Gregg's Seameal, Sea-jell, Seameal Dessert Custard*. This was based upon seaweed-derived gelatine and promoted the value of seaweed for its anti-goitre properties (Anon c.1930a & b).

National organisations and networks

From the late 1920s, coinciding with the developing Depression, an increasing proportion of cookbooks arose from national, as opposed to local, groups. Organisations such as the New Zealand Women's Institutes (NZWI), the Women's Division of the New Zealand Farmers' Union (WDNZFU), the Plunket Society,

About 1929 Merle Blackmore published a comprehensive manual covering a wide range of seafoods, and drawing on current nutritional expertise. H. Leach Collection.

and radio programmes such as that hosted by Maud Basham ('Aunt Daisy') provided mechanisms whereby large networks of women could communicate and therefore collaborate in the production of national publications. Whereas the NZWI linked women within small townships, the WDNZFU reached out to more remote farming areas, and Aunt Daisy's radio network spanned both rural areas and main centres. Collectively, the reach of these organisations was enormous. It is likely that, alongside technological advances in oven design and controllability, these expanding complex networks of women contributed greatly to the creativity of the 1920s and early 1930s, when many of New Zealand's 'iconic' baked products such as the Pavlova originated and when recipe book production was increasing rapidly.

The NZWI and WDNZFU (later to become Women's Division of Federated Farmers – WDFF) generally reflected a home-grown New Zealand cuisine, whereas Basham's later publications from the 1940s and 1950s suggest that a more urban network of women were contributing recipes, many of which had American or European origins. It is possible that many of Basham's listeners were recent immigrants to New Zealand, and taking into account her own love affair with the United States, the wartime limitation of printing, and the growing number of imported cookbooks – especially those from the United Kingdom – her later recipe compilations probably assisted the influx of international recipes into New Zealand during the late 1940s and early 1950s.

Basham's books vary in their fish content from a mere 1.5 per cent in her first *Aunt Daisy's Cookery Book of Approved Recipes*, with only a single recipe for a specified species of fish – mullet (Basham [1934]), to 7–8 per cent in editions of the 1938 *Aunt Daisy's Radio Cookery Book*, where varieties include flounder, gurnard, groper, hapuka, mullet and snapper (Basham 1938). Her later *Aunt Daisy's Favourite Cookery Book* is similar in its range (Basham 1952).

The New Zealand Women's Institutes' *Home Cookery Book* of 1939 devotes only 3 per cent of its recipes to fish, which included hake, sole, terakihi, groper, flounder, butterfish and blue cod (Anon 1939b). Similarly the WDFF's *New Zealand Women's Household Guide* devotes only 4 per cent of its recipes to seafood, again with a limited range of species including flounder, moki, snapper, sole and trevally (e.g. Anon c.1935b). The small fish sections of these books probably relate to the primary focus on baking, but may also reflect the inland nature of the communities and farms that would have contributed many of the recipes, as well as the ready availability of alternative home-killed protein sources, lamb and beef.

Overseas cookbooks reprinted in New Zealand

World War II saw declining numbers of locally produced cookbooks, but a significant number of English books being reprinted in New Zealand. Although it was common at the turn of the century for overseas books to be re-bound in New Zealand (for example the Canadian *Home Cook Book* (Anon 1892), and Payne's (c.1893) *Shilling Cookery Book*, re-bound as the *DIC Shilling Cookery Book*), few were reprinted in their entirety except for *Mrs Maclurcan's Cookery Book* (c.1930s). Between 1943 and 1946, at least seven English cookbooks were printed in New Zealand by Whitcombe and Tombs, including four by the wartime writer Ambrose Heath. Not surprisingly, these books have few if any indigenous species of fish, although Heath (1946) in *Good Savouries* uses fish or crustacea in 30 per cent of his recipes.

TRENDS IN NEW ZEALAND COOKBOOKS 1880–1950

I have already noted that the proportion of recipes devoted to aquatic species in some of the books prior to 1900 was large; the authored works of Broad, Murdoch, Carter and Tippler had over 10 per cent and, taking Miller into account, the average of these was 7.9 percent. After 1900 the overall mean figure falls to between 4 and 5 per cent and remains there until at least 1950.

Recipe books also became, on average, much smaller between 1920 and 1940. Between 1887 and 1920, the average number of recipe pages was approximately 130, but in the 1920s this had declined to 78 before slowly rising; by the 1930s it was 88, and in the 1940s 106 pages. The combination of decreasing book size and a declining proportion of fish content means that, where there was an average of 10 pages devoted to aquatic foods prior to 1900, with the passing of each subsequent decade the figure falls to 6.1, 5.7, 3.2, 3.6 and 4.6 pages. It is likely that these trends are the result of a combination of factors: primarily the high number of smaller booklets produced by commercial organisations and power companies, and the increasing focus on afternoon tea and baking.

Despite the development of the New Zealand fishing industry in the late nineteenth and early twentieth century, as well as the benefits of rapid rail transport and refrigeration, paradoxically, the recipe books do not show any increasing emphasis on fresh sea fish, and certainly no increasing sophistication in taste or technique as to the culinary properties of different species (Table 1). Although overall sea fish made up just under 50 per cent of all freshwater and marine recipes, there was a declining proportion of named species of sea and freshwater fish, and a

Table 1. Percentage of total fish, crustacean and shellfish recipes printed during each decade using each aquatic food group. (Numbers are rounded to the nearest integer and therefore very small quantities, less than 0.5%, are tabulated as 0.)

	Crustaceans	Shellfish	Fish pastes/ sauces	Salted fish	Smoked fish	Tinned fish	Unspecif'd cooked fish	Unspecif'd fresh fish	Specified fresh sea fish	Fresh-water fish
1880–99	8	26	2	1	1	7	7	17	21	10
1900–09	10	15	3	0	4	8	11	7	35	7
1910–19	13	15	4	1	6	8	13	6	27	7
1920–29	5	18	3	0	6	7	18	15	21	7
1930–39	4	12	5	0	4	8	24	19	20	4
1940–49	3	25	2	0	7	7	21	17	12	6

corresponding rise in the proportion of unspecified fresh or leftover cooked fish up to 1950. The proportion of sea fish recipes with named species falls from a range of 47–66 per cent between 1887 and 1920 to 24 per cent in the 1940s. Recipes for unspecified, previously cooked fish make up an increasing proportion of recipes over the period, possibly related to the economic need to use leftovers during the Depression and World War II.

At all periods, the single most common seafood recipe ingredient was the oyster, followed by tinned salmon. The oyster showed a slight decline over the period with tinned salmon increasing from the 1920s. These trends parallel the oyster boom in the late nineteenth century and the increasing quantity of tinned salmon being imported from North America in the twentieth century.

Sea fish diversity

The paradoxical decline in species-identified sea fish recipes as the fishing industry became established is coupled to a remarkable decline in sea fish diversity over the early part of the twentieth century. By 1950, 75 per cent of all fresh sea fish recipes were concentrated on only seven species: sole, flounder, cod, snapper, groper, herring and terakihi. In contrast, in the period 1880–1910, over twenty species had made up 75 per cent of the recipes. The decreasing diversity almost certainly relates to the transition between a period when catch size was small and varied, to a time when the industry concentrated on the catching of specific species using the trawl. Even in 1972, a Marine Department publication notes that whereas forty-

Table 2. Percentage of each species in all recipes using small pelagic fish species, printed during each decade. The bloater is a preserved herring that has not been split; it was often used as a paste.

	Anchovy	Sardine	Herring	Sprat	Bloater	Pilchard
1880–99	42	17	25	12	4	0
1900–09	27	39	21	10	2	1
1910–19	29	48	20	1	2	0
1920–29	22	54	23	1	0	0
1930–39	16	47	29	0	2	0
1940–49	21	51	24	0	2	2

two food fishes were known to be caught locally, only seven were being marketed regularly (Watkinson and Smith 1972).

Several sea fish species showed noticeable regional variation: in particular cod was most common in Canterbury and Otago books, whereas snapper was most common in Auckland, Hawke's Bay and Wellington, and absent in Otago. These variations are entirely consistent with the regional coastal distribution of these species (Paul 2000).

Smoked fish and small pelagic fish

In smoked fish recipes prior to 1900, 'haddock' was invariably given as the species, but from 1900 the fish began to be unspecified such that by 1920, 80–90 per cent of recipes simply recommended 'smoked fish'. From 1920 the herring made up 50–60 per cent of species where one was named, with the remainder 'kipper', cod or snapper. There were notably few recipes for smoked eel.

Although New Zealand has commercial numbers of pelagic fish such as the sardine and anchovy, commercial interest in these was variable and the introduction of specific fishing methods such as purse seining did not occur until the 1940s. Although pre-1900 cookery books do provide recipes for fresh herring, it is likely that, where the small pelagic fish are specified in recipes, they were for the most part preserved and imported varieties (Table 2). The most noticeable trend is the declining proportion of anchovy recipes coupled to the rising proportion of sardine.

Table 3. Percentage of each species in all recipes using freshwater fish, printed during each decade.

	Trout	NZ Trout	Whitebait	Salmon	Eel
1880–99	19	3	9	11	58
1900–09	27	0	32	36	5
1910–19	34	0	39	15	12
1920–29	20	0	41	13	26
1930–39	29	0	51	12	8
1940–49	21	0	53	18	8

Salted fish and freshwater fish

There was a decline in the proportion of salt-fish recipes from the turn of the century, presumably as better refrigeration allowed increased supplies of fresh seafood as well as increasing emphasis on tinned varieties, in particular salmon. Salt-fish recipes were always uncommon, making up 1 per cent or fewer recipes in each decade. Where species names were given, ling, mackerel and cod made up the majority of these.

The most obvious trends in freshwater fish recipe content were the rising proportion using whitebait, and the falling proportion using eel (Table 3). With some sporadic variation, the proportion of recipes for fresh salmon and trout were reasonably constant.

Because of the increasing numbers of recipes using tinned salmon, the relative ratio of fresh to tinned salmon declined markedly between 1920 and 1950. Prior to 1910 fresh and tinned salmon were approximately even, but by the 1930s, 93 per cent of all salmon recipes were using the tinned product.

Shellfish

Since the first cookbooks, oysters have dominated the shellfish sections, and were the largest single variety of named aquatic food in recipes over the period up to 1950 (Table 4). Of note is the increasing number of toheroa recipes from the 1920s, a relative dearth of paua recipes and an almost complete absence of scallop recipes, except in books by overseas authors and several from Maud Basham.

Table 4. Percentage of species, in all recipes using molluscs, printed during each decade. Scallop recipes made up less than 0.5 per cent at all times.

	Oyster	Toheroa	Pipi	Cockle	Paua	Mussel
1880–99	86	0	1	5	0	6
1900–09	98	0	0	2	0	1
1910–19	98	0	1	1	0	0
1920–29	87	3	4	3	2	1
1930–39	83	9	4	1	1	2
1940–49	79	10	4	2	1	4

Crustacea

The meaning of the term lobster is unclear in many recipes. Although some specified tinned lobster (especially pre-1920), lobster in some instances may have simply referred to the 'rock lobster', another name for crayfish. Lobster recipes were more common before 1920, and crayfish thereafter. Notably, there were very few recipes for crab, other than during the 1930s, and most of these came from books written by overseas authors and printed in New Zealand (e.g. Futter c.1925 and Maclurcan c.1930s). A very small number of crab recipes also reappeared in the 1940s, again from overseas authors such as Heath (1946).

SEAFOOD AND COOKBOOK GENRES

Some cookbook genres had minimal seafood content; however where books did contain recipes, different genres tended to have a similar proportion of recipes devoted to each type of seafood. The exception to this was in a small number of military manuals, and in nutritional and educational texts, where the proportion of unspecified compared to specified species of fish was considerably greater.

Overall an average of about 5 per cent of recipe pages were devoted to aquatic foods. This proportion was slightly higher in publishers' and authored books, compared to books produced by local and national organisations or companies. The larger the seafood section within a book, the greater the proportion of those pages that were devoted to shellfish and crustaceans, and the fewer devoted to unspecified fresh or cooked, or 'tinned fish'. Thus the more a compiler of the book emphasised seafood, the more discerning they were as to the species recommended.

Many complex factors have interacted to influence the aquatic species that eventually found their way into New Zealand's early recipe books. The most important of these were: a) changes in the availability of fish relating to importation, the local industry, methods of preservation, timely distribution and cost; b) changes in the perception and value placed on fish as food, and c) the complex spectrum of the cookbook genre, which was in turn influenced heavily by the individual motives of authors, organisations and commercial manufacturers.

Although few copies of New Zealand's nineteenth-century cookbooks have survived, their contents show a sophistication and serious attempt to define the best possible use for each species of sea fish. Despite the development of an efficient catching and distribution network, recipes subsequently show diminishing interest in species specificity, treating fish as a single commodity with little distinction between the texture and taste of individual varieties. As Merle Blackmore complains in *Cooking of New Zealand Fish and other sea foods,*

> In New Zealand, except at a few expensive hotels and boarding-houses, very little variation is shown in the cooking of fish. Frying and boiling are the only two methods in general use. (Blackmore 1929:16)

The apparent decline in culinary sophistication was paralleled by a decreasing content of fish recipes, and an increasing use of tinned salmon, one of New Zealand's most commonly used aquatic food recipe ingredients prior to 1950.

The reasons for this apparent decline are many. Certainly we must include a depression, two world wars, and increasing commercial drives to market cheap processed foods. Compilations of contributed recipes, especially relating to baked products, were also clearly different to those more balanced cookery books driven by a single author. It is also possible that the dominance of educational instructors as cookbook authors after the turn of the century transformed what were essentially sophisticated middle-class cookery books devoted to the pleasure of eating into volumes epitomised by the title of Elizabeth Miller's successful *Economic Technical Cookery Book*. Whatever the reasons, highly significant changes did occur in the recipe content of cookery books and these provide interesting and perhaps paradoxical contrast to the commercial development of fishing in New Zealand.

7

Guiding the Culinary Tradition: the School of Home Science

Raelene Inglis

For more than seventy years, the University of Otago's School of Home Science provided an outstanding service to the women of New Zealand. As an academic institution, the School played an invaluable role in the creation of fresh opportunities, as it produced well-trained graduates who found new careers as home science teachers, academics, demonstrators and institutional managers. The School also had a significant influence, as it began to transmit home science information into the community through its extension services during the 1920s. Led by an inspirational American home science professor, Ann Gilchrist Strong, staff and students at the School of Home Science gave lectures to mothers' groups, toured with the rural Extension Service, and provided practical solutions to the home science problems of women. This chapter discusses the emergence of the School of Home Science and examines the scope and impact of its various outreach services.

HOME SCIENCE IN NEW ZEALAND

During the late nineteenth and early twentieth centuries, home science became a widespread social movement in many Western nations. However, in New Zealand only one university ever developed a faculty of home science. The School of Home Science at the University of Otago in Dunedin owed its establishment to the vision and generosity of one man, Colonel John Studholme, a Canterbury landowner. While travelling in the United States, Studholme had observed the work of home economics departments and considered that this was a branch of education that merited a university degree or diploma in New Zealand. Initially, Studholme offered to establish a chair in Domestic Science at Canterbury College, Christchurch. The proposal was approved and the position of Professor of Home Science was offered first to Miss A.G. Gilchrist, who declined because of her impending marriage, and then to a Miss Hedges. When illness prevented Miss Hedges from coming to New Zealand, the proposal languished for lack of a suitable substitute. After three years, Colonel Studholme transferred his offer to the University of Otago.

The University of Otago agreed to Studholme's proposal. Although many supporters of the introduction of home science to the University were similar to Drs Batchelor and King, in advocating the philosophy that a woman's education should conform to her natural role in life, the New Zealand Government considered it to be an academic subject with a scientific basis (Thompson 1919:239–43; Strong 1937:3–6; Anon 1962:7). Joseph Ward, in a letter on behalf of the Minister of Education, emphasised that the course should focus on the academic aspects of domestic science such as laboratory work testing foods, and the scientific principles underlying the practice of cookery, rather than just duplicating instruction in cooking and sewing (classes which could be found at any technical school) (Thompson 1919:242).

THE SCHOOL OF HOME SCIENCE, UNIVERSITY OF OTAGO

In 1911, the University of New Zealand established the degree of Bachelor of Science in Home Science and the Diploma of Associate of the University of Otago in Home Science. From 1911–86 the School of Home Science was directed by five female deans: strong, dedicated women who challenged the academic community to recognise their discipline as worthy of a place within the University's environs. The deans guided their Department (later Faculty) of Home Science to create an academic environment that, over the next several decades, would produce graduates who would go on to have careers as academics, teachers, dietitians, nutritionists, appliance demonstrators, industry researchers and scientists. The School made a significant contribution to the women of New Zealand, as it taught generations of students advanced cookery and dressmaking, and provided the nation's housewives with helpful domestic advice.

Despite being allocated a substandard building and lacking crucial teaching equipment, the Faculty of Home Science thrived (Strong 1937:9). From the days of the 'Tin Shed' in 1911, the ongoing lack of facilities for the increasing student numbers demanded solutions. Such was the calibre and character of the deans, staff, graduates and students that they overcame their many adversities through fundraising and community activities to create a world-class institution.

University of Otago School of Home Science students photographed with the first Dean, Professor Winifred Boys-Smith, in 1919. Consumer and Applied Science Administration, University of Otago.

The First Dean: Winifred Boys-Smith 1911–1920

The first Dean at the School of Home Science, Miss Winifred Boys-Smith, had previously been a science lecturer at Cheltenham Ladies' College in England (1896–1910). Miss Boys-Smith was familiar with home science teaching, as she had spent the winter of 1906 travelling in America studying methods of teaching science and domestic science, thanks to the Frances Mary Buss Memorial Travelling Scholarship (*Evening Post* 27 January 1911:9; Thompson 1919:244). Professor Boys-Smith was a firm believer that the study of home science at university level was a positive influence for the higher education of women and in an address at the University of Otago she stated, 'It is my part to prove to a concourse of those interested in this University and its welfare that Home Science is a subject worthy of a place in a university curriculum' (Boys-Smith 1911:5). Professor Boys-Smith proceeded to defend the introduction of this discipline and answered objectors to the introduction of scientific methods in the home by saying, 'if science had not been applied to medicine and surgery we should still be treated by quacks and charms' (Boys-Smith 1911:8–9). Professor

A.G. Strong (1937:11) later reflected that the most important gain of Professor Boys-Smith's time at the School was the waning of prejudice and scepticism for the course throughout the University.

When the University of Otago's School of Home Science opened its doors in 1911, Professor Boys-Smith found five students waiting for her – two for the three-year degree course and three for the two-year diploma course. After suitable publicity, twenty-one additional women embarked on one or more of the courses, such as Applied Chemistry or Practical Cookery (Thompson 1919:245; Strong 1937:9). The School was situated in the discarded old Mining School building, known as the 'Tin Shed'; this provided a chemical laboratory and lecture room. Cookery was taught at the North Dunedin Technical School, then later at the King Edward Technical College, while laundry work took place at the Professor's residence. Later, laundry classes were held in the rear premises of Knox College on Saturday mornings and then in Studholme House.

Helen Rawson: Dean 1920–1923

The second Dean, Helen Rawson, had been involved in setting up the School's programmes and lectured in Chemistry, Applied Chemistry and Household and Social Economics. Like Professor Boys-Smith, Helen Rawson was scientifically trained and had also visited American institutions to observe home science teaching. During her brief time as Dean (the University insisted that she retire after she married Dr Noel Benson, Professor of Geology), the length of the degree course was extended from three to four years and the diploma to three years (Strong 1937:11–12).

Ann Monroe Gilchrist Strong: Dean 1924–1940

With the appointment of Ann Gilchrist Strong to the School of Home Science, an American influence began to make its presence felt. One of the pioneers of home economics in America, Ann Strong was educated at Bucknell University, and Columbia Teachers College. As Professor of Home Economics at the University of Tennessee, she started their rural extension programme. Later, when teaching at the University of Cincinnati, Professor Strong introduced experimental cookery coordinated with applied chemistry. During a year's leave of absence from the University in 1917 she visited Baroda, India (now also known as Vadodara), and was persuaded to remain and organise a graduate course in Home Science at what is now the University of Baroda (Anon 1957:6; Anon 1962:36; Thomson and Thomson 1963:67–9; Mitchell 2003:158). Nearing the

Professor Ann Gilchrist Strong, Dean of the School of Home Science from 1924 to 1940, was one of the pioneers of home economics in America.

Consumer and Applied Science Administration, University of Otago.

end of her contract in 1920, she was convinced by Colonel Studholme to leave India and come to New Zealand as Professor of Household Arts in 1921. After Helen Rawson's marriage at the end of 1923, Ann Strong became the third Dean of the Faculty of Home Science.

In contrast to the scientific focus of the British deans, Professor Strong encouraged a greater emphasis on practical work. After her arrival a number of substantial changes were made to the degree course, and in 1926 a Master's degree was introduced into the graduate programme. Professor Strong travelled twice to America during her tenure to locate additional staff for the Department, eventually securing Dr Lillian Storms to lecture in chemistry and nutrition and Miss Gladys McGill to teach textiles and clothing (Strong 1937:13). Professor Strong's continuing connections with the United States provided opportunities for students to undertake postgraduate study in America, many of whom returned to Otago filled with new ideas and techniques. Books published in America, such as *The Boston Cooking School Cook Book* (Farmer 1918), were used as teaching materials in class (Smale 1977:14). S.D. Sherriff remembered that as a student in 1921 she assisted Professor Strong in the afternoons, noting 'Many of the meanings about food were quite different, for example an American pie is a very different article from New Zealand pie and at that time, no-one knew anything about American cookery apart from Professor Strong herself' (Sherriff 1951:53–4).

145

Professor Strong was a firm believer in making home science a living force in the community. Her work with community and rural women's organisations was extensive and made a major contribution to the transmission of home science knowledge into the public arena. Evidence of her willingness to circulate information about cookery can be seen through her contributions to community cookbooks. For example, in *Dainty Recipes* (Anon 1926), published by the North East Valley Presbyterian Church, Dunedin, Professor Strong supplied a section entitled 'Salads and Salad Dressings', which provided information about the nutritional benefits of salads and several recipes such as Waldorf Salad (p. 18). Altogether Professor Strong contributed twelve recipes to *Dainty Recipes*, including Bran Muffins (p. 34), Ginger Cup Cakes (p. 58) and Tomato Sauce (p. 74). The appearance of the Bran Muffins recipe in *Dainty Recipes* identifies a pathway of culinary transmission from overseas because, as Leach (2006:9) explains, this particular recipe is identical to the Bran Muffins recipe in Emma Matteson's *A Laboratory Manual of Foods and Cookery* (1916), written in America. Leach (2006:9) maintains that we can be confident that Professor Strong used this source because a 1927 edition survives in the University of Otago Library. Professor Strong's recipes continued to be published in later editions of *Dainty Recipes* and interestingly, the fourth edition (Anon 1930) also included two contributions from Miss D. Little. Dora Little was the Assistant Warden of Studholme House for several years and her recipe for Banana Cream Pie (p. 85) shows a clear American influence.

Elizabeth Gregory: Dean, 1941–1961

Elizabeth Gregory was a graduate of the University of Otago Home Science faculty, gaining her Master's degree in nutrition in 1929. After attaining her PhD in biochemistry at University College, London, in 1932, Dr Gregory returned to the Otago Home Science School as a lecturer in chemistry and nutrition. In 1940, a Carnegie Visitor's Grant enabled her to visit universities in the United States and compare ideas and developments. After the retirement of Professor Strong, Elizabeth Gregory was appointed Professor of Home Science and Dean of the Faculty. During her time as Dean, Professor Gregory continued the extension work, made notable contributions in her field of human nutrition, and extended the School's teaching curriculum, introducing zoology, institutional management, design, methods of teaching, botany, and large-quantity cooking (*School of Home Science History* 1962:37–8).

Professor Elizabeth Gregory,
Dean of the Home Science
Faculty at the University of Otago
(1941–61), played a major role in
setting nutritional goals for all
New Zealanders during the 1940s
and 1950s.

Courtesy of the Consumer and Applied Science
Administration, University of Otago; original
portrait by W.A. Sutton.

Patricia Coleman: Dean, 1962–1986

Patricia Coleman was the last female Dean of the Faculty of Home Science. Graduating from the University of Otago's Home Science School in 1943 with a Diploma in Home Science, she taught in secondary schools in the Auckland province as a clothing teacher for six years before returning to Otago University as a tutor in the Department of University Extension. Periods of study followed, first in Paris (1953–4) on a French Cultural Scholarship, then at the School of Home Economics at Texas Technological College (1957–8), where she obtained her Master of Science degree. Patricia Coleman became the fifth Dean of Home Science at Otago in 1962 following the retirement of Elizabeth Gregory. After guiding the Faculty through to its seventy-fifth Jubilee in 1986, Professor Coleman retired and the form of the Faculty of Home Science altered significantly. The new Dean, David Buisson, was the first male to hold that position at Otago's School of Home Science. There was a shift in emphasis in course structure and core subjects as the School was split into two departments: Consumer and Applied Sciences and the Department of Nutrition (Coleman 1986:62–3; Laing and Putterill 1987:49–50).

A Permanent Building

One of the early challenges for the School of Home Science was the provision of suitable teaching premises. The original building allocated to Home Science, the discarded Mining School 'Tin Shed', was neither wind- nor weather-proof and its combined classroom and laboratory was inadequate for the size of the classes. Students were taught in rooms throughout the University and cookery classes were taken at the North Dunedin Technical School. Professor Boys-Smith was tireless in her efforts to get a permanent purpose-built building for the School and in 1919 construction started on an area of ground known as Tanna Hill, directly opposite the then main entrance to the University (Anon 1923:6). The new school building was opened in the middle of 1920, and included laboratories with associated kitchen, fabric room, and laundry as well as a library (Hercus 1955:71). The new building alleviated the space problem for a while, but soon classes had to be held in the attic. In 1947, a second Foods Laboratory was built in an American Army Hut. In 1961, a new two-storey teaching block (now four storeys), known as the Gregory Building, was opened by Miss Annie E. Stevenson, one of the first students to graduate from the School (Stevenson 1961:48–9; Anon 1962:17, 19).

Studholme House

Studholme House was established in 1915 to provide accommodation for students and a practice house for housekeeping. Originally the 'House' consisted of two 35-year-old houses joined by a new dining room, common room, laundry and kitchen, but over the next few decades the School of Home Science's facilities became a series of purchased and rented premises. The School had to contend with growing student numbers and ageing buildings (Anon 1922:6). By 1950, Lower Studholme House had been condemned as a residence but continued to be used for Food Service classes until 1959. In 1961, fifty years after the School of Home Science first opened, a new purpose-built six-storey hall of residence was completed (Anon 1962:20).

THE ASSOCIATION OF OTAGO UNIVERSITY HOME SCIENCE ALUMNAE

The Association of Otago University Home Science Alumnae, also known as the Alumnae Association, was formed in 1921 to keep graduates in touch with the School of Home Science through annual bulletins published by the alumnae, refresher courses and conferences. The bulletins kept the School's alumnae in touch about their teaching and work experiences, international study leave and home

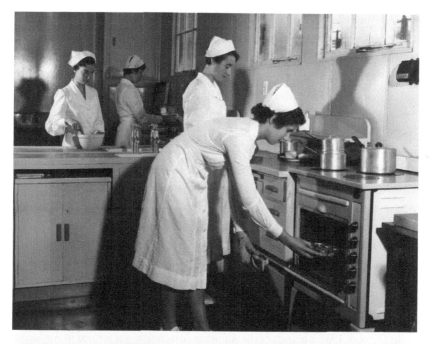

In 1957, the Publicity Division of the Tourist and Publicity Department, Wellington, photographed Home Science students in their practical Foods Laboratory class. Preparation was undertaken at island benches. Consumer and Applied Science Administration, University of Otago.

lives. Alumnae associations were more common in the United States and Professor Strong had proposed the formation of such a group soon after she arrived in New Zealand (Anon 1928:11). Professor Rawson approved the idea and it was decided to instigate it before the departure of Professor Boys-Smith. The first meeting was held at Studholme House, where Professor Rawson was elected the Association's first President, and Professor Boys-Smith a permanent Vice-President (Anon 1928:11).

The first annual conference was held at the University at the end of August, 1922 (Anon 1923:8). Sessions were held in the Home Science building where participants discussed their varying experiences, the difficulties of teaching home science, and the extension work begun since they had left the University (Anon 1923:8). The opening address was given by Professor Rawson who spoke about the aims and methods of teaching home science and the growth of the Home Science School at the University (Anon 1923:9). Professor Rawson then appealed to the Home Science graduates to share their knowledge with the home-makers in their districts, and encouraged them to recognise their qualification as an opportunity to give service to the community (Anon 1923:10). During the first evening of the conference Professor Strong spoke of the necessity for extension work (Anon 1923:10).

In October 1932 a branch of the Alumnae Association was formed in Auckland and by 1937 there were branches in Invercargill, Dunedin, Christchurch, Nelson, Wellington, Wanganui and a Havelock North-Hastings-Napier combined branch (Anon 1933:16; Anon 1937:5). Local branch meetings allowed members to discuss contemporary issues and provided a network of people with similar concerns. The activities of the branches were varied. For example, the Wellington Alumnae were invited twice in 1937 to afternoon tea with well-known cookery teacher Miss A.D. Rennie, and were shown over the Wellington Technical College's new Home Science wing and new flat (Anon 1937:7). Branch members participated in the Alumnae Association's, and also the School's many undertakings to share their home science knowledge with the community at large. However, throughout New Zealand one of the most essential functions of the Association was the ongoing task of fundraising at both local and national levels.

HOME ECONOMICS ASSOCIATION

One of the key attributes of the School of Home Science was the number of staff who were passionate in their desire to share their knowledge with the general public. In 1922, Professor Rawson and Marion Whyte organised a series of lectures for business girls at the School of Home Science. These lectures were popular and well attended, dealing with topics such as diet, clothing, exercise and balancing budgets. At one lecture, a Mrs Cooper asked why similar lectures and demonstrations were not given to housewives. It turned out Mrs Cooper had been instrumental in forming a small group of neighbours into the Mothers' Mutual Help Club in 1921. Meetings were held at different homes, where the mothers exchanged experiences and information, but by 1922 it was deemed that the scope and activities of the club needed to be expanded (Anon 1923:18–19; Emerson c.1972:4; University of Otago Hocken Collections MS 90-163, Box 5).

At the first annual conference of the Home Science Alumnae Association at the University of Otago in August 1922, Professor Strong described the St Kilda Mothers' Mutual Help Club and outlined the assistance that the School proposed to give the Club. At first, Professor Rawson and Professor Strong went to St Kilda to give their talks, but then arranged for six lectures to be given in the Home Science buildings under the auspices of the Mothers' Mutual Help Club. The first lecture in September in the Home Science buildings was enthusiastically attended by 100 women; at the second lecture over 200 turned up (Anon 1923:10; Anon 1928:17–18). After each lecture Professor Strong and her dietetics students gave a demonstration of cooking and food preparation to illustrate the practical applications of theory from the lecture. At the end of the final lecture the Home Science buildings were thrown open to inspection by the 200 visitors, who were most interested in the rooms and equipment.

On Professor Strong's recommendation it was unanimously agreed that the St Kilda Mothers' Mutual Help Club become the Otago Home Economics Association (OHEA). Professor Strong became the Association's first President, and then later its Patron, a position she held until her death in 1957 (Anon 1923:18; Emerson c.1972:4, 16; University of Otago Hocken Collections MS 90-163, Box 5). In 1923 new branches were formed in a number of Dunedin suburbs including St Kilda, Mornington, Caversham, Roslyn and North Dunedin (Anon 1923:18; Emerson c.1972:4, 21). Lectures were held monthly in the Home Science School, while branches arranged meetings at their own venues. Annie Stevenson, one of the first two Home Science degree students, joined the North Dunedin branch in 1924 and was the secretary for the OHEA for many years. Miss Stevenson maintained that the 'Home Economics Association was founded to let the University come to the housewife and to give them a true picture of food values and nutrition' (Emerson c.1972:12).

Branches held fundraising projects such as thrift exhibitions and the proceeds went towards a variety of worthwhile projects. For example, funds raised paid part of the salary of an extension worker (Emerson c.1972:16, 20–21). In 1938, donations were collected for the new Studholme House fund. During the war years, money was channelled to patriotic purposes and after the war, to food parcels for Britain. A Seacliff patient was 'adopted' in 1950 (Seacliff was a psychiatric hospital near Dunedin) and from 1952 a French boy was sponsored for some years. In 1956, donations from branches helped with the building of the new Home Science Extension demonstration kitchen at 835 George Street, Dunedin (Emerson c.1972:16). From 1955 to 1971 however, the branches no longer held fundraising activities but continued to support worthwhile causes from the balance that had accumulated over the years (Emerson c.1972:16).

RAISING FUNDS FOR THE SCHOOL OF HOME SCIENCE

The lack of suitable premises for teaching and student accommodation made it necessary for the Home Science staff, alumnae and students to find various ways of raising funds to meet their needs. Their frequent efforts were rewarding financially and offered the additional benefit of raising the profile of home science in the public arena. The School of Home Science was aided in these endeavours by the Home Economics Association and the Alumnae Association.

Fundraising ventures included operating Studholme House as a hotel when large numbers of out-of-town visitors required accommodation: for example, during the New Zealand and South Seas Exhibition (1925); a Medical Congress (1927); and a Mining Conference (1951) (Anon 1928:18; *Evening Star* 22 April 1952; Hercus 1955:71; Anon 1962:20). Exhibitions and fairs were also a common method of raising funds and publicising the activities of the Home Science School. One example in 1938 was held in the Dunedin Town Hall Concert Chamber to raise funds for a new wing for Upper Studholme House. Professor Strong welcomed those present and asked the Mayor, Mr Allen, to open the exhibition. The Mayor expressed gratification at the large attendance then went on to talk about the record of the Home Science School, its graduates and the purpose of the fair (*Otago Daily Times* 7 September 1938).

Professor Strong and Dr Elizabeth Gregory made three tours of New Zealand during their holidays in 1938, talking to organisations and holding public meetings explaining the work of the School (Anon 1962:20). Open days, held at the School of Home Science, proved a popular way to educate the public about home science and increase funds. For example, the *Evening Star* (11 July 1946) reported that hundreds of women and quite a few men spent an entertaining time viewing the work of the students and watching demonstrations of various activities. There was a bread-making demonstration, with the cooks turning out loaves and rolls and although the chemistry and nutrition laboratories attracted interest, it was the foods and clothing laboratories that caught the attention of the visitors.

Gifts, donations and bequests also helped to increase the resources in the building fund. For example, Annie Stevenson gave £10,000 in 1948, a substantial sum at that time. The Otago Home Economics Association donated £200 and the Sargood Trust £500 (Anon 1962:20). The National Council of Women promised support, as did many women's organisations throughout the country and the New Zealand Government offered a subsidy after £48,000 had been accumulated (*Evening Star* 22 April 1952; Anon 1962:20). In 1961 the new Home Science building was opened, rather appropriately, by Miss Stevenson.

HOME SCIENCE EXTENSION SERVICE

The School of Home Science made a significant contribution to improving the lives of many New Zealanders, particularly women. There is little doubt that the School's degree and diploma programmes provided graduates with new career pathways, but perhaps the School's most important role was through its involvement with extension activities. In 1909, Colonel Studholme wrote to the University of Otago Council stating, 'I believe the most valuable part of the work of the Professor [Strong] will be her extension work among teachers and other women who are not regular University students' (Anon 1962:14). Studholme's words would prove to be prophetic. Professor Strong was passionate about conveying information about home science into the community. At the first conference of the Alumnae Association, Strong explained 'We have such vital facts that we cannot keep them to ourselves, we must give them to others' (Anon 1923:10).

Professor Strong was eager to start a rural extension programme in New Zealand. In 1923 she enlisted the support of Mr R.B. Tennant, Director of Agricultural Instruction in Otago, and Mr Cameron, Secretary of the Farmers' Union, to help her to make contact with rural women. In turn, they asked her to accompany them to their meetings of 'Practising Farmers' Schools' held throughout the province. For two years Professor Strong accompanied these men at nights, after school, in weekends and during the holidays to various places throughout Otago, such as Lawrence, Poolburn and Owaka (Home Science Extension Work in New Zealand: University of Otago Hocken Collections MS 90-163, Box 5). Mr Tennant was enthusiastic about having a Home Science graduate work with rural women so Catherine Landreth, from the Home Science School, was sent in 1925 to the Iowa State College of Agriculture to study rural extension work with the aid of a fellowship from the American Federation of University Women (University of

Otago Hocken Collections MS 90-163, Box 5). Miss Landreth secured her Masters in Extension teaching and wrote a thesis concerning the organisation of extension work for women in New Zealand. Unfortunately, Professor Strong's efforts to interest the Minister of Agriculture or the head of the College of Agriculture in extension work were to no avail. The Principal of the College assured her that 'the women of New Zealand did not require such assistance' (University of Otago Hocken Collections MS 90-163, Box 5).

In 1926, Mrs Polson, the wife of the Dominion President of the Farmers' Union, organised a large group of women in the North Island as members of the Women's Division of the Farmers' Union (WDFU). Professor Strong wrote to Mrs Polson to discuss the benefits of extension work and to persuade her to unite with the Women's Institutes (WI) for this purpose. However, Mrs Polson was adamant that members of the Women's Division were to aid the Farmers' Union and that their name should reflect this. Professor Strong agreed to assist the organisation of WDFU groups in Otago and travelled with Mrs and Mrs Cameron to the first meeting of the WDFU in Milton, South Otago. For the first time, women met in a separate room from their husbands and sons. After the advantages of the organisation were explained, one woman rose and said 'I have lived in this district for six years but I do not know a single woman in this room' (University of Otago Hocken Collections MS 90-163, Box 5).

Dean Russell, a representative of the Carnegie Corporation, an American philanthropic organisation, visited New Zealand in 1928 and met with Professor Strong and Professor James Shelly, Director of Adult Education at Canterbury College. Russell was impressed with their plans for a rural extension programme and recommended to the Carnegie Corporation that aid should be granted to the University. Colonel Studholme (in England) was also invited by the Corporation to report on the matter and he endorsed the project as well. The board granted funds to both institutions, with the University of Otago to receive £1500 per annum for the next five years to form an Extension Service within the Home Science Department (Anon 1932:9; Anon 1957:7; Hocken Collections MS 90-163, Box 5).

The Home Science Extension Bureau was established in November 1929 and work began in January 1930 with three staff (all with either Home Science degrees or diplomas from the University of Otago), a Director (Professor Strong), an Information Bureau and a car (named Elizabeth). Professor Strong invited representatives from both the Women's Division of the Farmers' Union and the Women's Institutes to a meeting to discuss closer cooperation between the two organisations. However the meeting failed to achieve its objective and

The Home Science Extension advisors ready to load the cars with their equipment, c.1930s.
Courtesy of the Consumer and Applied Science Administration, University of Otago.

unfortunately succeeded in antagonising both parties. It was decided that the rural extension service would liaise with both groups separately.

Twelve country areas were chosen as 'lecturing centres' and 'Elizabeth' was packed with the demonstration kit for talks with titles such as Food Preservation, Basic Nutrition, House Planning, School Lunches (Anon 1932:9–10; Coleman 1975:26). Information about home science was passed on to the public through weekly fifteen-minute radio programmes, newspaper articles and through boys' and girls' clubs (Anon 1932:10). In 1934, a further five-year grant from the Carnegie Corporation made extension work possible in both Canterbury and Otago and the service was able to include a rural travelling library service. The joint service was named the Association for Country Education (ACE) (Anon 1957:7).

The association between the WDFU and the School of Home Science continued. The *New Zealand Dairy Exporter and Farm Home Journal* (November, 1936:69) described a Country Girls' Educational Week that had been held recently by the Otago Provincial Executive. Eighty girls, from almost all the branches of the executive, attended lectures at the School of Home Science and at the Karitane Harris Hospital (training hospital for Plunket nurses). The *Otago Daily Times* reported in 1938 that through the ACE the Home Science Department was one of the few University institutions directly benefiting the community (*Otago Daily Times* 7 September 1938).

The staff of the Home Science Extension Bureau made significant contributions to New Zealand farming journals over a number of years. For example, during the 1930s, articles in *The Journal of Agriculture*, in the Farm Home and Kitchen section, contained information about diet and nutrition, advice for the home and family, and recipes. Violet Macmillan, BHSc., wrote in 1938 'In almost every talk on nutrition given by this Department during the past eight years we have advised people to see that their diets contain generous amounts of fruit, vegetables, milk, eggs, and whole-grain cereals, and to watch and if necessary reduce the meat and the sweet and the starchy foods made from refined cereals' (Macmillan 1938:484). In the same issue, Macmillan also discussed American research on 'Food Fallacies and Nutritive Quackery' and supplied recipes for Wholemeal Bread, Wheatmeal Eggless Cake, Xmas or Birthday Cake, Meringue Cake, Raisin Puffs, and Wholemeal Shortbread (Macmillan 1938:484–6).

In 1940, the service reverted to the title of Home Science Extension. Although the impact of war limited the extensive tours and fieldwork throughout the countryside, there were numerous other activities undertaken. Staff of the School of Home Science and the extension service contributed significantly to the war effort as the constraints of food shortages, then later food rationing, began to impact on New Zealanders. Under the auspices of the Women's War Service Auxiliary (WWSA), classes in canteen management were given by staff of the School and members of the extension service. The notes and schedules for these classes prepared by Catherine MacGibbon were later published as books (see Table 3). In March 1942, four days were spent in Ranfurly preserving a crop of peas in 140 large tins for the WWSA. All the tins were supplied at cost price by Irvine and Stevenson. The Dairy Research Institute requested recipes using dried butter-fat, and recipes for cooking dehydrated meat in large quantities were developed for the Department of Scientific and Industrial Research. Lectures were given to a variety of organisations: for example, branches of the Home Economics Association; the WWSA in the suburbs and Mosgiel; the Home Science group of the YWCA, and the Young Citizens Club. A series of six talks on nutrition were given to the staff of the Roslyn Woollen Mills. A menu and food lists were drawn up for an Air Force Cadets' Camp held at Waikouaiti at Easter (ACE Brief Report for 1942, University of Otago Hocken Collections MS 90-163, Box 5; Anon 1962:27–8).

Despite the petrol shortage, field work was still taking place. In 1943 lectures on 'Eating for Victory' were given to twelve WDFU or WI groups (a total of 244 women), mainly throughout North Otago. Similar groups in seventeen locations heard the lecture on 'Wartime Substitutes' (362 women) (ACE Report of Work for 1943, University of Otago Hocken Collections MS 90-163, Box 5). A garden tutor was appointed for the 'Dig for Victory' campaign (Anon 1962:15). In February

Table 1. Estimated number of people contacted by Home Science Extension

Activities	Number
Letters received	3,653
Boxes to meetings – 98 (attendance at 20 each meeting)	1,960
Packets to meetings – 145 (attendance at 20 each meeting)	2,900
Packets and books issued to members	454
Magazines issued to members	1,305
Miscellaneous loans	354
Radio talks – 64 (audience at 500 each*)	32,000
Lectures	430
Show judging (can't estimate)	–
Classes	1,259
Total	**44,315**

* *This figure is based on 600 requests for a leaflet after a broadcast [Annual Report of Home Science Activities for 1954:4].*

1944 an urgent request was received from the Director of Talks at the National Broadcasting Service for special radio talks giving advice on meat rationing. Violet Macmillan wrote a series of nine special talks and 23 five-minute talks on meat-rationing recipes and tips. These talks were additional to the usual twice-weekly talks. Miss Macmillan also contributed further information and a meal outline to a booklet being prepared for the Food Controller (ACE Report of Work for 1944, University of Otago Hocken Collections MS 90-163, Box 5).

In 1948, Departments of Adult Education were set up at all four New Zealand universities to provide a general adult education service. At the University of Otago, home science extension work was now part of this new adult education initiative, but the responsibility for providing information services on a national scale remained with Otago (Anon 1962:15). Staff numbers increased to six, a list of publications was developed and a monthly press release was introduced for over 100 newspapers and magazines throughout New Zealand (Carpenter 1977:17).

A report from 1954 highlights how many people the Extension Department made contact with during that year. Table 1 shows the figures calculated for the number of people contacted.

In May 1956 the Extension Department opened a new demonstration kitchen at 835 George Street, Dunedin. This new resource contained a lecture room and plans included demonstrations on cookery, lectures on foods, nutrition, the use of kitchen equipment and applied topics. Such was the new kitchen's popularity that during the 1950s the staff of six had classes booked for the next three years (Coleman 1975:26). With the dissolution of the University of New Zealand in 1963, each university became fully responsible for its own education activities and the name was changed to Department of University Extension (Carpenter 1977:17–18). Over several decades, the Extension Department transmitted information on subjects such as food, catering, home making and appliances to the public through feature articles in newspapers (Table 2) and by publishing leaflets and bulletins (Table 3). As well as operating its information and advisory service for the general

Table 2. Examples of Home Science feature releases in newspapers.

Date	Title
1957	Out of Your Store Cupboard: How to Make a Meal in an Emergency
1958	Serve Bananas Often: Some Useful Recipes
1959	Feeding the Multitudes: Catering and Cooking for Numbers
1962	Convenience Foods: Changing Food Habits
1966	Versatile Tree Tomatoes: Rich in Vitamin C
1966	Mysterious Milk: Yoghurt. What it is, How to Make and Serve it.
1966	Teflon: Non-stick Finish
1967	Saving Wisely: Using Low Cost Foods
1969	Boysenberries and Loganberries: Two Unusual Berry Fruits
1969	Using Foreign Cookbooks: Equivalents and Substitutes
1972	Cooking with Metrics

Table 3. Examples of publications by the School of Home Science, or by Home Science graduates.

Date	Title
1941	Canteen Management
1942	Cooking for Canteens
1949	Preserving
1955	Journal of Agriculture Cookery Book
1960	New Zealand Dishes and Menus
1961	What Judges of Home Produce Look For
c.1974	In a Nutshell: A Recipe Guide to Almonds, Chestnuts, Hazelnuts & Walnuts
c.1980	Meals without Meat
c.1981	Microwave Ovens
1986	Preserving Food. Freezing, Bottling, Drying
1991	Low Cost Healthy Meals for All Ages

public, the Extension staff worked with governmental and statutory bodies like the Consumers Institute and the Metric Advisory Board (Carpenter 1977:17–18). During the early 1990s, the Department of University Extension was reduced to a single staff member answering consumers' queries. It closed in 1994.

THE SCHOOL OF HOME SCIENCE AND OAKHILL POTATOES

The School of Home Science made a significant contribution to the development of New Zealand's culinary history. As discussed above, the School used a variety of methods to transmit home science knowledge and recipes throughout the country. While it can be difficult to trace the pathways of cooking information, a distinctive recipe name, concept or ingredient in a recipe can help in the identification and tracking process. One such example can be seen in the recipe concept of Oakhill Potatoes. This was a dish probably introduced to New Zealand from the United States through the auspices of the School of Home Science, that attained some popularity, appearing in community cookbooks for a number of years.

One of the earliest versions of the recipe for Oakhill Potatoes is in the *Boston Cooking-School Cook Book* (Farmer 1896:286). This recipe appears again in the 1918 edition used by the School of Home Science (Farmer 1918:286). The dish consists of layers of sliced cooked potatoes and sliced hard-boiled eggs, which are then covered with a white sauce and a topping of buttered cracker crumbs and baked in the oven. The students of the School of Household Arts at the University of Cincinnati included a recipe for Oak Hill Potatoes in their cookery book (University of Cincinnati 1916:12), only the topping is different, with the crackers replaced with breadcrumbs. This recipe identifies a transmission pathway because Professor Strong had taught at the University of Cincinnati and there is a copy of this recipe book in the University of Otago Library. By the early 1940s, a recipe for Oakhill Potatoes is present in the Laboratory Manual used by students at the University of Otago's School of Home Science for their Foods 1 classes (Naylor 1944:20). The name and concept of this recipe are still the same but now bacon is layered with the other ingredients and grated cheese is sprinkled over the top of the breadcrumbs. There is also the additional option of using a cheese sauce instead of the white sauce.

This recipe concept was taught to at least one school cookery class because it appears in handwritten form in a copy of the *Home Science Scholar's Note Book* (Anon 1953), appropriately reduced in size for school cookery and without the breadcrumbs. Further instances of this recipe continue to appear in cookbooks, for example it was considered a popular luncheon dish by Mrs Ian Rutherford, who contributed it to a community cookbook (Farqharson and Jarvis 1961:11), and was modified in 1981, appearing as 'Oakle Potato' (Anon 1981:25), where the eggs and breadcrumbs are omitted. Former home science graduate and well-known television cook and author Alison Holst also included a recipe for Oakhill Potatoes in *Let's Cook with Alison Holst* (Holst 1983:31). This recipe may have achieved its early popularity because of its introduction and association with graduates from the School of Home Science.

CONCLUSION

The School of Home Science at the University of Otago was an academic institution unique in New Zealand. The School overcame doubts from the academic community about its validity and rose above the paradox of providing women with new academic and professional opportunities in a gendered subject that educated other women in work concerning the home. The School triumphed over the obstacles of inadequate facilities through the courage and determination of every Dean, staff member and graduate who passed through its halls. The School of Home Science became possibly the most important vector of culinary knowledge throughout New Zealand for most of the twentieth century. The inspiration for such transmissions was primarily about helping women in their homes. Throughout the country small improvements would occur, for example, with helpful bottling advice to preserve a season's excess fruit and vegetables, or budget help to feed the family healthy meals on a limited income. Through the passion and dedication of women like Ann Strong, the School of Home Science reached out into the communities of New Zealand and provided information and structure through which domestic kitchens were made more efficient, more scientific, diets were improved and menus extended. This chapter has only highlighted the cookery and foods section of Home Science teaching; dietetics and clothing were also key areas of Home Science.

If success is measured through providing information to the public, then the School of Home Science was successful. Through its fundraising ventures, Extension Service, Home Economics Association and Alumnae Association, there were a number of avenues through which communications about home science passed. This was not a one-way process – interested members of the public actively requested information, purchased booklets and attended fairs and open-day activities. The School of Home Science reached out into the communities of New Zealand, and the public responded.

8

Cooking on a Dais: From Daisy to Daish

Michael Symons

Like so many other words, 'dais' has a food-related origin. The name for a low platform in a hall, usually supporting a table or lectern, derives from the medieval French, 'table', and earlier Latin *discus* for a 'disc' or 'dish'. Aunt Daisy (Maud Ruby Basham, 1879–1963) and Lois Daish (1940–) are among New Zealanders who have elevated domestic cookery to public view. The contrasts between their recipes and presentations, as well as some similarities, provide a focus for reflections on two culinary epochs, the modern and what might have to be termed the postmodern. These spokespeople provoke discussions of marketing, domestic life, food intellectuality and the shifting sands of human authenticity.

FIRST, COOK YOUR PEAS

One vexing culinary custom that shows up repeatedly in old New Zealand cookery books is that people used to overcook their peas. I throw fresh peas into boiling water for approximately one minute and they are done. Yet culinary authorities used to advise boiling green peas for twenty minutes or more. An early edition of Edmonds' *The 'Sure to Rise' Cookery Book* recommended 'Peas: 20–30 minutes' (Anon [c.1930]:60). *Whitcombe's Modern Home Cookery and Electrical Guide* warned that vegetables 'are rich in vitamins, and should never be overcooked', and yet wanted cooks to 'Boil [peas] from 30 to 45 min. (as little water as possible)' (Anon [1939]:83, 89).

Cookery books show that cooking times generally shortened over the twentieth century, so that where early editions of Whitcombe and Tombs' *Colonial Everyday Cookery* wanted: '… from 20 to 30 minutes, depending on the age of the peas' (Anon [1907]:133), after a half-century, later editions trimmed five minutes off the estimate, suggesting boiling 'peas or beans 15–25 minutes' (Anon [1948?]:125).

In 1973, *Food for Flatters* advised novice cooks, 'Peas–10–15 mins', and by the time Michael Volkerling followed up with *More Food for Flatters*, peas required '8–10' minutes (Volkerling 1978:24; 1989:41).

One explanation for advocating as much as forty-five minutes might be that, until the 1970s, peas were picked much older. Ahead of her time, Helen Cox's recommendation in *The Hostess Cook Book* was to braise 'for about 8–10 minutes … Old peas will not be so successful, and they will take about 25 minutes (they are hardly worth cooking anyway)' (Cox 1952:248). Yet a much earlier book, Mrs E.B. Miller's *Economic Technical Cookery Book*, specified: 'Peas should be boiled quickly, cover off, with a sprig of mint added; from twenty minutes for young peas' (Miller [c.1907]:175).

The parallel experience in America worried scholar Jessamyn Neuhaus, who credits the deliverance from 'water-logged, overcooked vegetables' somewhat implausibly upon improved varieties, adding that 'we in the age of genetically engineered food have to remember that these authors dealt with fresh ingredients of vastly different quality' (Neuhaus 2003:115). As another possibility, the rapid mushiness of frozen peas might have encouraged a rethink, and yet Digby Law wrote in *A Vegetable Cookbook*: 'To [Braise] Frozen Peas … cover tightly and gently cook for 15 minutes' (Law 1982:132). Many participants at the conference on New Zealand culinary history in Dunedin in November 2007 remembered overcooked vegetables, but no one could come up with a winning explanation.

My suggestion is that the reduced cooking times resulted from a combination of factors, so many that they amounted to a culinary revolution. The greater respect for fresh peas is only one adjustment that can be pinpointed with surprising consistency to the early 1960s. That was when magazine cookery writer Tui Flower still received readers' complaints about recipes using garlic and olive oil – viewed as 'foreign muck' (Flower 1998:149–150). Seventy years earlier Isobel Broad might have made mayonnaise from 'yolks of two raw fresh eggs … eight tablespoonfuls of good olive oil … few drops of tarragon vinegar' (Broad 1889:143), but the standard method for several decades until the early 1960s involved cans of condensed milk (Basham 1954:109). Many people were good cooks, but their priorities were often different.

The two periods – before and after the revolution of the early 1960s – are investigated here through a comparison of the works of two much-loved writers, Maud Ruby ('Aunt Daisy') Basham and Lois Daish. Both women put home cooking 'on a dais'; yet they belong to two profoundly different worlds. In her later works, *Aunt Daisy's Favourite Cookery Book* (1954), and *Aunt Daisy's Ultimate*

GREEN PEAS

Shell and cook in boiling salted water with sugar to taste and a few sprigs of mint tied together for easy removal. Time, from 15 to 20 minutes according to age. Strain and serve with a little butter and pepper.

Buttersteamed green peas

At least once a year it's good to sit outside in the sun and shell a kilo of sweet green peas. It'll take half an hour and provide only two cupfuls, but it'll be worth it to be reminded that the texture and flavour of the best freshly harvested peas are unmatched by the frozen variety. It's a pity though, that the quality of fresh peas is so inconsistent. Many are allowed to overmature before picking, or simply take too long to get from farmer's field to consumer's table.

The optional lettuce leaves intensify the flavour of the peas and ensure that all will be evenly cooked under their leafy cover. If you don't use the lettuce leaves, the peas should be covered with water.

2 cups freshly podded peas
sprigs of mint
1 tbsp butter
water
lettuce leaves (optional)
salt and pepper

Put the peas in a small pot and add the mint and butter. Add water to half cover the peas, placing the lettuce leaves on top. Put on a lid and cook over a moderate heat for 2–5 minutes after the water boils, depending on the tenderness of the peas. Remove the lettuce leaves, lightly salt and serve in a warm bowl.

Serves 4.

Top: In *Aunt Daisy's Ultimate Cookbook* (1959, p. 80), published four years before her death in 1963, Aunt Daisy recommended that green peas should be boiled for up to twenty minutes.
Bottom: In *Dinner At Home* (1993, p. 130), Lois Daish wrote that green peas should be tender after two to five minutes' cooking. H. Leach Collection.

163

Cookbook (1959), Maud Basham included two differing instructions. The first was: 'Green Peas ... Time, from 15 to 20 minutes according to age' (Basham 1954:90; 1959:80). She wrote separately: 'shell just before cooking ... Boil 8 to 20 min' (Basham 1954:411). By contrast, Lois Daish edges towards minimal cooking, stating in *Dinner at Home*: 'Put on a lid and cook over a moderate heat for 2–5 minutes after the water boils, depending on the tenderness of the peas' (Daish 1993:130).

An early authority might cook green peas for twenty minutes, and a late one for two. Given that no simple physical explanation seems sufficient, the suggestion is that the two approaches belong to two entirely different culinary worlds. What lies behind these enormous changes? Trying to understand Daisy vs Daish means thinking about not just the kitchen but the food industry, pleasure, and authenticity. Being so in touch with the intricacies of daily life, personal aspirations and the wider economy, cookery books are capable of opening our eyes to the 'modern' in Daisy's time and the 'postmodern' (among other names) in Daish's.

AUNT DAISY

Broadcaster Aunt Daisy retains a special place in New Zealand hearts (Fry 1957; Downes & Harcourt 1976). For three decades until her death in 1963, at nine o'clock each morning after the radio played 'Daisy, Daisy, Give me your answer do ...', she piped up, 'Good Morning Everybody!', and delivered a rapid-fire half-hour monologue on domestic matters. In Nelljean M. Rice's words, such 'radio homemakers' served as a 'talking compendium of domestic advice. ... These women projected a community cookbook of the air' (Rice 1997:175). Standing at the elbow of housewives, when husbands had gone to work and children to school, Daisy became an early mass-media celebrity with not only her radio show, but also newspaper and magazine columns and series of cookbooks.

Born in London, Maud Ruby Taylor arrived in New Zealand in 1891, and in 1904 married Frederick Basham, whose drinking became an increasing liability. Becoming a singer and school teacher, she found her way into experimental radio transmissions and, by 1930, calling herself 'Aunt Daisy', worked on children's and classical music programmes, shifting between radio stations (including to 1ZR Auckland in 1932 and moving to 2ZB Wellington in 1937). These were turbulent years for broadcasting and, after its election at the end of 1935, the Labour Government removed restrictions on advertising. Often under the guise of purveyor of useful recipes, Daisy stole into kitchens each morning, hypnotically extolling one commercial product after another.

On 23 April 1940, the popular 2ZB radio personality Aunt Daisy (Maud Basham) compered the Wellington finals of a nationwide apple pie contest in the Wellington Town Hall. The national finals took place on 26 April at the Centennial Exhibition assembly hall. Alexander Turnbull Library, Wellington, New Zealand; New Zealand Freelance Collection; Ref. No. G–100928–1/2.

Her first book, the *'Aunt Daisy' Cookery Book: Containing Over 700 Recipes and Hints* (Basham [1934a]), was so successful that it helped pay for the first of three visits to the United States, as well as leading to further works. Her next books, from probably late 1934 until around 1951 were numbered No. 2 to No. 6, to be followed by *Aunt Daisy's Favourite Cookery Book* in 1952 and *Aunt Daisy's Ultimate Cookbook* in 1959. She also published collections of handy hints, and, towards the end of her reign, a series of booklets of sentimental wisdom from her radio programme, advising on the folly of fretting and the need for courage and humility.

Her cookbooks were almost devoid of radio chattiness and were formulaic lists of ingredients and instructions more typical of the time. Her selection suggests a seemingly endless round of family meals and perhaps afternoon teas. The early books were especially in touch with baking. As she wrote in her first, having recently left for 1ZB, her 'souvenir' recalled the 'jokes we had, – of the Cream Lily Controversy, the Custard Tart Contrariness, the Mysteries of Meringues' (Basham [1934a]:Foreword). Even more indicatively, it opened with sections on Biscuits,

Aunt Daisy at her desk at Station 1ZB, Auckland. This portrait appeared in *The N.Z. 'Daisy Chain' Cookery Book* (1934), her second volume of recipes sent in by members of the 'Daisy Chain' throughout New Zealand. S09-509, Hocken Collections, Uare Taoka o Hakena, University of Otago.

Bread and Yeast, Cakes (large) and Cakes (small), and relegated unusually short sections on Fish, Soup and Vegetarian to the back.

The early books were based on contributions from her followers, so that Daisy dedicated her first, a roughly edited jumble of grass-roots expertise, to 'all "the Girls" in the big "Family" … of our dear old Station 1ZR'. Such contributors as 'Ex-Sailor', 'Robin Redbreast', 'Anon.', 'Marigold', 'Interested, Grey Lynn' and 'Pam of Remuera' (Basham [1934a]), belonged to the 'Daisy Chain' of 'thousands of women who rally round "Aunt Daisy", and who supply her with innumerable recipes, simple remedies, and household hints' (Basham [1934b]:Foreword). Detailing this recipe gathering, Raelene Inglis concludes that Daisy's 'management of knowledge movement sounds very similar to our modern day concept of a webmaster' (Inglis 2006:115).

Daisy's network ensured that her cakes and biscuits were highly fashionable, such as three similar recipes (each with a spelling error) for 'Cornflake Merringues', 'Kellog Meringues' and 'Meringues, Conflake', coming hot on the heels of the breakfast cereal's introduction to New Zealand (Basham [1934a]:47, 52, 55). I have compared 1930s cookery books by counting their numbers of ten presumed Antipodean inventions (Lamingtons, Anzac Biscuits, Meringue Cake, Pavlova, Louise Cake, Tango Cakes, Khaki Sponge and Billy Sponge/Loaf/Bread). Many community (fundraising) books scored well, showing that they were often quite responsive to local fashions, unlike domestic science textbooks, which were noticeably uninterested. Aunt Daisy's first book was the equal highest scorer, the earliest to include seven of the selected recipes (Symons 2006b).

Within a few years, *Aunt Daisy's Radio Cookery Book No. 4* (published around 1936–8) was already a less lively ragbag and more carefully constructed, so much so that it seemed like the product not of 'the Girls' in the 'Daisy Chain' but a single authority, Aunt Daisy. More conventionally ordered, opening with Soup, Fish and Savouries, it was still not a comprehensive textbook, and so not recommending vegetable cooking times, for example. Pertinently, the book still had thirty-five biscuit recipes, sixty-six small cakes and sixty-one large, with further sections on related topics, 'Icing, Fillings', 'Bread, Scones & Tea Cakes', and 'Pastry'. We shall inquire further into this attention to cakes and biscuits, so typical of Daisy's period, after introducing Lois Daish.

LOIS DAISH

Lois Daish grew up in an unusually globally oriented family – her public servant father took them to New York from 1947 until 1949, when he worked in the United Nations secretariat, and then back to New Zealand, where he was responsible for the Colombo Plan students from South East Asia. Often thirty or forty of these students would be invited home for meals. 'I remember great pots of rice,' Lois recalled in an interview. When she was nine or ten, 'mother would cook the main meal, which left desserts, cakes and biscuits. Ruth, my older sister, and I did that non-essential cooking. We were never told to; we wanted to.' Lois used her own money to purchase her first cookery book, *Betty Crocker's Picture Cook Book* (1950), when she was about twelve.

She followed a university lecturer to Kuala Lumpur in January 1960, initially intending to marry him, but nonetheless staying in Malaysia, teaching at a Methodist girls' school and living with a Tamil family for two years. 'The mother was a very accomplished cook. I made a few notes, which I still have.' Lois married a postgraduate scholarship holder and shifted to Berkeley, California, from 1964 to 1966, 'and I had another hit of America. The food was very much like the food I'd had in Long Island. I cooked a lot of things with ground beef.' She became an avid viewer of Julia Child's pioneering television show about French cuisine, which had commenced in 1963. 'I bought her book that I could barely afford. With *Mastering the Art of French Cooking*, I started to love to cook properly; I started to cook from first principles.'

On her return to Wellington, Daish did some part-time reporting for a local newspaper and some part-time professional cooking and, in 1978, bought her first café, Number 9 in Bowen Street, opposite the Parliament buildings. According to a contemporary report, Number 9 was:

> light-heartedly called the smallest restaurant in the world, but no-one seems to mind – everyone still goes there. The five women who run it on a co-operative roster style, are serene and agile, and good at cooking warming cheerful food that people sometimes eat squatting on a pew already full of bodies or leaning on the counter waiting for the next body to leave. (Clayton [c.1980]:42)

Lois went into partnerships at Mount Cook Café in 1983 and then Brooklyn Café & Grill from 1988 until 1997. Meanwhile, she began a fortnightly cookery column for the *Listener* in 1984, which went weekly in 1994 until she relinquished it in 2007 (Welch 2005). The magazine has had a distinguished list of cookery writers, including Aunt Daisy, Graham Kerr, Patricia Harris, Annabel Langbein and, after Daish, Martin Bosley. Her first book, *Good Food*, appeared in 1989, followed by *Dinner at Home* (1993), *Fuss-Free Food for Two* [Good Food Series] (1997) and *A Good Year* (2005).

AUTHENTICITY

Both Aunt Daisy and Lois Daish wrote for the same magazine, were worldly travellers, were forced to become breadwinners, and put cooking on a dais. They wrote for the domestic cook, providing a range of ideas for homely meals and wider entertaining. Both had a seeming intimacy with their audience, the former primarily through the radio and the latter through a weekly column. Both writers' books benefited from continuous feedback, with an emphasis on completeness

Lois Daish working in the kitchen of No. 9 in Bowen Street, Wellington, 1980. Photograph by Catherine Palethorpe, courtesy of Lois Daish.

of coverage in Daisy's case and accuracy and refinement in Daish's. Early in the latter's columnist life, a reader wrote along the lines: 'Dear Mrs Daish, you have just caused me to waste one egg, two cups of flour, two apples and a half a cup of sugar, not to mention half an hour of my time.' Lois commented: 'Ever since, I have remained strongly aware of the very powerful relationship between the person who writes recipes and the person who reads them' (Daish 1994).

Yet several differences between their two worlds are quickly apparent – Aunt Daisy was noted for her distinctive voice, yet her non-stop radio chatter did not carry over to her books, which followed the convention of unadorned instructions. Lois Daish's books are illustrated and otherwise more graphically captivating, and a commentary introduces each recipe. Her style is crafted with a matter-of-factness larded with gentle humour (seen in such headings as 'Beyond the Banana Cake').

Among other differences is an expanded range of ingredients. Daisy's first book distinguished merely between cheese and grated cheese, while her later works added such treatments as shredded, sliced, chopped and melted, and admitted two special types: sharp cheese and cream cheese. With recourse to a larger dairy cabinet, Lois Daish's first book specifies cheddar, mild cheese, tasty cheddar, cream cheese, cottage cheese, blue vein, colby, gruyère, feta, ricotta, parmesan and mozzarella. 'Thanks to television advertisements for pizza, the chewy strings of warm mozzarella cheese are familiar to almost everyone', she notes (Daish 1989:162). She refers to the expansion of New Zealand cheese-making from cheddar cheeses – ranging from mild to sharp – through the replication of various European cheeses, to now devising 'varieties which are not copies but are truly original' (Daish 1989:159).

A second obvious difference is the much wider cultural mix of recipes. Daisy gives her recipes standard Anglo-Saxon names such as 'Date Kisses', 'Pumpkin Scones', 'Fruit Cake (Nice)', and so on. By contrast, Daish started out by explicitly rejecting the style of cooking that Aunt Daisy represented, 'just as my mother rejected it in New York'. Daish's first book includes not only 'Spinach Omelette' and 'Treacle Pudding' but also 'Grilled Groper Kebabs', 'Kouzou Kzartma', 'Huancaina Papas' and 'Panforte di Siena'. She was on a mission to introduce unfamiliar cuisines, 'For example, foccaccia … although I don't think I even called it that. I was interested in expanding people's interests away from traditional New Zealand cooking.' She only returned to what she thinks of as British colonial cookery later, once others were 'trashing it'. She noted: 'At some point, probably in the late 1980s, people became worried by the blandness, and the overcooked-ness of the British style. I started perversely saying it's not so bad.'

Reaching beyond the obvious widening of ingredients and styles, I consider that the two voices (one as distant from me as the other a good friend) contrast in their authenticity. While the concept of authenticity might be falling out of favour, it is like 'goodness' and 'beauty' in being imprecise, yet indispensable. The endangering of the word might be blamed on its too narrowly cultural use, so that a dish has been deemed 'authentic' only if strictly resembling some presumed original. Under such a definition, Aunt Daisy's recipes might even seem the more reliable source of what was actually happening in kitchens.

However, authenticity is more usefully regarded as having more than a cultural dimension. Authenticity can suggest harmoniousness not only with some narrow recipe, but also with the dictates of society and nature. Today, cooks must know and respect other culinary traditions, and not end up making a parody of the original but create something sensible for their kitchens and their guests. Heritage recipes might have to be adjusted, or abandoned, to cope with a different ingredient, climate or social circumstance (discussed in Symons 1993:66–77). This careful adaptation is distinctive of Daish's approach. Three of her four book titles involve the word 'good', which suggests similar qualities to 'authentic'.

Lois Daish has always read widely – the book cover of *Dinner at Home* records that 'at home she spends more time reading about food than cooking it' (Daish 1993) – and she likes writers who have a real presence. 'This need to know the writer in such a personal way is a curious thing for a technical manual, which is what a cook book really is'. It need not be through an author photograph, 'but I do want to feel that they are talking to me in their own distinctive personal voice' (Daish 1994). This implies that the author is not just reciting standard recipes. Similarly, while connecting with her readers, Lois Daish also told me she does not write for them but for herself, and so what can that mean? She might be interpreted as not talking down, or pandering, to her readers, but relaying the recipes and commentary she would want herself. That is, she wants an honest or authentic connection.

As a good journalist, Daish exhibits abundant curiosity. When she started writing for the *Listener*, she expected to run out of things to say after about three months. 'Instead the opposite happened and each subject I tackled opened up a new cluster of topics' (Daish 1989:5). Her curiosity extends from the growers to the expected company and from the history of ingredients to their handling and taste. She has not stopped experimenting. 'I'm interested in the craft of doing it better next time. I am constantly slightly improving recipes. In Lamingtons, I find that you can parch the coconut beforehand. I probably noticed that somewhere, and found it worked. At least it seemed good at the time.' Where Daisy's recipes scarcely changed from book to book, Daish is constantly coming up with improvements to produce 'Wendy's Warm Lamb Salad' and 'Asparagus Tips with Whipped Cream, from Alice B. Toklas'. Her books are not organised around the standard meal format – with chapters following the sequence of soups, appetisers, meats, vegetables, desserts, cakes and preserves – but on the annual round: 'I try to emphasise the season even more than the weather requires.'

Among further aspects, she is concerned with a meal's immediate social setting. 'I always think of a recipe in a setting. Perhaps dining alone or for a picnic in front of the television on election night. I am dreaming up occasions such as when other people might arrive unexpectedly, or when they didn't turn up, or whatever.' She has written: 'I'm a cook mainly because I like to feed people. I'm never happier than when I've got a row of empty mouths to feed ...' (Daish 1994:1). Daish seems to love cooking, reading about it even more and, mostly, sharing the results. Perhaps it was after an exhausting career as a café cook, but she introduced *Dinner at Home* with the comment: 'All day I look forward to the evening when I can pull out a chair and sit down to dinner at home' (Daish 1993:ix). She is concerned not only with the immediate guests but also with wider social issues, such as supermarket prices being higher in less affluent suburbs.

In addition to respecting her readers, cultural antecedents, craft techniques, ingredients and social settings, if Daish has a primary focus, it is taste. Her quest: 'something that is delicious to eat. The prime, number 1, that it's going to be nice to eat.' Time and again, she reveals discoveries to make a more enjoyable meal. Her first book boasted recipes 'in which the flavour of the natural ingredients shines through', and so a reliance on 'simple' methods (Daish 1989:5). Speaking of warm, 'meal-sized' salads, she has written, 'I seldom enjoy fridge-cold food, probably because the flavours of most food are dimmed at very low temperatures' (Daish 1993:68). Where such bracketed adjectives as '(Nice)' and '(Delicious)' stick out occasionally in Aunt Daisy's recipe headings, Daish's commentary is forever praising the 'delicate flavour and gentle texture' and rejecting the 'dull and unappetising' (Daish 1993:107). In her introduction to *A Good Year* she confesses that, when 'talking about cooking, there's one word that I find myself using over and over again. That word is gentle – gentle handling, gentle mixing, gentle heat, gentle taste. ... This gentle approach grows out of my deep respect for the natural flavour and texture of our wonderful raw materials' (Daish 2005:6).

The increased stress on authentic tastes was not limited to Daish, since books shifted their emphasis from cooking (in Daisy's world) towards eating (in Daish's).

Significantly, the word 'eating' only showed up in New Zealand recipe book titles from 1963 (Symons 2009). An analysis of the vocabulary also shows that the many appearances of 'taste', 'tastes', 'tastefully', 'tasty' and 'tastier' only started in cookery book titles with Madeleine Hammond's bell-wether introduction to a finer way of cooking, *A Taste of France* (1963). Also appearing in the new period, the cluster 'dine', 'diner' and 'dinner' usually suggested a serious approach to eating, along with 'entertaining', the earliest being another landmark, *Entertaining with Kerr* (1963). Two potent four-letter words joined for several gastronomic-sounding appearances of 'good food', dishes taken back to their material roots most notably by three of New Zealand's most celebrated cookery writers, starting with Lois Daish with *Good Food* (1989), then Julie Biuso, *The Joy of Good Food* (1993), and *Alison Holst's Good Food* (1995).

Overall, Lois Daish has published recipes that are true to the ingredients and to the people making and eating them, a complex task that demands much knowledge, experience, curiosity and recipe tweaking. She has sought good food with taste rewards. Although arguably the nation's finest cookery writer of her generation, Daish is far from alone in carefully considering requirements. Nor did cookery writers lack expertise in Maud Basham's day, although many tended to relay the received wisdom of cookery schools. And not all cooking became more authentic in Daish's era, so that unlike her well-educated and otherwise privileged readers, other people ate industry's worst, divorced from nature, family, community and culinary heritage. However, the real objection to my promotion of the greater authenticity of Daish's world is that it merely begs the question what really changed? 'Greater authenticity' is an evaluation rather than an explanation. So, what had happened in broader terms to make Daish and her readers more concerned with the social, cultural and natural suitability of recipes?

THE REVOLUTION OF '63

Previous research has shown that a major shift in cooking globally was reflected in the publication of three significant New Zealand cookery books in the year 1963 (Symons 2006a). These were Graham Kerr's *Entertaining with Kerr*, Madeleine Hammond's *A Taste of France: French Cuisine for New Zealanders* and Noel Holmes's *Just Cooking, Thanks: Being a Dissertation on New Zealand Seafoods*. These different texts, each from Wellington-based publishers A.H. & A.W. Reed, belonged to a discernibly new era of cooking. In marked contrast to so many earlier books, they had scarcely any cake and biscuit recipes, for example. They tended to glorify French cuisine, encourage wine with meals, and admit men into the kitchen. Most obviously in Graham Kerr's case, they were aimed at dinner parties, it becoming desirable at least among certain sections of society to gather at meals for their own sake. This, in turn, provided mutual education at least as exciting as cake and biscuit recipe swapping in Daisy's day, and covered a greater repertoire.

The books represented what has been given the ugly name 'gourmetization'. American scholar Jessamyn Neuhaus gave credit for this move to Julia Child's 'The French Chef' television series that had so enraptured Lois Daish when in the United States. 'Child virtually single-handedly fostered new widespread appreciation for fresh ingredients and classic French cuisine. ... Bolstered in large part by Child, the 1960s saw the rapid "gourmetization" of United States food culture', wrote Neuhaus (2003:263). This was no minor social movement isolated to one nation, let alone to one key figure (Julia Child). Other culinary figureheads have been equally credited – Elizabeth David in Britain, for example. The rise in speciality shops, restaurant-going and, eventually, the Slow Food movement has occurred in many nations. This is the revolution that concerns us here.

Arriving from England in 1958 with experience in the management of hotel dining, Graham Kerr became involved, he reports, with the excitement of rethinking New Zealand cookery. As he saw it, the country lacked what he terms a 'culinary tradition', by which he meant no fancy cuisine of great chefs, gourmets, regional delicacies and classic dishes:

> I regard my move to New Zealand as the most important step in my life.
> New Zealand, unlike any other 'Western' nation, did not have a culinary
> tradition to return to – that is, apart from her rich farming heritage. There
> was no establishment to carp, criticize, or snigger. There was a desire to
> learn and, above all, a love for the practical. ... I lived and worked in this
> refreshing climate of opinion for seven years. (Kerr 1969:4)

Lois Daish has explicitly aligned herself with the authors from this revolutionary period. In a speech at the National Library of New Zealand in 1989, she might have ignored Graham Kerr as a foreign ring-in, but she honoured four predecessors, including those two other books just mentioned from 1963, Noel Holmes' *Just Cooking, Thanks*, and Madeleine Hammond's *A Taste of France*. Daish's other acknowledged influences were also aimed at taste pleasures around those years, namely, a collection of Elizabeth Messenger's newspaper columns, *Dine with Elizabeth* (1956) and Patricia Harris's *Accept with Pleasure. A Book about Food Written for Those who Like to Share the Good Things of Life with their Friends* (1969).

Latching on to Julia Child's book and television show in America, and admiring such local authors as Elizabeth Messenger, Madeleine Hammond and Patricia

Harris, Lois Daish identified from the start with a new approach that rejected the culinary style identified with Aunt Daisy and embraced foreign cuisines, a welter of specialist suppliers, sophisticated entertaining beyond the family, and sensual pleasures. Patricia Harris's title says it all – the pleasure of sharing 'good things' with friends. What lay behind this worldwide movement?

MODERNITY AND POSTMODERNITY

Many social scientists and other writers have contrasted Daish's to Daisy's epochs. For example, J.K. Galbraith wrote in 1958 about the arrival of *The Affluent Society* with the boom in private wealth. Sociologist Daniel Bell stressed the overshadowing of the manufacturing industry by the services sector in *The Coming of Post-Industrial Society* (1976). Ernest Mandel diagnosed *Late Capitalism* (1978), with transnational corporations insinuating themselves into almost every nook and cranny of our lives. Such ideas have been amplified by reference to the growth of an information or knowledge economy, the rise of the culture industries, consumerism, increased individualism (the 'me' generation) and, especially, globalisation, so that products and customs are both readily available worldwide.

Such characterisations have generally not been made in culinary terms, although they have cropped up as examples. According to sociologist Anthony Giddens, 'My decision to purchase ... a specific type of foodstuff, has manifold global implications. It not only affects the livelihood of someone living on the other side of the world but may contribute to ... ecological decay which itself has potential consequences for the whole of humanity' (Giddens 1994:57–58). Such concepts as affluence, post-industrialism and globalisation provide clues to New Zealand cooking, given that Daish's approach accords with depictions of cross-cultural fertilisation at the same time as the expanding service economy helps explain the rise of restaurants such as hers, serving more affluent populations. These decades also saw women more commonly joining the workforce, with the arrival of women's liberation being signalled by the publication of Betty Friedan's *The Feminine Mystique* in 1963. Friedan protested against the same housewife's role that Aunt Daisy so strenuously enforced.

The revolution in cooking also fitted another important interpretation of the change. The later epoch has been called 'postmodern'. As an example, David Harvey discussed the 'time and space compression' of everyday life speeding up and people interacting over wider distances under the title, *The Condition of Postmodernity* (1989), and Marxist critic Fredric Jameson spoke to the theme in *Postmodernism, or, the Cultural Logic of Late Capitalism* (1991). The concept of

The cover of *Aunt Daisy's Ultimate Cookbook* (1959) belied the unadorned modernist content –
recipes without commentaries or even contributors' names. H. Leach Collection.

The cover of Lois Daish's *Dinner at Home* (1993) was a postmodernist invitation to a cookbook with reflections on good eating as well as appealing illustrations. H. Leach Collection.

177

'postmodernity' arouses continuing debate about, for example, the extent to which it extends or replaces modernity. Yet the cluster of ideas has remained seductive, especially since they stress the mixing of cultures, seen in the furious juxtaposition of culinary traditions. The idea of postmodernity helps bring out how the new globalised culture could be both more homogenised and also more complicated. Jean-François Lyotard stressed the 'eclecticism' of *The Postmodern Condition* and, in a rare food reference, noted: 'one ... eats McDonald's food for lunch and local cuisine for dinner' (Lyotard 1984:76). On one hand, McDonald's represents a new era of one global culture and, on the other, widespread gastro-tourism and an explosion in food publishing provide new forms of empowerment.

If we divide the twentieth century into 'modernity' and 'postmodernity', then Aunt Daisy exemplifies modernity. She might seem old-fashioned to us now, but that would be a mistake because she actually represented the fast, the new, the modern. Daisy used the latest means of mass communication, radio. Her advertising of electric water heaters fitted an exciting feature of modernity, the electrification of urban households. 'To-day electricity is paramount. It is representative of modern life and modern thought, and ... will be looked upon as the force which typifies our age' (Anon [c.1936]:Preface). Her broadcast chats, recipes and homely wisdom reinforced the nuclear family as the desirable social unit of modern times. Even the way her books included highly rationalised recipes with precise measurements went back less than a century. Her style of cooking replaced earlier versions, when at least some writers assumed mayonnaise was made from egg yolks.

Similarly, the diagnoses of postmodernity, overlapping with ideas about late capitalism and so on, apply to Daish's world. For example, the rise of the culture industries (especially the use of television, magazines and mass-market books for sophisticated marketing) replaces utilitarian recipe books. Cookery titles proliferate, books move towards larger formats and stronger design values, publication is more international, recipe sources become globalised, authors become identified less with domestic than with restaurant and 'celebrity' cooking, and aside from some huge sellers, the market segments. Belying postmodern marketing, the glossy new books arouse desire.

Accordingly, where Daisy's recipes were graphically dull and never illustrated, Daish's early books have artists' sketches and the latest has Belinda Pope's luscious photos. Her recipes reveal characteristics that are often proclaimed as particularly postmodern, such as eclecticism, bricolage, playfulness and irony. For example, 'bricolage' comes from the French verb *bricoler*, and means to arrange various bits and pieces, to do odd jobs, to potter about. As we have seen, Daish picks up recipes from here and there, tinkers with them and then acknowledges the process by using gently humorous headings ('Fish without Chips').

Where Aunt Daisy might have accepted the label 'modern', Lois would presumably jib at being called 'postmodern', preferring to think of her work as more modest and homely than this might suggest (she has even described her cooking as 'plain'). And perhaps she is right. She has sought authentic methods to create authentic tastes for authentic conviviality, which seems quite the reverse of postmodern game-playing. So, perhaps this cooking is only 'postmodern' if to some degree the usual understanding is upended and reversed. One trouble has been that postmodernists have seen the world primarily as 'signs', that is, the cultural surface rather than in the cook's finer detail. They have marvelled at the colour photographs straying towards idealism. The understanding of recent cooking needs a more worldly interpretation, with which Lois might feel more comfortable.

So many of the diagnoses of late capitalism, postmodernity and the like readily apply to food – the globalisation of food corporations, products and cultures, the intensification of marketing through television and fast colour printing, the rise of the service sector in takeaways, restaurants and cafés, the noticeable increase in the playfulness of recipes, and so forth. Common ideas within sociology and cultural studies help explain why Daish's cooking can seem more interesting, satisfying and sometimes more elusive than Daisy's. However, the depiction can be further improved by making it more two-way. That is, seen from a gastronomic perspective, massive changes on the table help to give meaning to the prevailing notions of affluence, aesthetification, and the rest. The food industry has changed radically since providing the 'Daisy Chain' with the basic ingredients for cakes and biscuits, and these changes help explain the sensation of postmodernity.

THE FOOD INDUSTRY'S CULTURAL TURN

In exchanging the latest recipes for the Pavlova, Khaki Cake, Pumpkin Scones and so on, Aunt Daisy recorded a 'Golden Age of Antipodean Baking' (Symons 2008; 2010). This can be understood in terms of the then newly modernised food industry (Symons 1996; 2000:329–42). Britain had colonised New Zealand during the nineteenth century, as the industrialisation of agriculture boosted the world trade in raw commodities. The classic instance was sugar, worked by African slaves shipped across the Atlantic, to make a former luxury widely accessible in Europe (Mintz 1985). In the late nineteenth century, entrepreneurs moved decisively into not just producing but also processing these commodities for urban distribution.

The emergence of this mass market occasioned the tumult of cookery books, starting somewhere around the 1890s, that featured and advertised refined sugar, roller-milled white flour, dried fruits, and so on, and which the new generation of cooks turned into biscuits, fruit cakes, sponges, scones, puddings, pies and crumbles. The most emblematic product locally became Edmonds' baking powder (McKee 2005) and the most emblematic cook, Daisy.

Another requirement for this golden kitchen age was the mass production of iron stoves, which was typical of the coal-fired industrial revolution. Although wood and coal were long valued as fuels, gas was used in the nineteenth century and soon after, electricity. Mechanical refrigeration supported the distribution of fresh milk, and provided large blocks of ice to keep dairy products domestically, and then homes gained electric refrigerators from the late 1920s. Another often underrated piece of kitchen equipment was the hand-cranked, counter rotating, geared egg-beater, which greatly reduced the labour required for such tasks as beating eggs and whipping cream. Invercargill inventor Ernest Godward (1869–1936) had by 1900 patented an egg-beater that could prepare eggs for a sponge cake in three and a half minutes, where it previously took fifteen (Strachan 2007).

Scones, biscuits and decorated cakes emerged from the new industrialised kitchen, that triumph of modernity equipped with an iron stove, labour-saving gadgets and ever-ready ingredients, especially refined flour, sugar, desiccated coconut, baking powder, walnuts, cocoa and flavourings. The results were mainly keeping or stand-about foods, eaten at room temperature and suited to snacking and socialising beyond the family. Showing creations off to a wider circle, women exchanged knowledge, and this recipe reciprocity supported the rapid circulation of cake and biscuit fashions. No known individuals were ever responsible for such creations as Lamingtons, Anzac Biscuits and Afghans; they were social inventions, so that a cluster of recipes tended to converge in an iconic version (Symons 2008).

Aunt Daisy became a consummate salesperson for the modern, industrially supplied, mass kitchen. Supplementing her hard radio sell, a full-page advertisement in *Aunt Daisy's Radio Cookery Book, No. 4* opened with 'Aunt Daisy recommends BAK-O-MALT The New Baking Malt' (Basham [1936–39]:120). *Aunt Daisy's Favourite Cookery Book* (1954) showed Daisy using a 'Zip' water heater in a full-page photograph, signed 'Approved "Aunt Daisy"' (Basham 1954:opp. vii). Even before she became a commercial mouthpiece, she was an intermediary between housewives, relaying the latest creations of baking's golden age.

The capital-intensive, industrial approach to primary production, the so-called factory farming which has reorganised nature and uprooted traditional society since the eighteenth century, continued to escalate. Primary production was industrialised to create a vast, global source of often extremely cheap ingredients. From Aunt Daisy's lifetime and onwards, businesses distributed those primary products, often highly processed to increase portability, until foods were super-marketed at the end of Daisy's career. In the last years of her broadcasts, plastic packaging, long-distance trucking and the cold supply chain further exploited fossil fuels. So, too, the food processing and distributing industries connected virtually every farm and kitchen around the globe into an enormous social network.

As a further step, taken essentially during Daish's day, the food industry revolutionised the cultural realm. To sell factory-made meals, businesses asserted control through the communication media – the culture industries – especially with near-saturation advertising. Food corporations now cooked finished, and almost finished, dishes. They moved aggressively into selling a myriad of snacks and drinks, foods that were eaten outside family meals. To a more limited extent, home kitchens were also supplemented by small businesses, especially restaurants and cafés. Marketing has theoretically made not only any food but also any food idea available.

Both Daisy and Daish witnessed the rise of mass-distributing corporations. In terms of featured products, Daisy's recipes incorporated basic, processed commodities (white flour and sugar), whereas Daish employed an enormously expanded range of pastas, rice, fruits, vegetables and, as already noted, cheeses. Similarly, while Daisy's works contained advertisements for New Zealand's prototype supermarket chain, Self Help, Daish refers not merely to supermarkets (sometimes negatively out of concern at the expense of their fresh foods, for example) but also to a supplementary array of small makers and retailers. Daisy's yellowing newspaper columns, crackling radio broadcasts and drab-looking books can scarcely be compared with the glossy cultural milieu, known to Daish, of beautifully photographed specialist texts and magazines, multiple colour television programmes (including a dedicated Food Channel) and instantaneous internet.

Through the communications explosion, large corporations gained enormous control of food representations and images, providing an image-wrapped supply of sweet, bubbly, caffeinated cola drinks, pseudo-milks, 'fruit' bars, degraded vegetables and chips. Many streets, living rooms and even some classrooms were cluttered with McDonald's signs. Simultaneously, Lois Daish became witness not merely to the world's foods, but to the world's food cultures, readily available to individuals who were sufficiently inclined, educated and privileged. At least notionally, anyone could now access not only the cornucopia of foods but also the vast culinary library of worldwide expertise. Within a much more dynamic social milieu, friends could concentrate on shared taste pleasures. Daish's world is attractive, but in some ways it picks up the crumbs from the corporate domination of culture. With postmodernity, it became possible to eat both much better and much worse.

Lois Daish's ever-present recipe introductions show her fretting about cooking's links with the commercial environment (mentioning high-quality growers, artisan processors and specialist retailers), with convivial settings (lately a quiet meal at home), with craft skills (making ingredient substitutions, and playing with timing and temperature), with cultures (calling upon her, her neighbours' and her favourite authors' experiences around the world), with gastronomic expertise (her walls are covered in books), with seasons (her preferred organisation of her own books is according to months), and with tastes, which reign supreme.

Where Daisy had spoken to the great mass of domestic cooks, labouring in their standardised kitchens with canisters marked 'Flour', 'Sugar', 'Rice', 'Tea' and 'Coffee', Daish talked intimately to individuals about the sensory, social and cultural intricacies of dining. This was an extraordinary development, even if the private pleasures and authenticity have to be viewed against a background of cultural imperialism and planetary plunder.

TWO PEAS IN A POD

Daisy and Daish are publicly visible faces of two culinary worlds. A revolution occurred around 1963, to hazard a date, and not because Aunt Daisy died that year, nor just because Julia Child popped up on United States television. Three epochal New Zealand cookery books appeared then, too, those of Madeleine Hammond, Noel Holmes and Graham Kerr. With their and others' works, our grandmothers and great-grandmothers' cooking gave way to that of gourmets, who served meals beyond the family at dinner parties, and included wine. Engaging in a mutual education programme over the decades since then, foodies have made heroes of artisan producers and chefs, and supported such catch-cries as 'fresh', 'local', 'slow', 'passionate', 'creative', 'taste' and 'gentle'. In Daish's day, domestic cooks – at least those accessing refined culinary ideas – slashed the boiling time for peas from approximately twenty minutes to two. Remember the peas?

A many-layered explanation is needed to understand why green peas were cooked less. Perhaps new varieties were more tender. Perhaps some growers got younger peas to the market. Perhaps the flood of frozen peas encouraged quick plunges before everything went to mush. Perhaps the clamour of culinary discussion encouraged finer cooking. But the sale of fresh peas declined markedly, so that it was left to gourmets – as now wrote many of the cookery books – to hunt down peas in good fresh condition and to bring out their flavour and texture. Encouraged by fellow gourmets and serious professional cooks, food lovers wanted their pasta 'al dente', their beef 'saignant' and their vegetables treated 'with respect'. The ways human beings fed each other were revolutionised, and with that came a new sensibility.

The enormous upheavals of the food supply chain – which both alienated people from nature and from each other, and also provided the reverse opportunities for authenticity – accord with notions of late capitalism, globalisation and the rise of the culture industries. The emphasis shifted from food as mere 'fuel', at its worst, to sharing 'the good things of life' with friends (Harris 1969). Careful cooking in the interests of pleasure fits the often-remarked rise of consumerism, individualism and globalisation. The concomitant resort to culinary eclecticism and playfulness fits postmodernity.

Such theories explain elegantly cooked peas and also, and perhaps even more interestingly, vice versa. The highly material activity of cooking provides the ground for such theories. People wanted to enjoy excellent peas and so reorganised the global food industry and associated knowledge. That might sound an outrageous claim. It's less ambitious to assert that recipe books are so intricately in touch with the basic routines of daily life that they provide valuable insights into the major social and cultural transformations of the twentieth century. The changes in cooking and eating – visible in the works of Daisy and Daish – lie at the heart of the times. This is a green pea account of postmodernity.

Works Cited

CHAPTER ONE
Maori Cookery before Cook

Anderson, Atholl J., 2002, 'A Fragile Plenty: Pre-European Maori and the New Zealand Environment' pp. 19–34 in E. Pawson and T. Brooking (eds) *Environmental Histories of New Zealand*. Melbourne: Oxford University Press.

Chang, Kwang-chih, 1977, *Food in Chinese Culture. Anthropological and Historical Perspectives.* New Haven: Yale University Press.

Crook, William P., 1799, *Account of the Marquesas Islands*. Microform, Hocken Collections, Dunedin.

Firth, Raymond, 1957, *We, the Tikopia. A Sociological Study of Kinship in Primitive Polynesia*. London: George Allen & Unwin Ltd.

Houghton, Philip, 1996, *People of the Great Ocean. Aspects of Human Biology of the Early Pacific.* Cambridge: Cambridge University Press.

Kendall, Thomas, 1820, *A Grammar and Vocabulary of the Language of New Zealand*. London: Church Missionary Society.

Leach, B. Foss, 2006, *Fishing in Pre-European New Zealand*. New Zealand Journal of Archaeology Special Publication, Archaeofauna Vol. 15.

Leach, Helen M., 1984, *1,000 Years of Gardening in New Zealand*. Wellington: Reed.

Leach, Helen M., 1986, 'A Review of Culinary and Nutritional Adaptations involving Wild Plant Foods following Polynesian Settlement of New Zealand', pp. 133–42 in G.K. Ward (ed.) *Archaeology at ANZAAS Canberra*. Canberra Archaeological Society.

Leach, Helen M., 1987, 'In the Beginning', pp. 18–26 in J. Phillips (ed.) *Te Whenua, Te Iwi – the Land and the People*. Wellington: Allen and Unwin/Port Nicholson Press.

Leach, Helen M., 1989, The Traditional Background of Polynesian Foods. *Proceedings of the Nutrition Society of New Zealand* 14: 131–6.

Leach, Helen M., 2001, European Perceptions of the Roles of Bracken Rhizomes (*Pteridium esculentum* (Forst. F.) Cockayne) in Traditional Maori Diet. *New Zealand Journal of Archaeology* 22(2000): 31–43.

Leach, Helen M., 2003a, Did East Polynesians Have a Concept of Luxury Foods? *World Archaeology* 34(3): 442–57.

Leach, Helen M., 2003b, Fern Consumption in Aotearoa and its Oceanic Precedents. *Journal of the Polynesian Society* 112(2): 141–55.

Leach, Helen M., 2005, 'Ufi kumara, the Sweet Potato as Yam', pp. 63–70 in C. Ballard, P. Brown, R. Bourke and T. Harwood (eds) *The Sweet Potato in Oceania: A Reappraisal.* Ethnology Monographs 19, Oceania Monograph 56.

Leach, Helen M., 2007, 'Cooking with Pots – Again', pp. 53–68 in A. Anderson, K. Green and F. Leach (eds) *Vastly Ingenious. The Archaeology of Pacific Material Culture in Honour of Janet M. Davidson.* Dunedin: Otago University Press.

Leach, Helen M. and Chris Stowe, 2005, Oceanic Arboriculture at the Margins – the Case of the *Karaka* (*Corynocarpus laevigatus*) in Aotearoa. *Journal of the Polynesian Society* 114(1): 7–27.

McGlone, Matt S., Janet M. Wilmshurst and Helen M. Leach, 2005, An Ecological and Historical Review of Bracken (*Pteridium esculentum*) in New Zealand, and its Cultural Significance. *New Zealand Journal of Ecology* 29(2): 165–84.

Mead, Hirini M. with Neil Grove, 2001, *Nga Pepeha a nga Tipuna. The Sayings of the Ancestors.* Wellington: Victoria University Press.

Mintz, Sydney W., 1996, *Tasting Food, Tasting Freedom. Excursions into Eating, Culture and the Past.* Boston: Beacon Press.

Oliver, Douglas L., 1974, *Ancient Tahitian Society. Vol.1 Ethnography.* Honolulu: The University Press of Hawaii.

Ollivier, Isobel, 1985, *Extracts from Journals Relating to the Visit to New Zealand in May–July 1772 of the French Ships Mascarin and Marquis de Castries under the Command of M-J. Marion du Fresne.* Wellington: Alexander Turnbull Library Endowment Trust with Indosuez New Zealand Limited.

Revel, Jean-François, 1982, *Culture and Cuisine. A Journey Through the History of Food*, transl. Helen R. Lane. New York: Doubleday.

Salmond, Anne, 1997, *Between Worlds. Early Exchanges Between Maori and Europeans 1773–1815.* Auckland: Viking.

Smith, Ian W., 2004, Nutritional Perspectives on Prehistoric Marine Fishing in New Zealand. *New Zealand Journal of Archaeology* 24(2002): 5–31.

Su'a, To'aiga I., 1987, Polynesian Pudding Processes in West and East Polynesia. Unpublished M.A. thesis, Department of Anthropology, University of Otago.

Taylor, Richard, 1848, *A Leaf from the Natural History of New Zealand.* Wellington: R. Stokes.

Taylor, Richard, 1855, *Te Ika a Maui.* London: Wertheim and Macintosh.

Tregear, Edward, 1891, *The Maori–Polynesian Comparative Dictionary.* Wellington: Lyon and Blair.

Wilmshurst, Janet M., Atholl J. Anderson, Thomas F.G. Higham and Trevor Worthy, 2008, Dating the Late Prehistoric Dispersal of Polynesians to New Zealand using the Commensal Pacific Rat. *Proceedings of the National Academy of Sciences* 105(22): 7676–80.

Yate, William, 1835, *An Account of New Zealand*, 2nd edn, London: R.B. Seeley and W. Burnside.

CHAPTER TWO
Cookery In The Colonial Era (1769–1899)

Newspapers

Daily Southern Cross
Nelson Examiner and New Zealand Chronicle
New Zealand Spectator and Cook Strait Guardian
New Zealand Tablet
New Zealander
Otago Witness
Tuapeka Times

Published Sources

Anon [1901], *Colonial Everyday Cookery.* 1st edn, Christchurch: Whitcombe and Tombs Limited.

Barker, Lady (Mary Anne), 1956 [1870], *Station Life in New Zealand.* Christchurch: Whitcombe and Tombs Limited.

Beaglehole, John C., 1962, *The Endeavour Journal of Joseph Banks 1768–1771.* Vol. 1. Sydney: Angus and Robertson.

Beaton, Sophia, 2007, A Contemporary Maaori Culinary Tradition – Does it Exist? An Analysis of Maaori Cuisine. Unpublished Master of Arts thesis, Te Tumu School of Maori Pacific and Indigenous Studies, University of Otago.

Bennett, Joe, 2008, *Where Underpants Come From. From Checkout to Cotton Field – Travels Through the New China.* London: Simon & Schuster.

Broad, Isobel L.M., 1889, *The New Zealand Exhibition Cookery Book.* Nelson: Bond, Finney, & Co.

Crawford, Fiona, 2006, Stocking the Colonial Kitchen. A Case Study from Dunedin, 1848–1860. Unpublished BA Hons research essay, Department of Anthropology, University of Otago.

Drummond, Alison and L.R. Drummond, 1967, *At Home in New Zealand. An Illustrated History of Everyday Things Before 1865.* Auckland: Blackwood and Janet Paul Ltd.

Fitzgerald, Caroline (ed.), 2004, *Letters from the Bay of Islands. The Story of Marianne Williams.* Auckland: Penguin Books.

Forster, George, 2000, *A Voyage Round the World* (eds N. Thomas and O. Berghof). Honolulu: University of Hawai'i Press.

Fuller, David, 1978, *Maori Food and Cookery.* Wellington: Reed.

Hursthouse, Charles, 1861, *New Zealand, the 'Britain of the South',* 2nd edn, London: Edward Stanford.

Inglis, Raelene, 2007, The Cultural Transmission of Cookery Knowledge. From 17th-century Britain to 20th-century New Zealand. Unpublished PhD dissertation, Department of Anthropology, University of Otago.

King, Michael, 2003, *The Penguin History of New Zealand.* Auckland: Penguin Books (NZ) Ltd.

Leach, Helen M., 1983, Model Gardens and the Acceptability of New Crops to Polynesian Horticulturalists. *New Zealand Journal of Archaeology* 5: 139–49.

Leach, Helen M., 1984, *1,000 Years of Gardening in New Zealand.* Wellington: Reed.

Leach, Helen M., 1997, The Terminology of Agricultural Origins and Food Production Systems – a Horticultural Perspective. *Antiquity* 71(271): 135–48.

Leach, Helen M., 1999, 'Food Processing Technology: Its Role in Inhibiting or Promoting Change in Staple Foods', pp. 129–38 in C. Gosden and J. Hather (eds) *The Prehistory of Food. Appetites for Change.* London: Routledge.

Leach, Helen M., 2001, European Perceptions of the Roles of Bracken Rhizomes (*Pteridium esculentum* (Forst. f.) Cockayne) in Traditional Maori Diet. *New Zealand Journal of Archaeology* 22(2000): 31–43.

Leach, Helen M., 2006, The Story of New Zealand Gems. *Pen & Palate* (New Zealand Guild of Food Writers) June 2006: 1, 8–9.

Leach, Helen M., 2007, 'Cooking with Pots – Again', pp. 53–68 in A. Anderson, K. Green and F. Leach (eds) *Vastly Ingenious. The Archaeology of Pacific Material Culture in Honour of Janet M. Davidson.* Dunedin: Otago University Press.

Leslie, Eliza, 1847, *The Lady's Receipt Book. A Useful Companion for Large or Small Families.* Philadelphia: Carey and Hart. Accessed on Feeding America http://digital.lib.msu.edu/projects/cookbooks/

Leys, Thomson W., 1883, *Brett's Colonists' Guide and Cyclopaedia of Useful Knowledge.* Auckland: Brett.

Martin, Mary Ann (Lady), 1869, *He pukapuka whakaatu tikanga mo nga rongoa mo nga kai.* Auckland: St Stephen's College.

Miller, Elizabeth B., 1890, *Cookery Book. Lessons Given at the Dunedin Exhibition and Under Auspices of the Technical Classes Association.* Dunedin: Mills, Dick & Co.

Parloa, Maria, 1882, *Miss Parloa's New Cook Book, A Guide to Marketing and Cooking.* Boston: Estes and Lauriat. Accessed on Feeding America http://digital.lib.msu.edu/projects/cookbooks/

Petrie, Hazel, 2006, *Chiefs of Industry. Maori Tribal Enterprise in Early Colonial New Zealand.* Auckland: Auckland University Press.

Polack, Joel, 1838, *New Zealand … 1831–1837.* 2 vols. London: Richard Bentley.

Porter, Frances (ed.), 1974, *The Turanga Journals 1840–1850. Letters and Journals of William and Jane Williams Missionaries to Poverty Bay.* Wellington: Price Milburn for Victoria University Press.

[Pratt, W.T.] 'An Old Colonist', 1877, *Colonial Experiences; Or, Incidents and Reminiscences of Thirty-Four Years in New Zealand.* London: Chapman & Hall.

Salmond, Anne, 1991, *Two Worlds. First Meetings Between Maori and Europeans 1642–1772.* Auckland: Viking.

Savage, John, 1807, *Some Account of New Zealand; Particularly the Bay of Islands, and Surrounding Country.* London: J. Murray & A. Constable.

Scammell, Henry (ed.), 1885, *Cyclopedia of Valuable Receipts A Treasure-House of Useful Knowledge.* St Louis, Missouri: Planet Publishing Company.

Soper, Eileen, 1978, *The Otago of Our Mothers.* Christchurch: Capper Press.

Thomson, Arthur S., 1859, *The Story of New Zealand: Past and Present, Savage and Civilized.* 2 vols. London: John Murray.

[William, Mrs] 'A Lady', 1883, *Facts: Or, the Experiences of a Recent Colonist in New Zealand.* Yalding, Kent: Mrs William.

Williams, William, 1844, A *Dictionary of the New Zealand Language and Concise Grammar.* Paihia: Church Mission Press.

CHAPTER THREE
Culinary Traditions in Twentieth-Century New Zealand

Newspaper
Otago Witness

Published Sources
Anderson, Eugene N., 2005, *Everyone Eats. Understanding Food and Culture*. New York: New York University Press.

Anon 1908, *300 Choice Recipes. Souvenir of All Nations Fair*. Gisborne: Te Rau Press.

Anon 1929, *Recipe Book. Souvenir of the Jubilee 1879–1929* [Harlesden Parish Church]. Harlesden: [Leveridge & Co. Ltd].

Anon 1932, *Souvenir Cookery Book of Tried & Tested Recipes* [Hastings Methodist Church]. Hastings: Painter & Wattie Ltd.

Anon 1955, *Recipes* [St Cuthbert's Old Girls' Association Scholarship Fund]. Auckland: Unity Press Ltd.

Anon 1960, *The Scottish Women's Rural Institutes Cookery Book*. Edinburgh: The Scottish Women's Rural Institutes.

Anon 1962, *Cookery Book* [New Zealand Country Women's Institutes]. Levin: Kerslake, Billens & Humphrey Ltd.

Anon 1965, *Carefree Cooking*. Feilding: Feilding Free Kindergarten Committee.

Anon 1975, *Recipe Calendar 1975* [Maori Women's Welfare League]. Dunedin: Otago Daily Times.

Beaton, Sophia, 2007, A Contemporary Maaori Culinary Tradition – Does it Exist? An Analysis of Maaori Cuisine. Unpublished MA thesis, Te Tumu School of Maori Pacific and Indigenous Studies, University of Otago.

Beeton, Isabella, 1899, *The Book of Household Management*. New edn, London: Ward, Lock & Co. Limited.

Brandon, L.E. (Miss) and Miss Christine Smith, 1905, *'Ukneadit.' Home for the Incurables Bazaar, July, 1905*. Wellington: Geddis and Blomfield.

Burton, David, 1992, Changing Tastes: The Food Revolution in New Zealand. *New Zealand Geographic* 13: 18–39.

Cwiertka, Katarzyna with Boudewijn Walraven (eds), 2001, *Asian Food. The Global and the Local*. Honolulu: University of Hawai'i Press.

Goody, Jack, 1982, *Cooking, Cuisine and Class. A Study in Comparative Sociology*. Cambridge: Cambridge University Press.

Jewry, Mary (ed.), 1893, *Warne's Model Cookery with Complete Instructions in Household Management*. London: Frederick Warne & Co.

Leach, Helen M., 1993, Changing Diets – A Cultural Perspective. *Proceedings of the Nutrition Society of New Zealand* 18: 1–8.

Leach, Helen M. (ed.), 2003, *St Andrew's Cookery Book* Facsimile Edition. [1st edn 1905]. Dunedin: Hamel Publishing.

Leach, Helen M., 2006, From Dunoon to Dunedin. What Two Distant Charitable Cookbooks Reveal about the British Tradition of Soups. *Petits Propos Culinaires* 80: 33–59.

Leach, Helen M., 2008a, *Culinary Treasures of the Hocken Collections*. Hocken Lecture 3, 2007. Dunedin: Hocken Collections, University of Otago.

Leach, Helen M., 2008b, The English Pilau. *Petits Propos Culinaires* 85: 61–8.

Leach, Helen M., 2008c, 'Translating the 18th century pudding', pp. 381–96 in G. Clark, F. Leach and S. O'Connor (eds), *Islands of Enquiry. Colonisation, Seafaring and the Archaeology of Maritime Landscapes.* Terra Australis 29. Canberra: The Australian National University E Press.

Leach, Helen M., 2008d, *The Pavlova Story: A Slice of New Zealand's Culinary History.* Dunedin: Otago University Press.

Longone, Janice B., 1997, 'Tried Receipts': An Overview of America's Charitable Cookbooks, pp. 17–28 in A.L. Bower, (ed.) *Recipes for Reading. Community Cookbooks, Stories, Histories.* Amherst: University of Massachusetts Press.

Miller, Elizabeth B., c.1903, *Elementary Cookery.* Dunedin: [Mills, Dick & Co.]

Miller, Elizabeth B., c.1917, *Economic Technical Cookery Book.* [7th edn?] Dunedin: Mills, Dick and Co.

Mintz, Sydney W., 2000, Sows' Ears and Silver Linings. A Backward Look at Ethnography. *Current Anthropology* 41(2): 169–77, 186–9.

Panayi, Panikos, 2008, *Spicing Up Britain. The Multicultural History of British Food.* London: Reaktion Books.

Ronald, Mary, 1895, *The Century Cook Book.* London: T. Fisher Unwin.

Simpson, Tony, 1999, *A Distant Feast. The Origins of New Zealand's Cuisine.* Auckland: Godwit.

Symons, Michael, 2000, *A History of Cooks and Cooking.* Urbana: University of Illinois Press.

Symons, Michael, 2006, Grandmas to Gourmets. The Revolution of 1963. *Food, Culture & Society* 9(2): 180–200.

Symons, Michael, 2008, 'The Cleverness of the Whole Number': Social Invention in the Golden Age of Antipodean Baking, 1890–1940. *Petits Propos Culinaires* 85: 31–60.

Wu, David Y.H., 2002, 'Improvising Chinese Cuisine Overseas', pp. 56–66 in David Y.H. Wu and Sidney C.H. Cheung (eds) *The Globalization of Chinese Food.* Honolulu: University of Hawai'i Press.

CHAPTER FOUR
Changing Kitchen Technology

Newspapers
Canterbury Standard
Daily Southern Cross
Otago Daily Times

Published Sources
Angus, John H., 1973, *The Ironmasters. The First One Hundred years of H.E. Shacklock Limited.* Dunedin: John McIndoe Ltd.

Anon 1897, *The Cyclopaedia of New Zealand, Wellington Provincial District, Vol. 1.* Christchurch: The Cyclopaedia Co. Ltd [New Zealand Electronic Text Centre www.nzetc.org/tm/scholarly/tei-Cyc01Cycl-tl-body-d4-d48-d17.html downloaded 6 January 2009].

Anon 1902, *The Cyclopaedia of New Zealand, Auckland Provincial District, Vol. 2.* Christchurch: The Cyclopaedia Co. Ltd.

Anon 1903, *The Cyclopaedia of New Zealand, Canterbury Provincial District, Vol. 3.* Christchurch: The Cyclopaedia Co. Ltd.

Anon 1905, *The Cyclopaedia of New Zealand, Otago and Southland Provincial District, Vol. 4*. Christchurch: The Cyclopaedia Co. Ltd.

Anon 1925, *St Andrew's Cookery Book*. 11th edn, Dunedin: Otago Daily Times and Witness Company Ltd.

Anon c.1927a, *Moffats Cook Book*. Toronto, Canada: Moffats Ltd.

Anon c.1927b, *Moffats Gold Medal Electric Ranges Catalogue No 103*. Canada: Moffats Ltd.

Anon 1930, *Radiation Cookery Book*. 11th edn. London: Stationers Hall.

Anon c.1933, *The 'All Gas' Domestic Tariff. Gas Appliances in the Home*. Christchurch: Christchurch Gas, Coal and Coke Company Ltd.

Anon 1947, *Cooking by Electricity*. Hawkes Bay Electric Power Board.

Anon 1951, *Atlas Cookery Book*. 3rd edn. Christchurch: Whitcombe and Tombs Ltd.

Anon 1963, *Atlas Cookery Book*. 10th edn. Christchurch: Whitcombe and Tombs Ltd.

Anon 1984, *Everyday Recipes* [New Brighton Sub-branch of The Royal New Zealand Plunket Society]. [Christchurch.]

Anon 1990a, *A Kaleidoscope of Recipes* [CFC Netball Club]. [Christchurch.]

Anon 1990b, *Family Favourites* [Burnside Primary School PTA]. Christchurch.

Anon 1992, *Centennial Cook Book* [Anglican Methodist Family]. Whakatane: Mann Printing Ltd.

Anon 1993, *Orana Park Recipe Book* [Orana Park Volunteer Group]. Christchurch.

Anon 1995a, *Cook Book* [Congregation of St Martin's Spreydon]. Christchurch: Outreach Press.

Anon 1995b, *Family Recipe Book* [St Ninian's Presbyterian Church]. Christchurch.

Anon 1996, *Country Flavours: A Collection of Recipes* [Supporters of St Joseph's Primary School, Pleasant Point, South Canterbury]. 2nd edn. Timaru: Herald Communications Ltd.

Anon c.1996, *Healthy Eating (with Sinful Sections)* [North Otago Herb Society]. Oamaru: Avis Business Communications.

Anon 1998, *Cook Book* [Temuka Rata Free Kindergarten]. Timaru: Fuji Xerox.

Anon c.1998, *Recipe Book* [St Joseph's School Papanui]. Christchurch: Outreach Press.

Anon 2001, *Budget Recipes for Students*. Christchurch: Budget Advisory Services University of Canterbury.

Anon 2006, *Woodbury School Community Recipe Book*. Woodbury School.

Anon nd a, *700 Recommended Recipes*. 1st edn and revised and enlarged 2nd edn. Auckland: Abel, Dykes Ltd.

Anon nd b, *700 Neeco Tested Recipes*. 3rd and 4th edns revised and enlarged. Auckland: Abel, Dykes Ltd.

Anon nd c, *Best Stoves and Where they are Superior* [Atlas Foundry Scott Bros Ltd.]. Christchurch: Lyttelton Times Co. Ltd.

Anon nd d, *Electric Cookery*. Wellington: Technical Publications Ltd.

Anon nd e, *Everyday Meals for Everyday Kiwis* [marketed by 'Students with Taste', Manukau Polytechnic]. Auckland.

Anon nd f, *Home Economics Recipe Book*. Phillipstown School Technology Centre Co. Ltd. [Christchurch].

Anon nd g, *Microwave for Mother … Cookbook* [Radio Marlborough]. Blenheim: Blenheim Print.

Anon nd h, *Microwave for Mother … Cookbook* [Radio Nelson]. Nelson: General Print.

Anon nd i, *Robertshaw Measured Heat Cook Book*. Auckland: Abel Dykes Ltd.

Anon nd j, *St John's Scouts' Celebrity Cook Book* [St John's Scout Group]. Dunedin.

Anon nd k, *The Engine House Dunedin Gasworks Museum*. Dunedin.

Anon nd l, *Whitcombes Modern Home Cookery and Electrical Guide*. 3rd edn, revised and enlarged. Christchurch: Whitcombe and Tombs Ltd.

Antique stoves.com. Cook Stoves and Ranges www.antiquestoves.htm downloaded 9 January 2009.

Barrington, E., 1940, *Centennial Recipe Book*. New Plymouth: Taranaki Daily News Co.

Bennett, V., D. McKnight, G. Schibli, and A. Stewardson nd, *Home Economics*. Phillipstown Manual Training Centre. [Christchurch].

Bilton, Jan, 1984, *The New Zealand Microwave Cookbook*. Whitcoulls Publishers.

Blake, Vivienne nd, *Viv Blakes Microwave KnowHow*. Hastings: Photolithox Printing Ltd.

Booth, Ken (ed.), 1996, 'Marianne Williams Missionary', pp.465–6 in *For All the Saints: A Resource for the Commemorations of the Calendar*. The Anglican Church in Aotearoa, New Zealand and Polynesia.

Boyd, Winifred (comp.), c.1994, *Heaton Intermediate School Home Economics Recipe Book*. Christchurch.

Boyles, Les, 1988, *Turnbull & Jones*. Wellington: Cory-Wright and Salmon.

Chatterton, L. nd, *Modern Cookery Illustrated*. London: Oldhams Press Ltd.

Cowan, J., 1910, *Official Record of the New Zealand International Exhibition of Arts and Industries Held at Christchurch 1906–7 A Descriptive and Historical Account*. Wellington: John Mackay Government Printer.

Crawford, Fiona, 2006, Stocking the Colonial Kitchen: A Case Study from Dunedin 1848–1860. Unpublished BA Hons Dissertation. Anthropology Department, University of Otago.

Electrical Development Association of New Zealand nd, *Facts about Microwave Cooking*. [Distributed by Electrical Supply Authority.]

Fitzgerald, Caroline (ed.), 2004, *Letters from the Bay of Islands The Story of Marianne Williams*. Auckland: Penguin Books.

Finlay, Isabella, c.1933, *The Osborne Cook Book* 2nd edn. [Dunedin?: np].

Galletly, Peggy, 1994, *St Andrews Co-operating Parish Recipe Book*. Timaru: Aoraki Polytechnic.

Gill, Mrs Patrick, c.1905, *A Practical Cookery Book. The New Zealand International Exhibition Cookery Book*. 2nd enlarged edn. Christchurch: Horace J Weeks Ltd.

Godley, John Robert (ed.), 1951, *Letters from Early New Zealand by Charlotte Godley 1850–1853*. Christchurch: Whitcombe & Tombs Ltd.

Glendinning, Anne, 2008, Gas cooker. *Victorian Review* 34(1): 56–62.

Good Housekeeping Institute (comp.), 1950, *Good Housekeeping's Cookery Book*. 5th impression. London: The National Magazine Company Ltd.

Griffiths, Penelope, 1982, Some Notes on Dating Whitcombe & Tombs Publications, 1882–1960. *Bulletin of the Bibliographical Society of Australia and New Zealand* 6(2): 71–4.

Hargreaves, Ray P. and Terry J. Hearn, 1978, *Letters from Otago 1848–1849*. Victorian New Zealand, A Reprint Series No 4 Hocken Library. Dunedin: John McIndoe Ltd.

Henderson, Jenny, Pam Isitt, Joan Russell, and Lois Siepkes nd, *Conventional and Microwave Culinary Capers*. Christchurch: Resource Education Base.

Henry, Glenys, 1991, *The New Zealand Step-by-Step Microwave Cookbook Combined Edition*. Auckland: C J Publishing Ltd.

Holst, Alison, 1974, *More Food without Fuss*. Wellington: Hicks, Smith & Sons Ltd.

Holst, Alison, 1986, *Alison Holst's Cooking Class*. Auckland: Beckett Publishing.

Holst, Alison, 1987a, *Alison Holst's New Microwave Cookbook*. Auckland: Beckett Publishing.

Holst, Alison, 1987b, *The New Toshiba Microwave Cookbook*. Auckland: Beckett Publishing.

Holst, Alison 1991, *Alison Holst's Microwave Menus A Collection of Vols 1 & 2*. Lower Hutt: Imprint Limited.

Holst, Alison, 2007, *The Best of Alison Holst*. Auckland: New Holland Publishers (NZ) Ltd.

Holst, Simon and Alison Holst, 1998, *Alison Holst's Best Mince Recipes.* Dunedin: Hyndman Publishers.

Hughes, Gwen L. (comp.) nd, *Perfect Cooking, A Comprehensive Guide to Success in the Kitchen.* London: Parkinson Stove Co. Ltd.

ITG [Informational Technology Group], Ministry of Economic Development, 2003, *Statistics on Information Technology in New Zealand* (updated to 2003) [last updated 16 December 2005] www.mwd.govt.nz/templatesMultipageDocument Page_9975.aspx

MED [Municipal Electricity Department], c.1927, *Consumers' Guide and Cookery Book.* Christchurch: Whitcombe and Tombs Ltd.

MED [Municipal Electricity Department], c.1935, *Consumers' Guide and Cookery Book.* Christchurch: Whitcombe and Tombs Ltd.

MED [Municipal Electricity Department], c.1938, *Consumers' Guide and Cookery Book.* Christchurch: Whitcombe and Tombs Ltd.

MED [Municipal Electricity Department], 1951, *Electrical Guide and Cookery Book.* Christchurch: H W Bullivant & Co. Ltd.

Miller, Elizabeth Brown, 1898, *Cookery Book Lessons Given at the Dunedin Exhibition and Under the Auspices of the Technical Classes Association.* 4th edn. Dunedin: Mills, Dick & Co.

Murdoch, F., 1888, *Dainties; or How to Please our Lords and Masters.* 2nd enlarged edn. Napier: Dinwiddie, Walker & Co.

Parry, Gordon, 2005, Memory Lane Kitchen warmly remembered as the home's heart. *Otago Daily Times* 13 February 2005.

Peel, Constance S. nd, *Radiation Recipe Book with Household Hints and other Useful Housekeeping Information.* London: Radiation.

Pollard, John S., 1987, *Requiem for a Gasworks.* University of Canterbury Publication No 38. Christchurch: Griffin Press.

Porteous, Sheila nd, *Electricity and the Home.* Palmerston North: Crawford Print.

Porter, Frances (ed.), 1974, *The Turanga Journals 1840–1850. Letters and Journals of William and Jane Williams Missionaries to Poverty Bay.* Wellington: Price Milburn for Victoria University Press.

Raffills, Glennys, 1988, *Microwave The New Zealand Way.* Reprint. Christchurch: Flour Power Press.

Reilly, Helen, 2008, *Connecting the Country. New Zealand National Grid 1886–2007.* Transport New Zealand Ltd Aotearoa New Zealand/Steele Roberts Publishers.

Rennie, Neil, 1989, *Power to the People: 100 years of Public Electricity Supply in New Zealand.* Electricity Supply Association: Shoal Bay Press Ltd.

Sinclair, F., 1929, *McClary Electric Range Cookery Book.* Wellington: Geo W. Slade Ltd.

Stanton, William Moses 1841–1904 [Reminiscences] The Nelson Provincial Museum/Tasman Bays Heritage Trust, Bett Collection MS STA.

Starky, Suzanne, 2007, 'Barnes, Henry William 1827?–1918,' in *Dictionary of New Zealand Biography*, updated 22 June 2007 www.dnzb.govt.nz/

Sherwood, Andrew and Jock Phillips, 2008, Coal and Coal Mining. *Te Ara – the Encyclopaedia of New Zealand*, updated 4 December 2008. http://www.teara.govt.nz/en/coal-and-coal-mining downloaded 9 January 2009.

Teal, Jane, 2006, 'Mrs Liebert's Cocoanut and Amy's Toffee: The Recipe Books of Grandma Winnie', pp. 84–96 in Kate Hunter and Michael Symons (eds) *Eating In, Dining Out, Proceedings of the New Zealand Culinary History Conference, 2nd Wellington Symposium of Gastronomy, 2005.* Wellington: Victoria University.

Thompson, George Edward nd, *Official Record of the New Zealand and South Seas International Exhibition Dunedin 1925–1926*. The New Zealand and South Seas Exhibition Company Ltd. Dunedin: Coulls Somerville Wilkie Ltd.

Todhunter, E. Neige, c.1933, *'Champion' Cook Book*. Dunedin: Robertson, McBeath Ltd.

Todhunter, E. Neige, c.1940, *Champion Cook Book*. Dunedin: Robertson, McBeath Ltd.

Todhunter, E. Neige, c.1945, *Champion Cook Book*. Dunedin: Robertson, McBeath Ltd.

Warburton, E.I., 1929, *Instruction and Recipe Book for Users of Orion Electric Ranges*. H.E. Shacklock Ltd. Dunedin: Coulls Somerville Wilkie Ltd.

Waterman, Pauline, 1985, *The Genius National Microwave Oven Cookbook*. Japan: Matsushita Electric Trading Co. Ltd.

Waterman, Pauline, 1987a, *Panasonic Microwave Oven New Zealand Cookbook*. Japan: Matsushita Electric Industrial Co. Ltd.

Waterman, Pauline, 1987b, *Panasonic the Genius Microwave Oven New Zealand Cookbook*. Matsushita Electric Industrial Co. Ltd.

Waterman, Pauline, 1988a, *New Zealand Microwave Cooking with Pauline Waterman*. Auckland: CJ Publishing Ltd.

Waterman, Pauline, 1988b, *Panasonic Microwave Oven New Zealand Cookbook*. Japan: Matsushita Electric Industrial Co. Ltd.

Waterman, Pauline, 1989, *My First Microwave Cookbook*. Auckland: CJ Publishing.

Webster, John, 1987, Coal Ranges in Auckland Trust Properties. *Auckland Regional Committee Newsletter* 16(3), New Zealand Historic Places Trust.

Woods-Dalloway, Julie, 2006, pers. comm. Atlas Cookery Book. Braille Awareness Consultant, Royal New Zealand Foundation for the Blind, South Dunedin.

CHAPTER FIVE

The Uptake of Nutritional Advice in the Twentieth Century

Anon 1905, *St Andrew's Cookery Book*. [Facsimile 1st edn 2003. Dunedin: Hamel Publishing.]

Anon 1907, *Colonial Everyday Cookery*. 5th edn. Christchurch: Whitcombe and Tombs Ltd.

Anon 1913, *The University of Otago. Affiliated to the University of New Zealand Calendar for the year 1913*. Dunedin: J. Wilkie & Co. Ltd.

Anon 1922, *The University of Otago. Affiliated to the University of New Zealand Calendar for the year 1922*. Dunedin: J. Wilkie & Co. Ltd.

Anon 1935, *Hints on Diet*. Wellington: New Zealand Department of Health.

Anon c.1936, *New Zealand Women's Household Guide* [The Women's Division of the New Zealand Farmers Union]. [5th edn?] Wellington: Lankshear's Ltd.

Anon 1939, *Home Cookery Book*. 1st edn new series. [New Zealand Women's Institutes.]

Anon 1943, *Rationing Without Tears*. Auckland: The League.

Anon c.1943a, *War Economy Recipe Book*. Christchurch: Whitcombe and Tombs Ltd.

Anon c.1943b, *The Red Cross War-Time Rationing Cookery Book*. Wellington: Roycroft Press Ltd.

Anon 1944, *Stretching the Meat Ration in New Zealand*. [New Zealand Dairy Exporter and Farm Home Journal.] Wellington: Whitcombe and Tombs Ltd.

Anon c.1945, *Sanitarium Recipe Book*. Christchurch: Whitcombe and Tombs Ltd.

Anon 1947, *Calling all Cooks. A Book of Recipes and Modern Cooking* [New Zealand Women's Food Value League]. Auckland: Unity Press.

Anon 1950, *New Zealand 'Truth's' Cookery Book*. Christchurch: Coulls Somerville Wilkie Ltd.

Anon 1956, *Choosing and Cooking Meat* [Auckland Meat Coy. Ltd.]. Auckland: Harvison and Seymour Ltd.

Anon c.1958, *The Family Cook's Book* [New Zealand Family Planning Association]. Dunedin: Otago Daily Times and Witness Newspapers.

Anon 1965, 'Leave your Weight on the Plate' *Health* 16(4): 8. Wellington: Dept. of Health.

Anon 1969, *Edmonds Cookery Book*. [T.J. Edmonds Ltd]. Christchurch: Whitcombe and Tombs Ltd.

Anon 1971a, *What's for Lunch?* [Parnell Kindergarten Establishment Committee]. Auckland: The Magazine Press Ltd.

Anon 1971b, *Kitchen Kapers* [Stratford Methodist Young Wives' Group Committee]. Hawera: The Hawera Star Publishing Co. Ltd.

Anon 1973, *A Real Gem. Tried and Tested Recipes* [Eastern Bay of Plenty Country Women's Institutes]. Dargaville: Northland Times.

Anon 1980, *Recipes* [Compiled and produced by Palmerston Plunket Mothers' Club. Palmerston.

Anon c.1980s, *I'm Hungry Mum.* Dunedin: Dunedin Parents Centre.

Anon 1981a, *Balfour Playcentre Recipes.* Balfour.

Anon 1981b, *Dietary Goals for New Zealanders.* Nutrition Advisory Committee. Wellington: Dept. of Health.

Anon 1981c, *Tried and True* [Eskview Free Kindergarten Committee]. Hawkes Bay.

Anon 1981d, *Tried and True Fairfield Plunket Recipe Book.* Dunedin: Whitcoulls.

Anon [1982–86], *Home and Country Cook Book* [New Zealand Country Women's Institutes]. Levin: KBH Print.

Anon 1991, *Food for Health.* Nutrition Taskforce to the Department of Health. Wellington: Department of Health.

Anon 1992, *Edmonds Cookery Book.* 32nd edn. Auckland: Bluebird Foods Ltd.

Anon 1994, *Edmonds Cookery Book.* 36th edn. Auckland: Bluebird Foods Ltd.

Anon 1995a, *Recipes from the Heartland* [The Country Women's Institutes of New Zealand]. Auckland: Penguin Books.

Anon 1995b, *The Playcentre Collective Vegetarian Recipes* [Portobello Broad Bay Playcentre]. Dunedin.

Anon c.1997, *Jonathan Rhodes Kindergarten Recipe Book.* Dunedin: U-Bix.

Anon 2005, *Edmonds Cookery Book.* 55th edn. Auckland: Bluebird Foods Ltd.

Bell, Muriel E., 1952, Review of Nutritional Trends in New Zealand 1925–1950. *New Zealand Dental Journal* 48(233): 174–82.

Bell, Muriel E., 1957, Some New Zealand Aspects of Animal Fat Considered in Relation to Diet and Cardiovascular Disease. *Journal of New Zealand Dietetic Association* 11(2): 13–14.

Bell, Muriel E., 1960, *Notes on Normal Nutrition for Nurses.* 4th edn. Dunedin: John McIndoe Printer.

Bell, Muriel E., 1962, *Nutrition in New Zealand. Forty Years History 1920–1960.* Dunedin: John McIndoe Printer.

Bell, Muriel E., 1969, *Normal Nutrition. Notes for Nurses.* 5th edn. Dunedin. John McIndoe Printer.

Birkbeck, John A., 1977, *New Zealanders and Their Diet: A Report to the National Heart Foundation of New Zealand on the National Diet Survey.* Dunedin: Linz Activity & Health Research Unit, University of Otago for the Ministry of Health.

Cameron, Ethel M., 1929, *The Ideal Cookery Book* [Wellington Branch Plunket Society]. Wellington: Watkins Print.

Christie, Jan, 1971, *Favourite Recipes* [Concord-Green Island Kindergarten]. Dunedin: Otago Daily Times.

Gillies, Margaret and Yola Swindells (eds), 1986, *Today's Food – Tomorrow's Health*. Home Science Information Service. Dunedin: University of Otago.

Gregory, Elizabeth and Elizabeth C. Wilson, 1943, *Good Nutrition: Principles and Menus*. 2nd edn. Wellington: Government Printer.

Gregory, Elizabeth and Elizabeth C. Wilson, 1952, *Good Nutrition: Principles and Menus*. 4th edn. Dunedin: John McIndoe.

Harvey, Elsie, c.1936, *New Zealand's Leading Recipe Book*. 6th edn. Wellington: C.M. Banks Ltd.

Holst, Alison, 1991, *The Best of Alison Holst*. Auckland: CJ Publishing and Hodder Moa Beckett Publishers.

Hunter, John, 1960, Coronaries, cholesterol, and calories. *Journal of the New Zealand Dietetic Association* 14(1): 13–18.

Kamminga, Harmke, 1995, Nutrition for the People, pp. 15–47 in Harmke Kamminga and Andrew Cunningham (eds), *The Science and Culture of Nutrition 1840–1940*. Amsterdam: Rodopi.

Leach, Helen and Raelene Inglis, 2006, Cookbook Collections – From Kitchen Drawer to Academic Resource. *The New Zealand Library & Information Management Journal Nga Purongo* 50(1): 69–81.

Leys Thompson W. (ed.), [1883], *Brett's Colonists' Guide and Cyclopaedia of Useful Knowledge*. [Fascimile edn 1980. Christchurch: Capper Press.]

Millar, Alice B. (compiler), 1928, *The 'Violet Day' Cook Book* [Plunket Society (Christchurch Branch)]. Christchurch: Foster and Paul Ltd.

Miller, Elizabeth B., 1901, *Improved Economic Cookery Book*. 5th edn. Dunedin: Mills, Dick & Co.

Primmer, Mélanie S., 1926, *The Up-to-date Housewife*. Dunedin: Coulls Somerville Wilkie Ltd.

CHAPTER SIX
Putting Fish Back on the Menu

Abbott, E., 1864, *English and Australian Cookery Book; Cookery for the Many as well as the 'Upper Ten Thousand'*. London: Sampson Low, Son, and Marston.

Anon 1889, *Economic Cooking Lessons. Tested and Given by Different Ladies* [Women's Christian Temperance Union]. 3rd edn. Dunedin: Mills, Dick & Co.

Anon 1892, *Home Cook Book Compiled by Ladies of Toronto and Chief Cities and Towns in Canada*. 90th edn. Wellington: Clara Pinney Yerex and Toronto: Rose Publishing Company.

Anon 1893, *Practical Household Recipes; With Chapters on Garden Management and Legal Memoranda, Adapted to Colonial Requirements*. Christchurch: Whitcombe and Tombs Ltd.

Anon c.1900s, *Technical School*. Dunedin: Mills Dick and Co. Ltd.

Anon [1901], *Colonial Everyday Cookery*. Christchurch: Whitcombe and Tombs Ltd.

Anon 1904, *Coronation Cookery Book*. 2nd edn. Hawera: Hawera Presbyterian Church.

Anon 1905, *St Andrew's Cookery Book*. 1st edn. Dunedin: Evening Star Co. Ltd.

Anon c.1905, *Defiance Cookery Recipes*. Wellington: Joseph Nathan and Co Ltd.

Anon 1908, *The "Sure to Rise" Cookery Book* [T.J. Edmonds]. Christchurch: Smith and Anthony Ltd.

Anon 1912, *Householders Annual Of Useful Information And Directory Of Selected Business Firms For Householders to do Business with. With which is Incorporated The Household Annual*

Index and The Home Annual. Wellington edn. Dunedin: The Householder's Annual and Directory Limited.

Anon 1914, *Highlander Economical Cookery Book.* Invercargill: Murrays Ltd.

Anon c.1920, *Fendalton Cookery Book* [St Barnabas Memorial Church]. Christchurch: Reliance Print Co.

Anon 1927, *Eat More Fish: Hints for the Housewife and Cook on the Proper Treatment of Fish as Food* [Sanford Ltd]. Auckland: Abel, Dykes Ltd. (printer).

Anon c.1930a, *Recipe Book for Seameal, Sea-jell, Seameal Dessert Custard.* Dunedin: W. Gregg and Co. Ltd.

Anon c.1930b, *Recipe Book for Seameal, Seameal Dessert Custard, Diabetic Seameal Custard.* Dunedin: W. Gregg and Co. Ltd.

Anon c.1930s, *The Proteena Way to Health.* Proteena Milling Co. Ashburton. Whitcombe and Tombs Ltd.

Anon 1934, *Tenth Anniversary Souvenir Book of Cookery Recipes; Also the Romance and Facts of the Dry Cleaning Industry.* [New Zealand Dry Cleaning Co. Ltd]. Auckland.

Anon c.1935a, *Cookery Book Issued by The Auckland Gas Co. Ltd. for the Use of Students in Manual Training Schools in the Auckland Education District.* Auckland: Whitcombe and Tombs Ltd. (printer).

Anon c.1935b, *New Zealand Women's Household Guide* [Women's Division of the New Zealand Farmers' Union]. 4th edn. Wellington: Lankshear's Ltd. (printer).

Anon 1939a, *St Saviour's Book of Recipes and Household Information.* Christchurch: Bullivant and Co.

Anon 1939b, *Home Cookery Book.* New Zealand Women's Institutes.

Anon c.1940a, *Whitcombe's Everyday Cookery* (278th printing). Christchurch: Whitcombe and Tombs Ltd.

Anon c.1940b, *Enquire Within.* Palmerston North: W.J. Crawford.

Anon 1955, *Edmonds "Sure to Rise" Cookery Book.* Economy edn. Christchurch: T.J. Edmonds Ltd.

Arnold, Rollo, 1994, *New Zealand's Burning: The Settlers' World in the Mid 1880s.* Wellington: Victoria University Press.

Basham, Maud R., [1934], *'Aunt Daisy' Cookery Book: Containing over 700 Recipes and Hints.* Auckland: Harvison and Marshall Ltd.

Basham, Maud R., 1952, *Aunt Daisy's Favourite Cookery Book.* Christchurch: Whitcombe and Tombs Ltd.

Basham, Maud R., Fred G. Basham (compiler), 1938, *Aunt Daisy's Radio Cookery Book.* Christchurch: Whitcombe and Tombs Ltd.

Best, Elsdon, 1927, Fishing Methods and Devices of the Maori. Dominion Museum Bulletin No 12, Wellington.

Blackmore, Merle A., c.1929, *Cooking of New Zealand Fish and other Sea Foods.* Auckland: Whitcombe and Tombs Ltd.

Broad, Isobel L.M., 1889, *New Zealand Exhibition Cookery Book.* Nelson: Bond, Finney and Co.

Carter, C.G., 1891, *New Zealand Cookery Book and Colonial Household Guide.* Tauranga: C.G. Carter.

Finlay, Isabella, c.1932, *Cookery.* Dunedin. [Rebound under various titles including T*he Osborne Cookery Book, The Dunedin City Gas Department Cookery Book, Gas Cookery Book* (Timaru Gas, Coal and Coke Co. Ltd), edn bound by the Napier Gas Co. Ltd.]

Futter, E., c.1925, *Home Cookery for New Zealand.* Auckland: Whitcombe and Tombs Ltd.

Gard'ner, E., c.1920s, *Recipes for Use in School Cookery Classes.* Christchurch: Whitcombe and Tombs Ltd.

Gregory, Elizabeth and E.C.G. Wilson, 1940, *Good Nutrition: Principles and Menus.* ed. Muriel Bell. 1st edn. Wellington: Dept. of Health.

Heath, Ambrose, 1946, *Good Savouries.* [1st NZ printing]. Christchurch: Whitcombe and Tombs Ltd.

Hector, James, 1872, 'Notes on the edible fishes', in Frederick W. Hutton *Fishes of New Zealand.* Wellington: James Hughes (printer).

Hutton, Frederick W., 1872, Catalogue with Diagnoses of the Species, in Frederick W. Hutton *Fishes of New Zealand.* Wellington: James Hughes (printer).

Johnson, David (completed by Jenny Haworth), 2004, *Hooked: The Story of the New Zealand Fishing Industry.* Christchurch: Hazard Press for the Fishing Industry Association.

Leys, Thomson W. (ed), 1883, *Brett's Colonists' Guide and Cyclopaedia of Useful Knowledge.* Auckland: H. Brett, *Evening Star* Office.

Maclurcan, H., c.1930s, *Mrs. Maclurcan's Cookery Book: A Collection of Recipes Specially Suitable for Australia and New Zealand.* Wellington: Gordon and Gotch Propy Ltd.

Makarios, Emmanuel, 1996, *Nets, Lines and Pots; A History of New Zealand Vessels. Volume 1.* Wellington: IPL Books.

Makarios, Emmanuel, 1997, *Nets, Lines and Pots; A History of New Zealand Vessels. Volume 2.* Wellington: IPL Books.

Martin, Mary Ann, 1869, *He pukapuka whakaatu tikanga mo nga rongoa mo nga kai.* Auckland: Henry Hill at St Stephen's Press.

Miller, Elizabeth B., 1906, *Economic Technical Cookery.* 4th edn. Dunedin: Mills, Dick and Co.

Miller, Elizabeth B. and J. Archer Miller, c.1903, *Elementary Cookery Book.* Christchurch: Whitcombe and Tombs Ltd.

Murdoch F., 1887, *Dainties: Or How to Please Our Lords and Masters.* Napier: Dinwiddie, Walker and Co.

Murdoch F., 1888, *Dainties: Or How to Please Our Lords and Masters.* 2nd edn. Napier: Dinwiddie, Walker and Co.

Paul L., 2000, *New Zealand Fishes; Identification, Natural History and Fisheries.* Auckland: Reed Publishing (NZ) Ltd.

Payne A.G. (ed.), c.1893, *DIC Shilling Cookery Book.* Wellington: D.I.C. Co-operative Stores. [Rebound copy of *Cassell's Shilling Cookery* 1893. London: Cassell and Company.]

Renwick, Margaret L., 1916, *Primary School Cookery Book.* Auckland.

Sinclair, Florence, 1929, *McClary Electric Range Cookery Book.* Wellington: Samuel Brown Ltd.

Sherrin, Richard A.A., 1886, *Handbook of the Fishes of New Zealand.* Auckland: Wilsons and Horton.

Soyer, Alexis, 1849, *The Modern Housewife or Ménagère.* London: Appleton and Co.

Spencer, Evelyn and John N. Cobb, 1921, *Fish Cookery.* Boston: Little, Brown and Company.

Tippler, Henry, 1891, *Henry H. Tippler's Cookery Guide.* Wellington: Fredk. G. Routh (printer).

Titchener, Paul, 1981, *The Story of Sanford Ltd.* Auckland: Sanford Ltd.

Todhunter, E. Neige, c.1940, *Champion Cook Book; for 'Champion' Oven Regulated Gas Cookers.* Dunedin: Radiation New Zealand Ltd.

Trent, Mildred, c.1920s, *Stevens' 'Cathedral Brand' Essences Cookery Book.* Christchurch: H.F. Stevens.

Warburton, E.I., 1929, *'Orion' Cookery Book; For 'Orion' Electric Ranges.* Dunedin: H.E. Shacklock Ltd.

Watkinson James G. and R. Smith, 1972, *New Zealand Fisheries.* Wellington: Government Printer.

CHAPTER SEVEN
Guiding the Culinary Tradition: the School of Home Science

<u>Newspapers</u>
Evening Post
Evening Star
Otago Daily Times

<u>Published Sources</u>
Anon 1922, The Home Science Alumnae. *Alumnae Bulletin* 1: 21–2.

Anon 1923, First Conference of the Alumnae Association. *Alumnae Bulletin* 2: 8–15.

Anon 1926, *Dainty Dishes* [North East Valley Presbyterian Church]. 1st edn. Dunedin: Empire Press Ltd.

Anon 1928, *Alumnae Bulletin* 3: 1, 11, 17–19, 40.

Anon 1930, *Dainty Dishes* [North East Valley Presbyterian Church]. 4th edn. Dunedin: Mills, Dick & Co. Ltd.

Anon 1932, Home Science Extension Service. *Home Science Alumnae Bulletin* 4: 9–10.

Anon 1933, Home Science Alumnae Conference. *Home Science Alumnae Bulletin* 5: 14–15.

Anon 1937, Alumnae News. *Home Science Alumnae Bulletin* 8: 5–7.

Anon 1947, The New Foods Laboratory. *Home Science Alumnae Bulletin* 16: 41, 43.

Anon 1950, *Home Science Alumnae Bulletin* 19: 9.

Anon 1953, *Home Science Scholar's Note Book.* Christchurch: Whitcombe and Tombs.

Anon 1955, Employment Opportunities. *Journal of the Association of Home Science Alumnae New Zealand* 24: 16.

Anon 1957, Ann Gilchrist Strong, O.B.E. *Journal of the Association of Home Science Alumnae New Zealand* 26: 6–8.

Anon 1959, Home Science Extension Leaflets. *Journal of the Association of Home Science Alumnae New Zealand* 28: 63.

Anon 1960, *New Zealand Dishes and Menus.* Wellington: Price Milburn.

Anon 1961, *Jubilee Journal of the Association of Home Science Alumnae New Zealand 1911–1961* 30: 93.

Anon 1962, *School of Home Science History 1911–1961.* Dunedin: School of Home Science, University of Otago.

Anon 1967, Employment Opportunities in New Zealand. *Journal of the Association of Home Science Alumnae New Zealand* 37: 67.

Anon c.1974, *In a Nutshell: A Recipe Guide to Almonds, Chestnuts, Hazelnuts & Walnuts.* Dunedin: University of Otago Extension.

Anon 1980, Focus for Home Economics. *Journal of the Association of Home Science Alumnae New Zealand* 49: 21–2.

Anon 1980, *Meals without Meat.* Dunedin: University of Otago Extension.

Anon 1981, *Coringa Country Club Recipes 1981.* Christchurch.

Anon c.1981, *Microwave Ovens.* Dunedin: University of Otago Extension.

Anon 1986, *Preserving Food: Freezing, Bottling, Drying.* Dunedin: Home Science Information Service, University of Otago.

Anon 1991, *Low Cost Healthy Meals for All Ages.* Dunedin: University of Otago FOCAS Information Service.

Borrie, Alice, 1978, 'In the Beginning ...' Alice Borrie (B.H.Sc. 1915–17). *Home Science: The Journal of the Association of Home Science Alumnae of New Zealand (Inc.)* 47: 15–16.

Boys-Smith, Winifred, 1911, A University Standard in Home Science. *The Otago University Review* May 1911: 5–10.

Carpenter, Emily, 1956, The H.S.E. Demonstration Kitchen. *Journal of the Association of Home Science Alumnae New Zealand* 25: 39–40.

Carpenter, Emily, 1961, *What Judges of Home Produce Look For.* Department of Agriculture Bulletin No. 401.

Carpenter, Emily, 1977, A Brief History of the Home Science Extension at the University of Otago. *Home Science: the Journal of the Association of Home Science Alumnae of New Zealand (Inc.)* 46: 17–18.

Coleman, Patricia, 1975, Home Science – Whence, Why and Whither. *Journal of the Association of Home Science Alumnae New Zealand* 44: 23–34.

Coleman, Patricia, 1986, Home Science – Whence, Why and Whither. *Journal of the Association of Home Science Alumnae New Zealand* 55: 62–3.

Cushen, Margaret A., 1949, *Preserving.* Home Science Extension Bulletin. Dunedin: Dept. of Adult Education/John McIndoe Ltd.

Emerson, Dorothy R., c.1972, *The History of the Otago Home Economics Association.* Dunedin: Robertson McBeath Limited.

Farmer, Fannie M., 1896, *The Boston Cooking-School Cook Book.* Boston: Little, Brown and Company.

Farmer, Fannie M., 1918, *The Boston Cooking-School Cook Book.* Rev. edn. Boston: Little, Brown and Company.

Farqharson, M.E. and H.A. Jarvis (comp.), 1961, *Selected Recipes.* Dunedin: S.N. Brown Ltd.

Favias, Avie, 1978, 'In the Beginning…' Avie Favias. *Home Science: The Journal of the Association of Home Science Alumnae of New Zealand (Inc.)* 47: 16.

Hercus, A., 1955, A Transition Period, 1918–1922. *Journal of the Association of Home Science Alumnae New Zealand* 24: 71.

Holst, Alison, 1983, *Let's Cook with Alison Holst.* Wellington: INL Print Publications.

Home Science Instructors, 1955, *Journal of Agriculture Cookery Book.* Wellington: A.H. and A.W. Reed.

Jeans, A., 1978 ,'In the Beginning…' *Home Science: The Journal of the Association of Home Science Alumnae of New Zealand (Inc.)* 47: 16.

Laing, Raechel and Megan Putterill, 1987, News from the Faculty. *Journal of the Association of Home Science Alumnae New Zealand* 56: 49–50.

Leach, Helen, 2006, The Story of New Zealand Gems. *Pen & Palate* June 2006: 1, 8–9.

MacGibbon, Catherine, 1941, *Canteen Management.* Christchurch: Whitcombe and Tombs Ltd.

MacGibbon, Catherine, 1942, *Cooking for Canteens: Including Recipes for Fifty Servings.* Christchurch: Whitcombe and Tombs Ltd.

Macmillan, Violet, 1938, Foods, Fads and Fallacies. Changes in Diet. *The Journal of Agriculture* 56(6): 484–5.

Matteson, Emma, 1927, *A Laboratory Manual of Foods and Cookery.* New York: The Macmillan Company.

Mitchell, Janet, 2003, Institutional Recipes as a Source of Information about Food Habits. *Food Service Technology* 3: 157–65.

Naylor, Ellen, 1944, Laboratory Manual for Foods 1. School of Home Science, University of Otago, Dunedin, New Zealand. Unpublished manual prepared by Ellen Naylor.

Sherriff, S.D., 1951, *Journal of the Association of Home Science Alumnae* 20: 53–4.

Smale, Clarice M., 1977, Reflections. *Home Science: The Journal of the Association of Home Science Alumnae of New Zealand (Inc.)* 46: 12–17.

Stevenson, Annie, 1961, Official Opening of the New Wing of the School of Home Science. *Jubilee Journal of the Association of Home Science Alumnae New Zealand 1911 to 1961* 30: 48–51.

Stevenson, Annie, 1978, 'In the Beginning...' Annie Stevenson. *Home Science: The Journal of the Association of Home Science Alumnae of New Zealand (Inc.)* 47: 13–14.

Strong, Ann M.G., 1937, *History of the Development of University Education in Home Science in New Zealand 1911–1936*. Dunedin: Coulls Somerville Wilkie Ltd.

Thompson, G.E., 1919, *A History of the University of Otago. 1869–1919*. Dunedin: J. Wilkie.

Thomson, Helen and Sylvia Thomson, 1963, *Ann Gilchrist Strong: A Scientist in the Home*. Christchurch: Pegasus.

University of Cincinnati, 1916, *Some Special Recipes: Compiled by the Students of the School of Household Arts the University of Cincinnati*. Cincinnati: University of Cincinnati.

Unpublished Sources
University of Otago Hocken Collections MS 90-163, Box 5

CHAPTER EIGHT
Cooking on a Dais: From Daisy to Daish

Anon [1907], *Colonial Everyday Cookery: Revised and Greatly Enlarged: Containing 930 Carefully Selected and Tested Recipes [etc]*. 5th edn. Christchurch: Whitcombe and Tombs.

Anon [c.1930], *The "Sure to Rise" Cookery Book: Containing Economical Everyday Recipes and Cooking Hints*. 5th edn. Christchurch: T.J. Edmonds.

Anon [c.1936], *Consumers' Guide and Cookery Book*. Issued by the Municipal Electricity Department, Christchurch, New Zealand. Auckland: Whitcombe & Tombs.

Anon [1939], *Whitcombe's Modern Home Cookery and Electrical Guide: Including a Selection of Cookery Recipes Especially Prepared for Electric Range Users*. 3rd edn. Christchurch: Whitcombe and Tombs.

Anon [1948?], *Whitcombe's Everyday Cookery for Every Housewife*. Rev. edn, 303rd thousand. Christchurch: Whitcombe & Tombs Pty Ltd.

Basham, Maud R., [1934a], *'Aunt Daisy' Cookery Book: Containing over 700 Recipes and Hints*. Auckland: Mrs D. Basham [Cover title: *Good morning Everybody! Aunt Daisy's Cookery Book of Approved Recipes*].

Basham, Maud R., [1934b], *The NZ 'Daisy Chain' Cookery Book: Containing Over 800 Recipes and Hints*. Christchurch: [np].

Basham, Maud R., [1936–39], *Aunt Daisy's Cookery Book of Selected Recipes: Broadcast by Aunt Daisy and Compiled by Fred G. Basham*. Auckland: Whitcombe & Tombs [Cover title: *Good Morning Everybody!: Aunt Daisy's Radio Cookery Book, No. 4*].

Basham, Maud R., 1954, *Aunt Daisy's Favourite Cookery Book: Over 1800 Favourite Recipes* [1st edn. 1952]. Christchurch: Whitcombe & Tombs.

Basham, Maud R., 1959, *Aunt Daisy's Ultimate Cookbook: Over 1300 Selected Recipes*. Christchurch: Whitcombe & Tombs.

Bell, Daniel, 1976, *The Cultural Contradictions of Capitalism*. New York: Basic Books.

Biuso, Julie, 1993, *The Joy of Good Food*. Auckland: Hodder & Stoughton.

Broad, Isobel L.M., 1889, *New Zealand Exhibition Cookery Book*. Nelson: Bond, Finney & Co.

Clayton, Pauline, [c.1980], *Eating Houses in Wellington, Drawings by Michael Fowler*. Wellington: Anchor Communications.

Cox, Helen M., 1952, *The Hostess Cook Book, with Line Drawings by Russell Clark*. Sydney: Angus and Robertson.

'Crocker, Betty', 1950, *Betty Crocker's Picture Cook Book*. New York: McGraw-Hill Book Co., Inc. and General Mills Inc.

Daish, Lois, 1989, *Good Food: Recipes from the Listener*. Wellington: Listener Ltd.

Daish, Lois, 1993, *Dinner at Home, Illustrations by Geoffrey Notman*. Wellington: Bridget Williams.

Daish, Lois, 1994, 'Books which Shaped our Appetites'. Talk at the National Library of New Zealand in association with 'Working Titles' exhibition, Wellington, 10 February 1994.

Daish, Lois, 1997, *Fuss-Free Food for Two*. Whangaparaoa: Chanel Publishers.

Daish, Lois, 2005, *A Good Year*. Auckland: Random House.

Downes, Peter and Peter Harcourt, 1976, *Voices in the Air: Radio Broadcasting in New Zealand: A Documentary*. Wellington: Methuen.

Flower, Tui, 1998, *Self-Raising Flower*. Auckland: Viking.

Friedan, Betty, 1963, *The Feminine Mystique*. New York: Norton.

Fry, Alexander S., 1957, *The Aunt Daisy Story*. Wellington: A.H. & A.W. Reed.

Galbraith, John Kenneth, 1958, *The Affluent Society*. Boston: Houghton Mifflin.

Giddens, Anthony, 1994, 'Living in a Post-traditional Society', pp. 56–109 in Ulrich Beck, Anthony Giddens and Scott Lash, *Reflexive Modernisation: Politics, Tradition and Aesthetics in the Modern Social Order*. Cambridge (U.K.): Polity Press.

Hammond, Madeleine, 1963, *A Taste of France: French Cuisine for New Zealanders*. Wellington: A.H. & A.W. Reed.

Harris, Patricia, 1969, *Accept with Pleasure. A Book About Food Written for those who Like to Share the Good Things of Life with their Friends*. Sydney: Angus and Robertson.

Harvey, David, 1989, *The Condition of Postmodernity*. Oxford: Blackwell.

Holmes, Noel, 1963, *Just Cooking, Thanks: Being a Dissertation on New Zealand Seafoods, with Illustrations by Neil Lonsdale*. Wellington: A.H. & A.W. Reed.

Holst, Alison, 1995, *Alison Holst's Good Food*. Auckland: Premier (Hodder Moa Beckett).

Inglis, Raelene, 2006, 'Aunt Daisy – The original webmaster: A Case Study of Synchronic Cultural Transmission in New Zealand in 1934', pp. 97–116, in Kate Hunter and Michael Symons (eds) *Eating in, Dining Out: Proceedings of the New Zealand Culinary History Conference, 14 & 15 November 2005*. Wellington: Victoria University.

Jameson, Fredric, 1991, *Postmodernism, or, the Cultural Logic of Late Capitalism*. London: Verso.

Kerr, Graham, 1963, *Entertaining with Kerr*. Wellington: A.H. & A.W. Reed.

Kerr, Graham, 1969, *The Graham Kerr Cookbook by The Galloping Gourmet*. Garden City, New York: Doubleday [originally 1966].

Law, Digby, 1982, *A Vegetable Cookbook*. 2nd edn. Auckland: Hodder and Stoughton.

Lyotard, Jean-François, 1984, *The Postmodern Condition: A Report on Knowledge*, transl. by Geoff Bennington and Brian Massumi. Manchester: Manchester University Press.

Mandel, Ernest, 1978, *Late Capitalism*, transl. by Joris de Bres. London: Verso.

McKee, Alison, 2005, 'A Grand Advertisement': Determining the Influence of the Edmonds 'Sure to Rise' Cookery Book on the Culinary Habits and Tastes of New Zealanders. Dissertation in partial fulfilment of requirements for Master of Arts (Gastronomy), University of Adelaide.

Messenger, Elizabeth, 1956, *Dine with Elizabeth: A Round-the-year Book of Recipes Written and Compiled by Elizabeth Messenger*. Wellington: Blundell Brothers.

Miller, Mrs Elizabeth B., [c.1907], *Economic Technical Cookery Book*. [5th edn?]. Dunedin: Mills, Dick & Co.

Mintz, Sidney, 1985, *Sweetness and Power: The Place of Sugar in Modern History.* New York: Viking.

Neuhaus, Jessamyn, 2003, *Manly Meals and Mom's Home Cooking: Cookbooks and Gender in Modern America.* Baltimore: Johns Hopkins University Press.

Rice, Nelljean M., 1997, 'A Tale of Three Cakes: On the Air and in the Books,' pp.173–88, 259–60 in Anne L. Bower (ed.) *Recipes for Reading: Community Cookbooks, Stories, Histories.* Amherst: University of Massachusetts Press.

Strachan, S.R., 2007, 'Godward, Ernest Robert 1869–1936', in *Dictionary of New Zealand Biography.* Updated 22 June 2007 [http://www.dnzb.govt.nz/].

Symons, Michael, 1993, *The Shared Table: Ideas for Australian Cuisine.* Canberra: AGPS Press.

Symons, Michael, 1996, 'The Postmodern Plate: Why Cuisines come in Threes', pp. 69–88 in David Walker (ed.) *Australian Cultural History 15 (Food, Diet Pleasure).*

Symons, Michael, 2000, *A History of Cooks and Cooking.* Urbana and Chicago: University of Illinois Press [originally *The Pudding that Took a Thousand Cooks* 1998].

Symons, Michael, 2006a, Grandmas to Gourmets: The Revolution of 1963. *Food, Culture, and Society* 9(2), Summer 2006: 179–200.

Symons, Michael, 2006b, Authentic Kitchen Voices? Internal Clues and Measures of the Historical Value of Community Cookery Books, pp. 117–35 in Kate Hunter and Michael Symons (eds) *Eating in, Dining Out: Proceedings of the New Zealand Culinary History Conference, 14 & 15 November 2005.* Wellington: Victoria University.

Symons, Michael, 2007, *One Continuous Picnic: A Gastronomic History of Australia.* 2nd edn. Melbourne: Melbourne University Press [originally 1982].

Symons, Michael, 2008, 'The Cleverness of the Whole Number': Social Invention in the Golden Age of Antipodean Baking, 1890–1940. *Petits Propos Culinaires* 85: 31–60.

Symons, Michael, 2009, From Modernity to Postmodernity: As Revealed in the Titles of New Zealand Recipe Books. *Food and Foodways* 17(4): 215–41.

Symons, Michael, 2010, The Confection of a Nation: The Social Invention and Social Construction of the Pavlova. *Social Semiotics* 20(2): 197–217.

Volkerling, Michael, 1978, *Food for Flatters, or How to Close the Edibility Gap.* Revised edn. Auckland: Reed Methuen [originally 1973].

Volkerling, Michael, 1989, *More Food for Flatters.* Auckland: Heinemann Reed.

Welch, Denis, 2005, Lois Daish: Perfecter of Passionfruit Meringue Sandwiches. *New Zealand Listener* 198(3387), 9–15 April 2005: 14.

About the Contributors

DUNCAN GALLETLY is Head of Surgery and Anaesthesia at the University of Otago: Wellington. Although his primary research interests are concerned with the control of the cardio-respiratory system, his passion is New Zealand culinary history. For almost twenty years Duncan has collected cookery books. With an international culinary collection of over 3000 volumes and a New Zealand collection of 600 works printed prior to 1950, Duncan attempts to apply scientific research methods to the analysis of his books. His presentations at New Zealand culinary symposia have included the changes in 'ecological' diversity in cake and biscuit 'species' over time, and the analysis of stains, wear and loose ephemera in cookery books.

RAELENE INGLIS graduated in 2009 with a PhD in Anthropology from the University of Otago. Her thesis was on the cultural transmission of cookery knowledge, from seventeenth-century Britain to twentieth-century New Zealand. Raelene's publications include an article on iconic New Zealand cookery expert and radio broadcaster, Aunt Daisy (Maud Basham), and co-authored works with Helen Leach on the Christmas Cake, New Zealand cookbook collections, and southern cheese rolls. Raelene currently works for the Ministry of Education in Wellington, while continuing her research into early New Zealand cookery teachers.

HELEN M. LEACH is an Emeritus Professor at the Anthropology Department of the University of Otago and a Fellow of the Royal Society of New Zealand. For over thirty years she has published articles and books on Polynesian and Maori prehistory, many focused on diet and horticulture. She has co-authored several cookbooks with her sisters and contributed articles on food history to the journals

Gastronomica, Food & Foodways and *Petits Propos Culinaires*. Her most recent book is *The Pavlova Story* (Otago University Press, 2008). From 2005 to 2008 she was the Principal Investigator of the Marsden-funded project on the development of New Zealand's culinary traditions.

JANET MITCHELL is a lecturer in the Food Science Department at the University of Otago and a registered dietitian. In 1995 she completed a MA thesis in Anthropology on change in New Zealand culinary history. Her publications and international conference presentations cover topics such as invalid cookery, institutional recipes and food reform. She joined the Marsden-funded project with a particular interest in using fund-raising cookbooks to evaluate the uptake of nutritional information by the community.

MICHAEL SYMONS is an independent food historian who gained his qualifications for this role by running a restaurant, working as a journalist, and gaining a PhD in Sociology. He is the author of *One Continuous Picnic*, the history of eating in Australia (1982, 2007), and the award-winning *A History of Cooks and Cooking* (2000). While living in New Zealand, he joined the Marsden-funded project, publishing his resulting papers in a range of international journals.

F. JANE TEAL completed an MA in Anthroplogy from the University of Otago in 1980 and a Dip Tchg from Dunedin Teachers College the previous year. She co-edited *Shaping a Colonial Church: Bishop Harper and the Anglican Diocese of Christchurch 1856–1890* and has recently co-authored *'We Kindle This Light'*, a history of St Margaret's College. Jane has been the Archivist for the Anglican Diocese of Christchurch, Christ's College and College House for many years.

Acknowledgements

HELEN M. LEACH

I wish to express my thanks to Karen Nero and the Macmillan Brown Centre for Pacific Studies for their invitation to present the lecture series in 2008. I am also grateful to Yanbin Deng, and Jim Williams, and to the members and associates of my Marsden research team for their assistance: Sophia Beaton, Fiona Crawford, Duncan Galletly, Raelene Inglis, Janet Mitchell, Michael Symons, Jane Teal and Renée Wilson.

F. JANE TEAL

My thanks to John Webster, Curator of Ewelme Cottage and Rose Young, Curator of History at the Auckland Museum for drawing my attention to stoves which are associated with Auckland historic houses and institutions. Lesley McLachlan from Fisher and Paykel gave permission to access the Shacklock files that are held at the Hocken Collections. Michael Davies, Heather Bundy and Margaret Holloway listened willingly as I tried out yet another idea, while the McPherson-Hames family of Brenda, Andrew, Joshua and Annie provided child-minding opportunities where the books could be spread all over their table without the competition of other projects. Raelene Inglis has been a very supportive colleague and friend throughout this project and Helen Leach has, as always, encouraged and challenged. The research on cooking technology would not have been possible without the aid of a Marsden Grant from the Royal Society of New Zealand.

JANET MITCHELL

I should like to thank the Royal Society of New Zealand's Marsden Fund, and fellow members of the research team for their support. Thanks are also due to the University of Otago for facilitating my attendance at overseas conferences.

DUNCAN GALLETLY

The author is grateful to Michael Symons, Helen Leach, Dave Veart and Raelene Inglis for invaluable guidance, encouragement and stimulating discussions. He would also like to thank the many friends and strangers who have contributed cookery books, and the book dealers and specialist auction houses that have managed to unearth battered but precious culinary treasures from late nineteenth- and early twentieth-century New Zealand. He would also like to thank his wife for the patience she has shown in allowing him to spend innumerable hours counting species of biscuit, stains, pages, and, of late, fish.

RAELENE INGLIS

I would like to thank the following people and organisations for their help towards the writing of this paper: The Royal Society of New Zealand Marsden Fund Te Pūtea Rangahau A Marsden, The University of Otago Research Committee, Emeritus Professor Helen M. Leach, Mrs Janet Mitchell, and Ms Jane Teal.

MICHAEL SYMONS

This chapter culminates research under the auspices of the Marsden Fund of the Royal Society of New Zealand. With especially grateful thanks to Professor Helen Leach for inviting me to join her enthusiastic team.

Index